TENNIS
MAESTROS

TENNIS MAESTROS

The Twenty Greatest Male Tennis Players of All Time

JOHN BERCOW

\B^b\

First published in Great Britain in 2014 by
Biteback Publishing Ltd
Westminster Tower
3 Albert Embankment
London SE1 7SP
Copyright © John Bercow 2014

ISBN 978–1-84954–512–9

10 9 8 7 6 5 4 3 2 1

A CIP catalogue record for this book is available from the British Library.

Set in Sabon by Soapbox

Printed and bound in Great Britain by
CPI Group (UK) Ltd, Croydon CR0 4YY

Contents

	Acknowledgements	vii
	Foreword by John Barrett	ix
	Introduction	xi
Chapter 1	Bill Tilden	1
Chapter 2	Fred Perry	15
Chapter 3	Don Budge	33
Chapter 4	Jack Kramer	43
Chapter 5	Pancho Gonzales	57
Chapter 6	Ken Rosewall	73
Chapter 7	Lew Hoad	91
Chapter 8	Roy Emerson	101
Chapter 9	Rod Laver	109
Chapter 10	Jimmy Connors	121
Chapter 11	Björn Borg	135
Chapter 12	John McEnroe	147
Chapter 13	Ivan Lendl	159
Chapter 14	Boris Becker	171
Chapter 15	Stefan Edberg	189
Chapter 16	Andre Agassi	205
Chapter 17	Pete Sampras	223
Chapter 18	Roger Federer	239
Chapter 19	Rafael Nadal	265
Chapter 20	Novak Djokovic	279
	The Greatest of the Greats	293
	Further Reading	311
	Index	313

Acknowledgements

THANKS ARE OWED to many people for their help with this book. It would have been wholly impractical for me to attempt to interview players or their representatives and, therefore, what follows is based upon personal observation and the existing stock of knowledge about great champions. Even though my sources are published in full at the end, I begin by thanking all who have written about the twenty champions. In preparing this tome I have had the pleasure of reading more than twenty books and, alongside thanks to those players who have penned autobiographies, I should like to thank those who have written biographies or other reference books on tennis that I have consulted over the past two years. They are John Barrett, Chris Bowers, Bud Collins, Frank Deford, Jon Henderson, Richard Naughton, René Stauffer and Stephen Tignor.

Iain Dale of Biteback Publishing readily offered to publish the book and I am grateful to him and his team for all of their support. Vivien Smiley undertook early research on the project with great skill and I am obliged to her as well as to Roger Draper and Bruce Phillips who recommended Vivien for the purpose. John Barrett, now retired from BBC commentary, has over six decades' experience of tennis and I have known him for nearly forty years. He has a more comprehensive knowledge of the sport than anyone I know and has been unstintingly generous in sharing his time and insights with me. Alan Little MBE at the Wimbledon Lawn Tennis Museum opened its doors to me and, supported by the excellent Audrey Snell, was happy to let me consult records there. Greg Rusedski, Barry Cowan and Neil Harman have all offered thoughts about particular players which I have appreciated. I am also grateful to the exceptionally talented Michael Cole for providing the excellent photographs in this book. Perhaps my biggest single thanks are due to Sadie Smith. After working as my parliamentary assistant, she could be forgiven for wanting respite outside of office hours. Yet she willingly volunteered to do research, by appointment with Biteback, and to type my manuscript on her computer. She has done so with typical efficiency and without complaint. Of course I am grateful to my wife, Sally, and our three young children, who have stoically put up with me working on the book. All are a tad amused by my passion for the game and preoccupation with its greats, but I appreciate their understanding. Finally, whatever views or advice people have offered, I am alone responsible for the contents of the book.

Foreword by John Barrett

FOR SPORTS LOVERS everywhere, it is the ultimate question. Whether we are passionate about football or boxing, cricket or baseball, golf or tennis, or indeed any of the other professional pastimes that are played for the entertainment of the masses, the one thing we all want to know is this: who was the greatest performer of them all?

It is a question about which we all have opinions – sometimes strong ones. Would you rate Muhammad Ali (alias Cassius Clay) ahead of Joe Louis, the 'Brown Bomber', as the world's greatest heavyweight champion? Or perhaps Jack Dempsey, Rocky Marciano, Joe Frazier or even George Foreman would be your choice?

What about the golfers? Where do you place Harry Vardon or Bobby Jones alongside Jack Nicklaus, Arnold Palmer or Tiger Woods?

The arguments are endless and inconclusive, simply because in most sports it is impossible to compare performers of different generations who never competed against one another. The exceptions, of course, are those sports like athletics and swimming where the clock and the tape measure are the ultimate judges of performance, regardless of era. Even then, there are problems. What about the improvements in performance due to technological advances in track and pool manufacture (yes, the swimmers insist that there are 'fast' pools and 'slow' pools), as well as innovations in equipment. Then there are the improved training methods enjoyed by today's athletes, plus greater knowledge about dietary supplements. How have they improved performances?

As he explains in this fascinating volume, John Bercow is aware of the pitfalls. In attempting to place the top twenty gladiators of men's tennis in ascending order, he realises that the game played by today's champions using modern equipment is very different from the one played by those from the era of wooden rackets. Playing surfaces, too, have changed and so have the tennis balls.

Nevertheless, John has bravely attempted to answer that ultimate question and for that we should all be grateful. His list is certain to promote protest and debate, a situation he is familiar with as Speaker of the House of Commons. Nevertheless, his arguments do have a certain logic. As he introduces us to the great players of the past and present (and each biographical sketch is very well researched), there are facts and figures aplenty to support his case, many of which will be unknown to the casual reader.

What emerges from all this is John's firm grasp of his subject. His love affair with tennis began early. I remember him as one of those promising young players, each of whom had won an official LTA age-group tournament, who were invited to attend the clinics I was organising in the mid-1970s for the BP International Tennis Fellowship. John was one of those determined and dedicated youngsters at our clinic in Ilkley. His speed about the court was commendable as John Lloyd played a tie-break against him and his enthusiasm was boundless. Clearly, he was relishing the challenge.

John brings that same energy and enthusiasm to his writing. As someone who has followed the game closely ever since those days of his youth, he has formed opinions about the players that he shares with us quite openly. Whether we agree with his conclusions is a matter for individual readers to decide.

'Order, order. Let the debate begin.'

Introduction

'WHY HAVE YOU written a book about tennis?' Several friendly acquaintances, who don't know me especially well, have asked that question, entirely reasonably. I have never been a professional player or commentator. In the tennis world there are a great many experts and I am not one of them. My name is almost entirely unknown in tennis circles and insofar as it is known, some might realise that I have two day jobs – as a local Member of Parliament and as Speaker of the House of Commons.

The truth is that I started playing and watching tennis at the age of eight in 1971 and I have been a passionate fan of the sport ever since. I played as a junior in north London until my late teens and was nowhere near good enough to contemplate a career as a competitor, but I had a lot of fun and qualified as a coach in the early 1980s. Today, I play for recreation and I adore the game more than ever.

More particularly, I have enjoyed watching the men's and women's singles finals at Wimbledon, overwhelmingly on BBC television and very occasionally in person, every year since 1972, when Stan Smith and Billie Jean King won the titles. I have had the pleasure too of viewing a great many other Slam finals and, in more recent years, I have watched matches on the professional circuit throughout the year thanks to Sky Sports and Eurosport. In short, when I am not working, relaxing with my wife and three children, swimming, watching Arsenal at the Emirates, or reading a book, the chances are that I am playing or watching tennis.

Of the twenty players covered in the book, I have had the privilege of watching eleven of them live, from Jimmy Connors onwards, playing at the peak of their powers. In addition, I have seen recordings of the other nine greats from Bill Tilden to Rod Laver.

So it is from the unashamed vantage point not of an expert but of an enthusiast that I have penned this book. Of course, there is no agreement, even between experts, as to the greatest player of all time and there will not even be a consensus as to who should be in the top twenty. Sure enough, the record book is an invaluable guide to who won what, and when. That said, there have inevitably been many players with similar numbers of titles to their names and the choice of a top twenty, unless decided by the narrowest statistical criteria, is inevitably subjective and, ultimately, personal. I have chosen in this volume to focus only on men simply because, other than in mixed doubles, women do not compete against men and, as a young man, I was first drawn to observation of the men's game.

The technique, styles of play and shot-making attributes of the twenty champions described in these pages have varied greatly. Yet all of them have been champions – winners of major titles, usually several times – and each and every one of them has been the leading player in the world as an amateur, a professional, or both. What I have attempted to do in each chapter is to capture the essence of the player's record, the distinctive features of his play, and the qualities, mental as well as physical, which enabled him to climb to the top of the tree. Naturally, I am conscious that some of the titans in this tome have distinguished track records in doubles as well as singles, but others either did not play doubles so dedicatedly or eschewed such competitions altogether. Partly for that reason, and because I am keen to focus on the supremacy of the lone competitor fending for himself, I have made assessments of players exclusively on the strengths of their records in singles.

Whether you are a dedicated aficionado of the sport or a casual reader picking up this book in a spirit of idle curiosity, I hope that you gain something from reading it and can share in my delight at the achievements, the skills and the sheer stubborn will to win of the greatest players ever to set foot on a tennis court.

Chapter One

Bill Tilden

POLL A THOUSAND people in the street today and precious few, certainly outside the United States, would correctly identify who Bill Tilden was. Yet in his heyday, the 1920s, 'Big' Bill Tilden, as he came to be known, was the undisputed master of tennis and one of a select group of sporting giants acknowledged across the world. For seven years Tilden was the world's number one player; he won ten Grand Slam titles, including three Wimbledon titles and seven US championship crowns, the World Hard Court Championships in 1921 and four Pro Slams, namely the US Pro in 1931 and 1935 – aged thirty-eight and forty-two – and the French Pro in 1933 and 1934. His amateur career spanned eighteen years, during which he won 138 of 192 tournaments he contested and enjoyed a match record of 907–62, a winning percentage of 93.6 per cent.

A slim man of athletic build, he stood at 6ft 1.5in. and typically weighed no more than 185lb. He played his tennis with a Bancroft wooden racket with a handle that measured 5⅜ inches in circumference and weighed 14¼ ounces, a comparatively heavy racket even in his era and positively leaden by the standards of the twenty-first century.

The youngest child of wealthy Philadelphian parents, having suffered the harrowing loss of three elder siblings, Tilden had a privileged, even cosseted, early life. He first started to play tennis at the age of five but there is no indication that he excelled and, rather, it appears that his elder brother was thought for a time to be a more likely prospective star. Herbert, six years Bill's senior, was an inter-collegiate doubles champion whilst at Penn and he it was who taught young Bill how to play. As Frank Deford emphasises in his captivating biography of Tilden, his ascent from obscurity to global dominance of tennis is remarkable. Indeed, though Deford does not say so explicitly, it is extraordinary and still largely unexplained just how, other than by dint of sheer belated application, he came to achieve greatness. There are at least three reasons why the meteoric rise would have seemed an implausible prospect.

Firstly, Tilden was thought to be anything but a fit, strong child. Allowing for the understandable anxiety of his parents, especially his mother, about health – an anxiety bordering on neurosis – there was a firm family conviction that he was not a well boy. It seems that he suffered only from the normal range of childhood afflictions, as well as some short-lived bladder problems. Nevertheless, according to Frank Deford, his mother judged that he was infirm. Overprotected, frequently kept away from school and evidently not given to much exercise, this was hardly an auspicious start to the career of a man later to be regarded as the greatest tennis player the world had ever seen. Recalling the child Tilden five decades later, neighbour Josephine Reeves Walton tells Frank Deford, 'It's amazing that he became this great athlete. June [as he was known then] was so very sickly. None of us could imagine that he would ever become this wonderful athlete.'

Secondly, although a great champion does not have to be at the front of the pack from the earliest of his competitive days, he or she will tend to be there or thereabouts, in an elite group or knocking on its door. Moreover, top sportspeople are usually champions at one level or another by the age of twenty. It is hard to overstate just how far Tilden was from such a position. Deford describes his transformation from someone who 'couldn't even make a very ordinary college varsity' to one of the greatest champions of all time as 'frog-to-prince'.

Indeed, such was his lack of prowess that when he entered the National Collegiate Athletic Association tournament as a sophomore, Tilden was routed 6–1, 6–3 in the qualifying round by a man named Eli Whitney, a Harvard student. In other words, Tilden could not get into the tournament proper. To place the matter in the sharpest focus, Little Bill Johnston, whom Tilden later came to dispatch regularly with consummate ease, reached the top ten in the US as a teenager and, aged twenty, was ranked number one in 1915. By contrast, Tilden, twenty-two that year, attained a ranking of seventy in the US. The following year he participated in the US Nationals but was dumped out of the tournament in the first round by Harold Throckmorton. Carl Fisher, who knew Tilden extremely well at this time, tells Frank Deford, 'If you had asked me around 1915–16 if I thought Bill Tilden would ever be national champion, I would have been stunned. I just would have replied, "Whatever would make you ask me a foolish question like that?"'

Thirdly, Tilden did not practise a healthy lifestyle and surely could not, by standards either conventional or modern, have been considered fit. His meal would begin with a large bowl of soup, or, alternatively, he would opt for a fruit cocktail or a honeydew melon. So far, so good, you might think. That, however, seemed to be his only concession to healthy living. Thereafter, to the modern dietician, let alone fitness coach, Tilden's approach was appalling to the point of recklessness. His unexceptional starter would be followed by a steak or two, accompanied by hash brown potatoes. He did not deign to consume salad or green vegetables. The main course of steak and potatoes satisfied his palate on its own and, having wolfed it down, he would invariably have ice cream for dessert. Even when he had cereal for breakfast, it would be drenched in thick cream.

What shocks above all is that he would not only consume such a meal, with monotonous regularity, perhaps twice a day every day, but that he would do so but an hour before he played tennis. Contemporary champions will eat a couple of hours before matches and will typically choose pasta, rice or sushi. Not Tilden. Objections to his diet were brushed aside by Tilden, who knew his own mind and believed he always knew best. 'You should have plenty of fuel in you,' he would insist, adding, 'Better to be slow for a few games at the start because you are full than it is to be weak-kneed and shaky at the climax because you are hungry.' As Deford notes, this outlook became a self-fulfilling prophecy as Tilden often started matches badly but finished them well. On top of his dietary habits, Tilden, though never keen on alcohol, smoked heavily and drank vast quantities of coffee.

So Tilden was thought by his family and neighbours to be weak and sickly, though he was certainly endowed with an athletic build; he performed unremarkably as a junior and into his twenties and he scorned a healthy lifestyle. We are bound, therefore, to ask two obvious questions: 'How did he become a great player?' and 'Why did he want to become a great player?'

Let us attempt to answer the second question first. In May 1911, Bill Tilden's life 'came completely apart', Frank Deford informs us, with the death of his mother. Despondent, nervous, given to shaking, making no mark academically at Penn, and almost friendless, Tilden was evidently an isolated, even unhappy young man. Surely a part of that unhappiness resulted from the fact that Tilden knew that he was gay when homosexuality was illegal, that this set him apart from his peers and that it differentiated him from most of American society. In short, Tilden was rudderless and lost. Just over four years later, in July 1915, his father, suffering kidney trouble and then urenic poisoning, died at the age of sixty. In the same year, Herbert, the elder brother Bill esteemed, distraught by his father's death, stepped up his already heavy drinking and then contracted pneumonia, dying in September at the tender age of twenty-nine. Paralysed by grief, languishing in self-pity, declining to do anything much with his time, Tilden was in danger of becoming a wretched figure.

The combination of a busy father and a mother who had become wheelchair-bound in 1908 had led to Big Bill being shunted off, aged about fifteen, to live with an aunt. Now he had lost both parents and brother. Unlike Herbert, who had mixed naturally with girls, Bill did not. Indeed, he recoiled from intimacy with anyone and was bereft of real company or support, save for that of his aunt. There were, however, two compensations. He had a substantial inheritance and a reporter's job with the *Evening Ledger*. Gainfully employed, not penniless, and with meals routinely dished up for him, Tilden had time to think and to decide what to do. This is the start of the answer to the first question of how he became a great player. What he decided to do was to excel at tennis. He was hungry for greatness. In the words of Carl Fisher, one of the few people who knew him well at this time, 'he suddenly was compelled to want to be supreme in the game of lawn tennis', and would work as hard as it took to achieve this aim.

From 1916, the year he had been beaten in the first round of the US Nationals, Tilden consciously chose to go back to first base and to contrive to develop a complete game. He was evidently convinced that he 'began tennis wrong'. His observation that 'my strokes were wrong and my viewpoint clouded' is as decisively self-critical as it is infuriatingly vague. It is not clear what overarching defects he was seeking to remedy. What we do know is that henceforth he would play every conceivable tournament open to him, no matter how minor or inglorious it might seem; that when not competing he would, so Deford tells us, 'hit endless balls against a backboard' to improve technique, accuracy and consistency; that whilst coaching at Germantown Academy he would consciously aim to learn from his pupils, trying to perfect his knowledge of why a ball behaved as it did, hitting a thousand or two to supply a satisfactory answer; and that, in particular, discontented with his inadequate defensive backhand, would work tirelessly to make it a far superior shot.

As Tilden belatedly developed his game, it contained immense strengths. He had a cannonball first serve which won him many cheap points, together with a dependable second delivery; he produced impressive groundstrokes off both wings which he could hit hard and flat but also, it appears, with all manner of spin, especially favouring the sliced and chopped strokes; he had good if not outstanding volleys, the ability to lob and dropshot, superb footwork, unrivalled stamina and a brain whirring at a rate of knots as he sought not merely to out-hit but to outwit his opponents.

Tilden once provided his nephew with a list of thirteen points which were neither narrowly functional nor a complete methodology for match-winning tennis. They were, however, a shrewd guide to potential players and an illuminating insight into what drove his own approach:

1. Tennis is a game of errors, so strive to avoid them.
2. Play to your opponent's strength to open up his or her weakness.
3. Avoid double faults through the development of a reliable second serve.
4. Focus as much on return of serve, played half of the time, as on serve.
5. Don't miss the easy shots as doing so gives your opponents two points – what would have been yours and is now theirs.
6. Try hardest at 30–15 or 15–30.
7. Approach a match with alternative plans of attack, i.e. a Plan B or C. (This is significant because on one occasion, irritated by a friend who saw him over-hitting balls out and called out, 'Take it easy', Tilden had hit back, 'Deacon, I'll play my own sweet game.' In fact, he became perhaps the canniest of strategists, probably more versatile and dextrous than any of his competitors.)
8. Never change a winning game.
9. Make it easy on yourself, e.g. getting a better angle for the shot you want to play.
10. Play the percentages in covering the court.
11. Choose results before form.
12. Deploy variety.
13. Be a sportsman, but with a killer instinct.

Through a combination of ambition, skill, practice and endurance, both physical and mental, Big Bill Tilden, for so long a journeyman in men's tennis, leapt into the premier league of the sport's competitors. This he demonstrated thrillingly and conclusively at Wimbledon, on Centre Court, in 1920 at the relatively advanced age (for a rising champion) of twenty-seven. In 1918 and 1919, Tilden, whose game had by then greatly improved, had been the losing singles finalist in the US National Championships. However, though an American, Tilden had not been popular with home crowds, who were much keener on his main rival, often known as 'Little' Bill Johnston. The latter had defeated Tilden in the US National Championships in 1919 in straight sets and many observers thought that the 1920 Wimbledon final would feature Johnston against the Wimbledon defending champion, Gerald Patterson. It was not to be, however, as Johnston was defeated early in the tournament by a solid British player, J. C. Parke. Tilden, on his first visit to the UK, disposed of Parke and immediately appeared to find favour with the British crowds, who regarded him with admiration as an impressive, even exotic, character. One observer noted approvingly that 'there is no stroke Mr Tilden cannot do at full speed and his is undoubtedly the fastest serve seen'. Tilden duly progressed to the all-comers final against the Japanese Zenzo Shimizu. Here, Tilden displayed a trait that was to recur throughout his career: he fell behind, only to recover. 1–4 down in the first set, Tilden won it 6–4. 2–4 down in the second, he took it 6–4. 2–5 down in the third, he eventually prevailed 13–11. Tilden was a great sportsman and a great competitor but he was also a great showman. He wanted to entertain, to impress when necessary, and to give the crowd what he judged to be their due: an intriguing encounter. Frank Deford quotes one observer, Paul Gallico, declaring, 'To his opponents it was a contest; with Tilden it was an expression of his own tremendous and overwhelming ego, coupled with feminine vanity.'

Tilden squared up against Gerald Patterson on 3 July 1920. At the time, Patterson, an Australian, was not only the defending Wimbledon champion but also a Davis Cup hero and the top player in the world. Others assumed, and he probably assumed, that he would walk away with the title. Blessed with a strong serve and a powerful forehand offset a tad by a relatively weak backhand, Patterson was accustomed to playing offensively, taking the game to opponents and imposing himself on them. We have already noted that Tilden liked to play to his opponents' strength in order to open up their weakness. He opted for this favoured stratagem now, but, initially at least, it did not bear fruit. The Australian champion romped through the first set 6–2 and the reaction elicited from Tilden was a telling theme of his career. He had invited an actress friend, Peggy Wood, and, having lost the first set so comprehensively, he nodded at her with a confident expression, for all the world as though he, not his opponent, had drawn first blood. This was Tilden personified. Losing, yet devoid of self-doubt, utterly convinced of the inevitability of his own ultimate victory. His display of confidence flummoxed Miss Wood, who could see no reason for it. Yet, she testified to Frank Deford, as soon as he had produced this expression, 'Bill proceeded to play.'

Thereafter the tables were turned, Patterson's winners became errors and Tilden took control. As he had emphasised in his book *The Art of Tennis*, 'The primary object in match tennis is to break up the other man's game.' That is what Tilden had done: played to Patterson's strength, extracted his best to a point beyond which it could be sustained, and left him with only the thin gruel of his weaker side on which to fall back. Tilden marched triumphantly through the next three sets for the loss of only nine games, 6–2, 6–3, 6–4. For the next six years, Tilden lost no major match and he dominated his sport in a way probably unsurpassed by any competitor in any sport at any time.

Two months after his triumph at Wimbledon, Tilden came up against 'Little' Bill Johnston, his fellow American, whom most tennis aficionados had thought would be in his place at Wimbledon. The occasion was the final of the US Championships, on grass at Forest Hills. 'Little' Bill was enthusiastically supported

by a legion of fans who firmly expected him to worst Tilden.
The pattern was not the usual. Tilden started strongly, deploying to full advantage the more offensive backhand that he had
so painstakingly cultivated. He took the first set 6–1, Johnston
fought back with effective lobs and won the second by the same
margin. Play was of a high quality as the two Americans locked
horns and plotted to establish ascendancy. Tilden won the third
set 7–5 but, squandering an advantage in the fourth set, he lost it
by the same margin. Interrupted briefly by the scary and surreal
experience of witnessing a plane crash nearby, the two Bills perse-
vered. Tilden, serving his cannonballs with great accuracy, was
the more assured with his own delivery. Classically, he kept up
the pressure and broke serve to enable him to close out the match
6–3 in the fifth set. Some had thought that the Wimbledon title
victory was a fluke and that 'Little' Bill would that day prove that
'Big' Bill was second best. In fact, the reverse happened. With his
second Slam in the bag, Tilden was now unarguably the world's
finest player.

Preparation for Wimbledon in 1921 was as far from ideal as
could be imagined. If anything, he had overplayed, competing
almost unremittingly over the previous year, travelling and playing, and having to undergo an operation to remove boils just
after he had won the Paris World Hard Court Championships.
Exhausted, on arriving in London, he went to a nursing home
to recuperate. Tilden had vociferously objected to the challenge
round system whereby the title holder did not compete but
received a bye to the following year's final to face the winner of
the previous rounds of the tournament. Enforced idleness was a
mixed blessing. It meant that Tilden could rest. Yet it also meant
that he was desperately short of match practice – or, indeed, any
meaningful practice – before having to fight, through the sudden
death challenge of one match, to retain his title.

To the evident satisfaction of the crowd, Brian Norton, a
diminutive but formidable South African, Tilden's opponent
in the final, raced to a two-sets-to-love lead, 6–4, 6–2. At this

point, the time and thought Tilden had devoted to gameplans, to rethinking his approach when it did not avail him, and to winning the psychological battle with his opponent, paid dividends. Abandoning the powerful drives which were his hallmark, Tilden took to chopping and slicing ball after ball after ball. Norton was fazed by Tilden's approach, which the crowd despised but which was entirely legitimate. Taking the pace off, applying spin, positioning the ball awkwardly, he gave the South African nothing off which to feed and took the next two sets 6–1, 6–0 to square the match at two sets apiece.

Curiously, at this point, when the momentum was running so strongly in Tilden's favour, Norton recovered himself, dug in, took a 5–4 lead and had two match points at 15–40 on Tilden's serve. On the second of these, something truly bizarre occurred. According to Deford, Tilden hit a ball that seemed destined to go way long and, realising this, ran to the net to shake hands with Norton, the winner. Norton thought that Tilden was coming to the net to volley and that his groundstroke must be going in. Norton hit the shot that was going out and hit the ball out himself, taking the score to deuce. Tilden then held serve, broke Norton's and held again to take the match 7–5 in the final set, winning the last Wimbledon final to be played at Worple Road. This was a legendary comeback and, later that year in the Davis Cup against Japan, Tilden provided a repeat performance of his Houdini act. Tilden was two sets down to Zenzo Shimizu and a break down at 5–4 in the third, the Japanese player serving for the match. Tilden fought back to take the set 7–5 and romped through the next two sets 6–2, 6–1. Tilden certainly enjoyed the drama of a tight match and made no secret of wanting to put on a show, but it is highly doubtful that he contrived to dice with death by going so perilously close to defeat. In any event, the irony is that the most extreme big-match example of a turnaround worked against Tilden. At Wimbledon, in 1927, aged thirty-four, Tilden faced the Frenchman Henri Cochet, almost nine years his junior. Firing on all cylinders, and keen to avoid a long, drawn-out struggle against the much younger man, Tilden took the first two sets 6–2, 6–4 and raced to a 5–1 lead in the third set. Astonishingly, the king of Spain and his retinue having arrived in the stands, Tilden completely lost concentration, delivered a spate of errors and lost six games in succession to drop the set 7–5. Cochet took the fourth and fifth sets 6–4, 6–3.

Tilden had always inveighed against the professionalisation of tennis and declared that it would not be for him. In the end, however, he succumbed. In 1931, at what for competitive sport was the staggeringly advanced age of thirty-eight, Tilden turned professional. At the time, the game was devoid of professional stars. In contrast to later decades, when the 'pros' were generally superior, the opposite was true in 1931. Tilden was not merely *a* star, but *the* star. He began by taking on and demolishing the pro champion, a Czech named Karel Koželuh, and did so time after time after time. Thereafter, Tilden played a series of ten matches against Vinnie Richards and won all of them. In September 1933, the former French Wimbledon champion Henri Cochet having just turned pro, Tilden trounced him in Paris in straight sets 6–3, 6–4, 6–2 in under an hour. Tilden was forty, Cochet just short of thirty-two. Subsequently, Tilden enjoyed victories over Ellsworth Vines, more than eighteen years his junior, and Don Budge, twenty-two years his junior.

It could not and it did not last. Astonishing though it had been that Tilden had blossomed late and remained at the pinnacle of world tennis for so long, a change of guard at the top was inevitable. Sure enough, those younger giants of the game established an ascendancy over Tilden. Still, as late as 1934, when Tilden was forty-one and Ellsworth Vines a mere twenty-three, Tilden won an estimated nineteen of their sixty matches that year. Even when he lost, he would often take a set or enjoy short spells of superiority and, crucially, the promoters knew that Tilden was the draw. The manner of his play, the shot-making, the tactical guile, the graceful movement, the showmanship – all these made Tilden matches box office material.

By all accounts, Tilden was a complex and, frankly, difficult man. He could be very generous, engaging, even warm. But he was stubborn, irascible, egotistical and determined to have his own way. He enjoyed the company of others, within limits – on his terms – but preferred his own. Throughout his career he had feuds with the United States Tennis Association. These covered a range of issues but to the fore was the USTA's determination to protect the amateur game and their insistence that Tilden, to retain that status, should not write for money about his sport, especially not about tournaments in which he was competing. Put bluntly, they never approved of Tilden and Tilden saw no reason to conceal his contempt for them.

For decades, Tilden enjoyed the company of much younger men, including minors, mixing with ball boys and coaching them in tennis. Therefore, although Tilden was not an 'out' gay man – after all, homosexual practice would remain illegal in California until 1976 – he was widely thought to be gay and rumours were often rife of his fraternisation with boys. Of what relevance is this, the reader might ask, to his prowess as a tennis player? It is relevant in one sense. Conscious that he was not like his peers, never having taken an interest in women, never mind getting hitched and having a family of his own, an awareness that his non-conformity met with disapproval almost certainly fuelled Tilden's desire to excel and his single-mindedness in ensuring that he did so.

Most modern observers would say that being gay is not a lifestyle choice but a matter of genetic predisposition. Today, it would be – and is – widely accepted and regarded less and less as a matter warranting comment, certainly not of a critical variety. In 1920s, 1930s and 1940s America, however, it was thought to be essentially abnormal, disgraceful, scandalous and a taboo subject for public discussion. Whether Tilden feared to proposition adults or simply preferred to engage sexually with minors, the fact is that he did the latter and eventually paid the price. In November 1946, he was arrested by Beverly Hills police and charged with 'contributing to the delinquency of a minor' for soliciting an underaged male, a fourteen-year-old boy whose genitals he was fondling in a car. He pleaded guilty, was sentenced to a year in prison and served seven and a half months. His strict parole conditions, prohibiting contact with minors, deprived him of the chance to earn income from tennis coaching. Just over two years after the first conviction, Tilden picked up a sixteen-year-old male hitchhiker and was arrested. He was subject to a probation sentence but, of much greater significance, Tilden was spurned and shunned by the tennis world.

To what extent Tilden was a prolific child abuser – which would rightly be condemned in any age – is uncertain. He undoubtedly broke the law and there is no doubt that he favoured the company of much younger men. However, there is also no doubt that he will have suffered from the homophobia of the society in which he lived. His homosexuality spurred him to prove that if he was different in one sense, he was also different – and better – in another, reigning in the tennis world for years without equal. The suspicion of him, and then his criminal convictions, damaged his reputation, made his final years miserable and lonely, and denied him the recognition that his sporting accomplishments deserve. For all that, the historical record speaks for itself. Tilden was the first great tennis champion. He bestrode the world stage as a colossus of the game for the best part of two decades. For as long as people write about the history of tennis and the pantheon of greats, the name Bill Tilden will always feature. As Tilden was not renowned for his modesty, we can safely say that he would both have welcomed that recognition and thought it only his due.

Chapter Two

Fred Perry

FRED PERRY IS the most successful British tennis player there has ever been. That is not a matter of opinion but a statement of fact. Beginning his trophy-winning sequence comparatively late at twenty-four, Perry won eight major titles – including the Australian Open, the French Open, Wimbledon (three times) and the US Open (three times) – as an amateur and two professional majors in the United States over a period of eight years. For seventy-six years, no British player after Perry won any of the majors until Andy Murray claimed the US Open title in 2012, and in 2013 he became the first Briton to take the Wimbledon crown since Perry had last won it, seventy-seven years earlier. On top of his Slam success, Perry four times led Britain to victory in the Davis Cup.

Born on 18 May 1909 in Stockport, Cheshire, Perry hailed from authentically working-class roots. His father, Samuel Perry, was a cotton spinner and a Labour activist in the north-west of England. There it was that Perry first went, according to his excellent biographer, Jon Henderson, to the junior school of Wallasey Grammar in Withens Lane, before moving aged nine to Brentham Garden Suburb in Ealing. As a child, Perry was keen on sports but turned to tennis relatively late. Young Fred enjoyed football, cricket and, above all, table tennis, in which he became world champion in 1929.

Just as Jack Kramer was later enthralled by the sight of elegantly attired men in the mid-1930s playing tennis, so Perry's fascination with the sport can be precisely traced. On holiday in Eastbourne, close to the tennis venue of Devonshire Park, in 1924, Perry was transfixed by the sight of young men in long, white trousers playing the sport. He also noticed the array of classy cars parked nearby, and the discovery that they were the property of the players provided an additional spur. He told his father of his excitement and Sam Perry promptly bought him a racket for five shillings. Perry would thereafter practise for hour after hour after hour both on court and against a wall at home. He loved it. He was hooked. He aspired not merely to be good, even excellent, but to be the best.

Initially, Perry played at the Brentham Institute and later at the Herga Club. Unlike most, though not all, of his fellow all-time greats, Perry did not enjoy an illustrious career in the junior ranks. After all, he started late – at least five, possibly nearer to ten years later than many other champions. He competed in some junior tournaments but his only notable success was a victory in the junior doubles at the Middlesex Championships in 1926. From his early days, of much greater interest than his prowess as a performer is the glimpse we obtain of the mores of the tennis establishment and of the character trait of stubborn non-conformity which was never far from the surface throughout Fred Perry's career. As a child, Perry went to the Queen's Club in London for a schools tournament. Henderson records Perry senior's account of young Fred's experience. Asked by an official whether he was from Eton, Marlborough, Harrow or Repton, Perry answered, 'Ealing County School.' The official, clearly a pompous twit and, it seems, a snob, replied, 'Never heard of it. Where is it?' To which Perry replied, factually, 'At Ealing.' Told that there was no allocated changing room for him, Perry responded matter-of-factly, 'Never mind, I can change on the floor.'

At the same tournament, Perry saw that the dressing room supervisor was a Mr Jenkins, a Brentham Club member known to him. Unsurprisingly and unexceptionably, he greeted the man as 'Mr Jenkins', only to be told sniffily, 'We don't address attendants like that here.' Splendidly, Perry replied that he had known Jenkins longer than he had known the Queen's Club and would address the man as he thought fit. In his own words, 'I was a determined young cuss even then and was very conscious that I was regarded as being from the wrong side of the tracks.' It was not that Perry sought to flaunt his difference from the others. Rather, he merely wanted to be himself. As he put it, 'I made up my mind that I wasn't going to let people tell me what to do or order me about. If they said "We would rather you didn't do that", there was no problem; but if they gave me an outright prohibition then I would deliberately find a way around it.' On his own admission, he was 'bloody-minded'. In his autobiography, published in 1984, Perry declares that at least some of the British tennis establishment looked down on him as a 'hot-headed, outspoken, tearaway rebel'.

His undistinguished career as a junior was doubtless attributable in large measure to the fact, already mentioned, that Perry took up the game much later than many of his contemporaries. Yet his progress early on was not helped, and was almost certainly hindered, by his lack of height. As was to be unconsciously replicated by the great American Don Budge just after him, Perry had a late growth spurt. At nineteen, he stood at only 5ft 3in., but he shot up nine inches to 6ft by the age of twenty-one.

Just at the time that Perry was growing physically, so he worked to grow his game, specifically by developing more penetrating strokes that would pressurise opponents, create chances and enable him to finish points in his favour. The forehand was his signature shot, his terminator, his lethal weapon, as it has long been and continues to be for so many great champions.

Fred's father, Sam, went to the All England Club one day to observe his son's practice session. Perry had been advised by Pop Summers but was now working regularly with a man who was to be a lifelong friend and the Voice of Wimbledon for decades, the coach turned commentator Dan Maskell. Henderson tells us that when the session had finished, Perry senior asked Maskell his opinion of Fred as a player. He told Maskell, 'He seems determined to take this game seriously. Do you think I should give him a year?' Maskell replied, 'All I can tell you, Mr Perry, is that Fred is the most promising player I've ever seen. He seems to have exactly the right attitude to the game and is prepared to do whatever it takes to succeed.'

These were far more than comforting words to a parent ambitious for his son. Maskell rated him and, critically, he did so not on the relatively superficial basis that he had one good shot or another. Rather, Maskell was making a character assessment and, from what we will observe in Perry's subsequent career, a very shrewd character assessment at that. Maskell declared of Perry, 'From the first I could see that he was single-minded ... he was a stubborn and sometimes truculent character who believed totally in his own ability.' Maskell also thought that Perry had guts, character and vision.

Pop Summers continued to advise on Perry's forehand, encouraging him to make it a more forcing shot, which Perry took on the rise either to finish a point or to approach the net. Refining a stroke, in this case by consciously taking it earlier, is not the work of an afternoon or even a week. It can take months of assiduous and focused practice. This was certainly the case with Perry. In 1929 he spent approximately five and a half months working on taking the forehand on the rise, thereby attacking the ball, denying his opponent time, and giving him the chance to dominate play. Whilst Summers had urged Perry to develop his forehand, Dan Maskell worked with Perry to bolster his backhand. It was not chronically weak but it was not the source of winners and was essentially a defensive stroke, ordinarily hit with slice. Maskell aimed to bring the shot up to standard not by forcing Perry to abandon the slice for a flat or topspin drive but by helping Perry to deploy the stroke more imaginatively, enabling him to use it to manoeuvre an opponent out of position and to set up a chance for Perry to unleash his preferred weapon, the forehand.

So, by the age of twenty-one, Perry was 6ft tall, a slim man of athletic build with extremely well-developed ball sense, a competent albeit not a ferocious service, adequate volleys, an unorthodox but effective forehand, sound footwork and an insatiable desire to win. That obviously sufficed to advance Perry to the fringes of the top class but definitive membership of that class would require more. Perry had by now been world table tennis champion. There was nothing left for him to achieve in that sport and all efforts, physical and mental, were now to be focused upon the improvement of his tennis. At Wimbledon in 1929, Perry qualified for the tournament and progressed through two rounds before losing to his fellow Briton John Olliff in four sets. Watching the defeat closely, Pop Summers decided that Perry's forehand, already his best stroke, required greater potency. This meant that Perry must step in, take the ball earlier and attack. It was one Sunday evening, after months of remorseless practice, that Perry felt everything gelled on the shot and that he had made an important advance.

The work involved in developing a new shot from scratch, or refining an existing stroke so that it yields better results, can be rewarding and, at times, fun. Yet even for a passionate enthusiast for his sport, which Perry undoubtedly was, it can also be lonely, frustrating, monotonous, at times even soul-destroying. Perry did the work because he knew he had to do it. The reason was simple enough. As he candidly acknowledged, 'I never could abide coming second. If I lost a table tennis match I was very upset for a couple of days and was so embarrassed that I would stay away from my friends. If I lost a tennis match, it was the end of the world.'

At the British Hard Court Championships in Bournemouth in 1930, Perry reached the final for the first time. His opponent was the then British number one, Bunny Austin. Perry lost in five sets but only after failing to convert a match point. It was no comfort to Perry, who had been the underdog, when people told him how well he had done to get that far, how splendid a fight he had put up and so on. To Perry it was painful to lose any match. To lose when he was a point from winning was insufferable. This was something he 'just couldn't stomach'. Winning would have been a career breakthrough – taking the title and overcoming his higher ranked Brit. Paradoxically, Pop Summers, his dedicated advisor who truly believed in Perry, was much more philosophical. He told a downcast Perry: 'I'm glad you lost that match. It would have come too early for you. The public would have been expecting something brilliant every time you came on court. It will also keep the press off your back. I think you'll be ready by the end of the year.' In fact, a big victory was to come somewhat sooner.

At Wimbledon in 1930, Perry progressed to the third round, where he met an Italian baron and veteran airman from World War I, Umberto De Morpurgo. At the time, the Italian was ranked fourth in the world behind Bill Tilden, Henri Cochet and Jean Borotra and was seeded seventh in the championships. Morpurgo was a formidable competitor with an impressive forehand and, though he lacked a striking net game, observers thought Perry's prospects were slim. Predictably, Perry fell behind 5–1 but he continued to go for forcing deep groundstrokes and to rush the net, helping him to save a set point, reverse his two breaks of service deficit and to claim the opening set 10–8.

A substantial crowd began to gather around Court 3 and, fortuitously for Perry, it included an LTA selection committee which was due to decide on the remaining place in a four-person team to tour the US and South America. Perry lost the second set 6–4 but raced through the third and fourth sets 6–1, 6–2 to achieve a major upset.

Naturally, Perry was delighted with his victory and, equally naturally, his proud father was one of those who came to the dressing room to congratulate him. Perhaps less naturally, another person in the changing room, described by Perry as 'an official' – whether of the LTA or the All England Club, we know not – was overheard by Sam Perry saying, 'Don't be surprised if you play terribly badly in the next match. You are bound to suffer a reaction.' Sam Perry, in a masterly understatement, said, 'It seemed to me undesirable to dampen confidence thus. Why not let a youngster carry on with faith in himself? If the reaction comes, then there is time to offer him consolation.' Of course, the intervention might have been well-intentioned but it came across as spiteful. It is one thing to say, 'Stay grounded. Take each match as it comes. Don't be disappointed if this triumph doesn't produce lift-off in your career straightaway.' It's quite another to say, to all intents and purposes, 'Your next match will be ghastly.' Anyway, Perry had the last laugh. Although he did lose in the fourth round to Dr Colin Gregory, a Davis Cup player, it was not because he played badly. At that stage, Gregory was better. More important was that Fred secured that last place in the touring team, achieving recognition and the opportunity for international experience.

In 1931, Perry won the Eastern Grass Court Championships in the United States. Thereafter, he beat seven of the top ten Americans without managing to win another tournament and in the course of a string of relative disappointments, Perry lost no fewer than four times to the emerging giant of the game, the tall and powerful American Ellsworth Vines.

In 1932, at the US Championships, Perry succumbed in five sets to Sidney Wood, having led two sets to love. It was no disgrace: Wood had won the Wimbledon singles the previous year and remained a top-flight competitor. Yet there was no concealing the fact that it was a bitter blow. The occasion – a major event – and the opportunity – to defeat a top player – would themselves have rendered it a big enough disappointment. What made it worse – more painful, but ultimately beneficial – was that it was the third match in three months that he lost in five sets.

Of course, it is in the reaction to a defeat or other setback that one can find the character of a competitor. Perry was mortified but he did not wallow in misery or merely resolve in a general sense to do better next time. Rather, he deduced something from these failures and resolved to act upon his deduction.

In short, he was failing to come on strong in the closing stages of tight matches. One way to maximise his chance of doing so in future would be to ensure that he was fitter than his opponent. 'So,' says Perry, 'I made up my mind that when I got back home from America I would set about making myself the fittest tennis player around.' His assessment was that in terms of the quality of his play he was at a level whereby no one was likely to take three sets in succession from him. He would win at least one, preferably the first so he had 'something to play with', and any opponent would be obliged to go four or five sets in order to beat him.

These days, each of the top players has a retinue, small or large, including coach, manager, agent and, very importantly, fitness trainer or dietician or both. All train hard but usually in conditions of closely guarded secrecy so that rivals don't know quite what they are doing. Perry's approach was different but both original and effective. He trained with Tom Whittaker, the Arsenal trainer, and the Arsenal team. Whatever they did together, it must have helped Perry. Already nimble-footed, he became still sharper and, of vital importance, his endurance improved. Perry knew that he was doing the right thing, though it was at the time unusual if not altogether novel to try to become supreme by being fitter than opponents. It is almost as if it was thought not to be the done thing – 'It's a jolly poor show if a chap is trying to get the upper hand by outlasting another chap rather than by a display of languid brilliance alone.'

Perry declared that tennis had always been something of an intellectual exercise. Now he wanted 'to make it a physical test, too'. He maintained that working with Arsenal 'put a lot of power' into him and that in big matches over four and five sets, 'I could just go on running', Henderson reports him saying. That was his own assessment, but at least as revealing is the verdict of others, most notably his contemporaries. Bunny Austin asked rhetorically whether anyone ever saw Perry unable to reach a dropshot or a lob over his head. His analysis, reported by Henderson, was that Perry never seemed to be running especially fast, 'but without apparent movement he is everywhere in the court at once'. George Lott, a distinguished American contemporary of Perry, reeled off a lengthy list of his great attributes, including his 'stamina, quickness and speed'. Indeed, referring to a prodigious five-set Davis Cup rubber between Perry and Cochet, Lott insisted that Perry was simply stronger and fitter. Indeed, as if to emphasise his conviction as to Perry's physical prowess, Lott's 1972 published essay on Perry, highlighted by Henderson, described him as 'the finest athlete I ever saw'.

Bill Tilden, a caustic and frequently provocative observer of events and of his competitors, was aghast at Perry's stroke-making technique, which he considered fundamentally wrong, but he was unstinting in his praise of Perry's strength and fitness, attributing his success to the strength in his right wrist, calling it 'strong as iron and abnormally supple'.

Finally, on the subject of Perry's condition, Robert Minton, in his *History of Forest Hills*, praised his speed and argued that he won his matches 'by outlasting his opponents'. 'His physical condition', said Minton, 'was second to none.'

Jon Henderson observes that 'the speed with which Perry reached the pinnacle of tennis was remarkable, even at a time when the number of players competing seriously was a fraction of today's figure'. He adds, 'Rarely can aptitude and commitment have been combined in such measure in one person.' Indeed they were. He had terrific ball sense, great hands, boundless energy and an indomitable determination to succeed. In particular, a determination, even a thirst, to do whatever was necessary to succeed. Enhanced playing skill, taking the ball early and bossing about his opponents, coupled with training to ensure he was the fittest player in the game, were the keys to his success. At the time of writing, there seems to be an almost uncanny parallel with Britain's Andy Murray, who has developed a more attacking style of play, sharply increased his upper body strength and acquired a physical endurance equal or superior to that of any of his rivals.

In 1933, despite improvements to his play and fitness, Perry performed relatively poorly in South Africa and at Wimbledon, where he crashed out to Norman Farquharson in the second round. That was his worst performance at the All England Club tournament. Yet within weeks he was to make huge strides for himself and for his country. Perry was the driving force of the British Davis Cup team which won the competition after a 21-year trophy drought. After beating Australia at Wimbledon and the USA in the Inter-Zone final in Paris, Perry was vital to success in the challenge round against France. Perry played two singles rubbers and won both of them. In a pulsating encounter with Henri Cochet – referenced earlier in this chapter – Perry prevailed in five sets, 8–10, 6–4, 8–6, 3–6, 6–1. In that contest, the sheer physical superiority of Perry over Cochet – the Frenchman being more than seven years older – was key. Then, in the decisive fifth match when the tie stood at two matches apiece, Perry overcame André Merlin in four sets, 4–6, 8–6, 6–2, 7–5. Success for his country was matched by the satisfaction of success for himself when Perry took the US Championship title, his first Slam victory. It was quite a tussle, Perry falling behind two sets to one but romping though the last two sets 6–0, 6–1 against the Australian Jack Crawford.

  1934 was to prove an *annus mirabilis* for Perry. Buoyed by his success in the Davis Cup and at the US Championship the previous autumn, it was as though Perry now went up a gear. He won the Australian Championship. He won the British Hard Courts title for the third successive year. In the French Championship quarter-finals, however, he damaged an ankle against his versatile Italian adversary, Giorgio de Stefani and, though he refused to default, was soundly beaten.

  Still worried about the ankle, Perry nevertheless competed at Wimbledon, where in the third round his opponent was the Czech Roderich Menzel. Perry lost the first set 6–0 and also trailed by two sets to one. We are indebted to Perry's biographer for a revealing account of what followed. His trainer, Hugh Dempster, had counselled that Perry should run for the first wide ball on his forehand side because if the ankle was to succumb it would do so one way or another and it was as well to put the matter to the test. In fact, Perry had resisted moving wide on his forehand but had thereby hampered his effectiveness. Eventually, a frustrated Dempster sent Perry a note with a blunt instruction: 'Either you go for the wide ones or I'll pull you off court.' Duly emboldened, Perry heeded the instruction, no injury was sustained, Perry took the last two sets and had no further concerns about his ankle. After a straight-sets defeat of Australian Adrian Quist, Perry beat George Lott in four sets in the quarter-finals. In the semi-finals, Perry came though an exacting five-set duel with the American Sidney Wood, triumphing 6–3, 3–6, 7–5, 5–7, 6–3. In the final, Perry faced Jack Crawford, the popular Australian he had beaten in five sets to win the US title – his first 'major' – and in three sets to win the Australian final in January of that year. This time, as in the contest in Australia, Perry was dominant, brushing aside Crawford with ruthless efficiency to claim his first Wimbledon title in one hour and ten minutes. The score was 6–3, 6–0, 7–5, Perry conceding one game less than in the battle on Crawford's home turf. Perry was the first Englishman to win Wimbledon in twenty-five years and he was justifiably proud of his efforts, as he played supremely well. Perry said, 'I don't think I have played better and I don't think I ever will again.'

George Lott was positively poetic in testifying to the quality of the Perry performance. 'On that particular day, in that particular match, I had seen the perfectly conditioned athlete play the perfect match … he reached the peak of his effectiveness.' Lott was not the only observer to wax lyrical about the majesty of Perry's performance on the All England Club's turf. Reporter Ferdinand Kuhn said of the triumph: 'Perry was always the complete master. He didn't make a half-dozen bad shots in the whole match. He was lithe as a panther, always holding the opponent in check and beating Crawford at his own cool, courteous game.'

Even though Perry was the first Briton to win the men's singles for a quarter of a century, Crawford received greater applause from the crowd. Sure enough, Crawford was very well-liked, possessed of a pleasing personality and regarded as a gentleman. Yet there is no escaping that it was not merely a matter of pro-Crawford sentiment but of some discomfort with, even disapproval of, Perry himself. A little incident, recorded both by Perry and by Henderson

in his biography, following his 1934 Wimbledon victory is revealing. Perry was bathing following his triumph. He heard in the
dressing room the voice of a committee member of the All England
Club, Brame Hillyard, talking to Crawford. 'Congratulations,'
said Hillyard. 'This was one day when the best man didn't win.'
Hillyard presented Crawford with a bottle of champagne. When
Perry emerged from the bath, he saw draped over the back of his
seat an honorary All England Club member's tie, the traditional
prize or acknowledgement to mark success in the championship.
Hillyard had not so much as troubled to present it to the winner
but, impersonally and cruelly, left it without a word. Perry's
reaction at the time was one of intense anger: he insisted on
an apology as a condition of him playing in the Davis Cup and that
apology was eventually, apparently grudgingly, provided. However,
the incident also understandably reminded him of so many earlier
experiences. As he put it, 'All my paranoia about the old-school-tie
brigade surfaced with a vengeance.'

Jack Kramer later said that no champion in any sport had
ever looked more like a champion than Fred Perry – presence,
authority, style and will combined to make him cut a formidable
figure. Yet, impressive champion though he was, he had not won
the affections either of the British tennis establishment or, more
widely, of the sports fans in his homeland. John R. Tunis, in an
article for *Esquire* magazine at the time, explained the froideur
towards Perry as a manifestation of Wimbledon snobbery.

> The members of that Holy of Holies ... seem to resent the fact
> that a poor boy without a Varsity background should have yanked
> himself to the front – even though in the process he yanked England
> back into the tennis from which she had been absent since 1909.
> Extraordinary people.

There is a danger in overanalysis. When all is said and done, snobbery is prejudice. A prejudice whose adherents believe that they
are superior because of who their parents are, which school they

attended, who they married, where they live etc. The sadness, almost the comic absurdity of it, is that the snobbery directed against Perry was based on others' notion that their status was superior to his. Of course, the snobs would rarely admit to quite such a base and loathsome prejudice. Rather, they would dress it up by claiming that Perry was cocky, abrasive, difficult etc., all of which may have been true and exacerbated their hostility but it will not have been its primary cause. In truth, as Perry observed, the establishment 'had never really seen an Englishman of this era who didn't like to lose'.

On his own admission, Perry hated losing, wasn't a particularly good loser, and strove to avoid losing at all times. In short, surprise of all surprises (not), as a competitive sportsman, Perry played to win. He battled tenaciously on the court and took the most elaborate, albeit legitimate, precautions off it. For example, he would not drive on the day of a match if at all avoidable as he thought it impaired his vision. He would conscientiously avoid shaking hands before playing, believing that it would undermine his feel and touch in the handling of the racket. He was not above modest gamesmanship before and during matches, dressing unexpectedly, knocking up with one racket, playing the match with another, driving opponents to distraction, calling out 'very clevah' when they hit a winning shot against him. Perry wanted to win and fought like an alley cat, as Pancho Gonzales was later to do, to ensure that he came out on top. 'Well,' said Perry, 'I don't think this was an approach generally followed in England at the time. It was un-English. It wasn't done, old bean. Not in tennis, anyway.'

There is no denying that, far from being relaxed about the snooty and condescending treatment he received, Perry was irritated by it. His autobiography, published fifty years after his first Wimbledon triumph, leaves readers in no doubt on that score. Yet, though it irritated him, Perry did not allow the snobbery to discourage or derail him, albeit it was certainly a pull-factor in attracting him eventually to live in the United States. In 1934, however, demonstrably scaling new heights, Perry ploughed on, proving for all to see his sheer worth as a competitive player.

A mere three weeks after his success at Wimbledon, Perry led Britain in the successful defence of their Davis Cup trophy. The challenge round at Wimbledon took place against the United States. Perry had two singles rubbers to play and he won both. The tussle with Sydney Wood was a five-setter, Perry coming from two sets to one down to win 6–1, 4–6, 5–7, 6–0, 6–3. His other match was against Frank Shields, whom Perry overcame in four sets, but it was a hard-fought affair towards the end, as the scoreline demonstrates. Perry was victorious: 6–4, 4–6, 6–2, 15–13.

From success for Britain in the Davis Cup, Perry achieved further glory at the US Championships in Forest Hills in September, claiming his fifth Grand Slam title. He cantered through the first five rounds to the semi-final without dropping a set against any of his American opponents and sacrificing a mere thirty games in the process, an average of only six games per match. In the semi-finals he dropped one set, and then he had an altogether more nerve-racking experience in the final. Having led Wilmer Allison by two sets to love, he dropped the next two sets heavily but squeaked home 8–6 in the final set.

In 1935, Perry claimed his first and only French Championship title. His progress through the draw after losing the first set in his opening match was seamless until the final. There, he met and conquered the German aristocrat Baron Gottfried von Cramm in four sets: 6–3, 3–6, 6–1, 6–3. Von Cramm was a fine player whom Perry nevertheless overwhelmingly dominated over the years but to whom he did lose in the French final in five sets the following year, 1936. At Wimbledon in 1935, Perry successfully defended his crown, defeating Crawford in four sets in the semi-final and von Cramm 6–2, 6–4, 6–4 in the final, bringing the total of Slam singles titles to six. In Australia and the US Championships, Perry fell in the final and the semi-final respectively to Crawford and Allison. Disappointing though this was for him, he had won two of the four majors that year and he triumphed again as the leading player in the British team which held on to the Davis Cup. Once again, the United States were the opponents in the challenge round and Perry looked after business for Britain to great effect. He defeated the rising American star, Don Budge, in four sets 6–0, 6–8, 6–3, 6–4. In his second singles match, he beat Wilmer Allison in four sets 4–6, 6–4, 7–5, 6–3.

1936, the final year of Perry's amateur career, was outstanding. He did not play in the Australian Championship, having won it in 1934 and been runner-up in 1935. In Paris, at the French Championship, he was defeated in a five-set final by von Cramm. Wimbledon and the US Championship at Forest Hills were his preferred stages and he performed exquisitely on each of them. At Wimbledon he sacrificed only one set in the entire tournament – to Don Budge in the semi-final – and trounced von Cramm 6–1, 6–1, 6–0 in the final. The match took less than forty-five minutes, was the speediest of the twentieth century and the second short-est of all time. Von Cramm had a groin injury – as Perry had discovered from the masseur who serviced them both – making it difficult for him to move wide on the forehand. Armed with this insider knowledge, Perry exploited it ruthlessly. This was Perry's third successive Wimbledon crown and his seventh major title.

Later that month, Perry heroically led the charge against the Australians in the challenge round of the Davis Cup. Once again, Britain was victorious – substantially due to Perry's match-winning prowess on big occasions. On the All England Club turf, Perry won both of his singles rubbers, defeating Adrian Quist in four sets 6–1, 4–6, 7–5, 6–2 and Jack Crawford with consummate ease, romp-ing home 6–2, 6–3, 6–3. The icing on the cake of his great year was victory in the US Championship. En route to the final Perry dropped only two sets, but faced an increasingly formidable oppo-nent in the final in the shape of Don Budge. It was hot and humid. Budge got off to a cracking start, taking the first set 6–2. Midway through the second set, the heavens opened and rain stopped play for thirty minutes. On resumption, Perry won the second and third sets 6–2, 8–6. In his autobiography, Perry tells us: 'Budge's tongue was hanging out; I knew I had him going.' The umpire, to Perry's fury, announced a ten-minute break. Perry remonstrated that such a break should be taken at the end of the third set only if there had been no earlier interruption, but his protest was to no avail. Perry lost the fourth set 6–1. Budge served for the match at 5–3 in the final set but Perry prevailed 10–8, later admitting that his winning serve on match point might have been delivered before Budge was ready. It was the eighth Slam for Perry and, as it proved, a triumphant finale to his amateur career.

For years, there had been speculation as to whether and, if so, when Perry would turn professional. Understandably, Perry wanted to be and remain the best in the amateur game for a goodly period, accumulating titles and playing for his country in the Davis Cup. He was spectacularly successful in his mission.

Yet the lure of big money was enticing. It would be, and had been, for many top players for years. For Perry, there were three attractions. First, he was not a man of means and the chance to make himself financially secure was too good to miss. Secondly, he wanted to pit himself against the best of the professionals. Thirdly, most of the professional matches were in the US, a country Perry had long admired and where he was not subject to the stuffiness of the British tennis establishment.

Ultimately, those three attractions were decisive for Perry and he turned professional at the end of 1936. Very soon he was pitted against Ellsworth Vines, with whom he played four tours. In 1937, they competed in the States sixty-one times, Vines prevailing 32–29. In England, they squared up to each other nine times, Perry winning six of them. In 1938, their major tour was won by Vines, forty-nine matches to thirty-five, the shorter English tour resulting in a tie of four victories apiece. In 1939, when Budge turned professional, he beat Perry twenty-eight matches to eight. To add to his eight majors as an amateur, Perry won the US Pro title twice – in 1938 and 1941.

Just how good was Perry? Jack Kramer, writing in 1979, put Perry in the premier league of champions, behind Vines and Budge, but suggested, perhaps mischievously, both that Vines 'carried' Perry on tour to keep the crowds interested and that Perry was given to throwing matches from time to time. Perry disputes both claims and I can find no independent corroboration of Kramer's verdict. Moreover, Kramer makes no attempt to disguise his dislike of Perry, denouncing his gamesmanship, alleged selfishness, and betrayal of the players in condemning the 1973 Wimbledon boycott. The only significant point is that, for all his personal dislike, Kramer acknowledges that Perry was a great champion.

So too does Bill Tilden. In a much-quoted and typically acerbic observation, Tilden said he often had difficulty deciding whether Perry was 'the worst best player or the best worst player,' and wondered at his ability to 'hit every shot wrong' and yet still notch up triumphs and trophies. Tilden concluded that he must have been one of the greats. 'You don't go on winning all the tournaments unless you are.'

Perry is candid about his qualities. He tells us in his autobiography that he was not the most gifted player 'by a long stretch'. Yet he had great strengths – that running forehand foremost amongst them – and deployed them ruthlessly. Above all, he had phenomenal determination, will to win and staying power. He was probably the most nakedly competitive player anyone had ever seen – matched in the Open era perhaps by a Connors, a Borg, a Lendl or a Nadal – and, he says, 'I gave no quarter.' Perry goes on: 'I never believed in taking prisoners on a tennis court. I was a great believer in getting my nose in front and making sure the other fellow's nose didn't catch up.'

Of course, as Perry himself states, quite apart from the advances in racket technology and string manufacture which help today's players, some rules have changed too. For example, in his day, at least one foot had to be on the ground when serving. That is not so now. This is one reason why comparisons across eras are difficult, though not necessarily impossible. The point Perry is at pains to make is that 'whatever the rules and whatever the era, a champion earns his fame because he possesses that extra something the other fellow doesn't'.

I second that proposition.

Chapter Three

Don Budge

IN THE GALLERY of tennis greats, the place of Don Budge is assured. He was the first male player to win the Grand Slam of Australian, French, Wimbledon and US titles – that is to say, all four in one year – and, three-quarters of a century later, he remains the only American to achieve that remarkable feat. In total, Budge won ten majors, of which six were Grand Slam titles and four were Pro Slams, the latter notched up on three different surfaces. He topped the sport first as an amateur and then as a professional, leading the pack for a total of five years.

Born in Oakland, California on 13 June 1915, Budge was the son of a Scottish immigrant and a former footballer. As a child, Budge junior played several different sports before turning to tennis. Until the age of eighteen, Budge was not tall – a mere 5ft 6.5in. Then, in one year, he grew six inches. When young and small, he learned to win by the simple but important expedient of repeatedly getting the ball back until his opponent broke down. His predecessor as world number one, Ellsworth Vines, in his book *Tennis: Myth and Method*, observed of Budge that 'once he started growing and adding power to his consistency he became virtually unbeatable – and consistency was to be the hallmark of his game'. Tall, slim and athletic, Budge developed a very powerful service and, such was his progress as a player that, having studied at the University of California in 1933, he soon left to play tennis with the US Davis Cup auxiliary team. Initially, Budge was far superior in performing on hard courts, to which he had become thoroughly attuned in California, and he found grass a much more difficult surface on which to excel.

Supported by a good coach and assiduous practice, Budge made big strides such that he could approach Wimbledon in 1937, aged twenty-two, with justified confidence. Seeded first, whilst Baron Gottfried von Cramm was seeded second, Budge motored through the draw without dropping a set until he reached the semi-final. There, he took on Frank Parker, to whom he lost the first set before coming through in four sets 2–6, 6–4, 6–4, 6–1. Von Cramm prevailed in a challenging four-set semi-final encounter against Jack Crawford to book his place in the final. Budge dominated his opponent in that contest, winning in straight sets 6–3, 6–4, 6–2. Then, in that year's Davis Cup, Budge again prevailed over von Cramm in the decisive rubber of the tie, but this time it was a vastly tighter affair as Budge clawed his way back from a two-set deficit to win 6–8, 5–7, 6–4, 6–2, 8–6. He went on to lead his country to success in the challenge round against Great Britain.

So 1937 was a successful year for Budge. He had been invited to turn professional but had decided to remain an amateur, not least out of a debt of gratitude to the game and to those who had helped him and his country, for whom he wished to perform in the Davis Cup, which was at the time an amateur-only competition. Budge decided that he would pace himself in order to ensure that he peaked for the big tournaments. In Budge's words, 'the Grand Slam then occurred to me as something of an afterthought'.

That strategic vision of aiming to achieve peak form for the big tournaments was realised to perfection in 1938. Now aged twenty-three, Budge enjoyed a gloriously successful year: it was in 1938 that he won the Australian, French, Wimbledon and US Championships. In Australia, he won the final over John Bromwich in straight sets 6–4, 6–2, 6–1, taking less than an hour for the purpose. In the French, Budge apparently suffered from diarrhoea, an experience not only physically unpleasant but more than a tad unnerving, as it recurred during the course of the event. In the third round, Budge was taken to five sets by Yugoslav left-hander Francisco Kukuljevik. Then, in the final, life was altogether more straightforward as Budge beat a 6ft 4in. Czech, Roderich Menzel, a first-class clay-court player, 6–3, 6–2, 6–4 in less than an hour.

His performances at the Australian and French Opens had been impressive. At Wimbledon, however, Budge rose to new heights of dominance as he cruised through the tournament to take the title without losing a set. Curiously, Bud Collins reports, at the outset of the event, Budge was anxious to the point of being panicky about his form. This was because he was having trouble with his backhand, the shot that has come to be regarded as the most superlative in his repertoire. The truth is that he was undercutting it, rather than getting the lift on the ball which is the foundation of a truly attacking stroke. One day, at the All England Club, he saw an older woman playing tennis, noticed that she was hitting her backhand with topspin and instantly realised what he should be doing. He then made the necessary technical adjustment, struck the backhand forcefully with topspin and reaped the benefit. Budge then won his second successive Wimbledon title, beating Britain's Bunny Austin in the final for the sacrifice of only four games, 6–1, 6–0, 6–3. This triumph remains one of the most comprehensive victories in any major final in the history of the game. Years later, John Bromwich, beaten by Budge in the Davis Cup and elsewhere, described him as 'the greatest player I've ever seen or played against'.

At the US Open, Budge cantered through the draw, enjoying straight-sets wins over Welby Van Horn, Bob Kamrath, Charles Hare, Harry Hopman and Sidney Wood to reach the final against his pal and doubles partner Gene Mako, who had upset John Bromwich in the semi-final 6–1, 7–5, 6–4. To suggestions that it was a neat set-up for Budge, he replied pointedly, 'Gene was as likely to roll over for me as peace was to come in our time.' Mako did win the second set, only the fifth Budge lost in the four Slam tournaments that year. Budge was adamant that he did not chuck that set. He wanted the title and wanted it badly. Moreover, as he put it, 'I had too much respect and affection for Gene to treat him as if he were an inferior player who could be given a set for his troubles, rather like a condescending pat on the head.'

Stunning season though it was for Budge, he was not to remain undefeated. In the semi-final of the Pacific Southwest tournament at Los Angeles, Budge was beaten 7–5, 6–2, 5–7, 6–3 by Adrian Quist. That loss ended his 92-match, fourteen-tournament run, which dated from a January 1937 defeat by Bitsy Grant at Tampa.

In the quarter-final of the Pacific Coast tournament, Budge also lost 6–2, 5–7, 6–1 to Harry Hopman. Yet, for two years, Budge won when it mattered and in 1938, the stellar year of his career, he won six out of eight tournaments, clocking up a 43–2 win–loss record. Before he had even won the Grand Slam in the autumn of 1938, the year had already acquired a special character both for Budge and for the sport. In June, in winning the French Open, he had become the youngest man in history to win all four majors – Wimbledon and the US Open had been won the previous year – in his career. He did so two days before his twenty-third birthday. Three months later, to become the first winner of all four in a single year was the icing on Budge's amateur cake.

The Grand Slam in the bag, and success in the Davis Cup achieved, it was the logical next step for Budge to turn professional. In 1939, he was pitched against the two giants of the professional game, namely Ellsworth Vines and Fred Perry. Just as Bill Tilden and others had done, and others later entering the professional ranks were to do, Budge played substantial head-to-head series against his rivals. His tussle with Ellsworth Vines was close, Budge prevailing by twenty-two matches to seventeen. The record against Fred Perry was much more decisive, as Budge won twenty-eight matches to eight. Alongside these triumphs, Budge won two important professional tournaments: the French Pro Championship, where he overcame Vines, and the Wembley Pro tournament over Hans Nüsslein. In 1940, Budge competed in seven significant professional tournaments, winning four of them, including the most prestigious, the US Pro Championship, and this series of successes enabled him to retain his status as the world's top player. In 1941, he was the heavy victor in a substantial tour with Bill Tilden, though this tells us little of their respective merits, as Budge was in his mid-twenties and Tilden forty-eight. The following year, 1942, Budge played his last big tour, besting Bobby Riggs, Frank Kovacs, Fred Perry and Les Stoefen. At the US Pro, he trounced Riggs 6–2, 6–2, 6–2.

War service then interceded and it hampered Budge in more ways than one. First, he was by definition unable to play with any regularity or intensity, and that was bound to impair his competitive capacity, though of itself it need not do so permanently. Secondly, and this really did for him, in early 1943, Budge, undergoing an obstacle course, tore a muscle in his shoulder. In his book, *A Tennis Memoir*, he explained that the resultant scar tissue made the injury even more serious, although he was unable to obtain leave from his military duties to receive treatment for it until two years afterwards.

It seems clear that the injury permanently impaired Budge, not least by depriving him of some of the power in his strokes, which had previously enabled him to dominate opponents, playing and winning points on his own terms. In 1945, Budge lost a five-match series against Riggs, winning the first two encounters and losing the next three. Budge was shocked by this reverse, and his disappointment can only have been compounded in 1946 when, once again, he was worsted in a lengthy tour by Riggs, albeit by the tightest of margins of 24–22, and Riggs then rubbed in his new supremacy at the US Pro final in Forest Hills. Riggs then repeated the victory over Budge in the US Pro final in 1947, though on that occasion he required five sets to get the job done. Riggs was by then the world number one. There had been a changing of the guard at the top of the game. Riggs was only three years younger and he was now at his peak, Budge beyond it.

By 1947, Budge was thirty-two, an age when most players in the Open era are past their best, but this was not predictably the case in the 1930s, '40s, '50s or even '60s. Therefore, it seems probable that his relative decline was more attributable to injury

than to age. His difficulty post-1945 against Riggs was the more
acute because the latter was a formidable match player and tactician. Though he played within the rules, he was ruthless and that
ruthlessness was exemplified by his approach to playing Budge
– Jack Kramer said of the match that Riggs 'lobbed him to death'.

The lob tactic was effective on two fronts. Its persistence led
Budge to close less tightly on the net, thereby opening the way for
Riggs to pass him either down the line or cross-court. In addition,
the lobs themselves were often deep and required Budge to run back
to the baseline, thereby sacrificing the initiative and being worn
down at the same time. In other words, the impact was physical and
psychological, affording Riggs an edge that Budge could not counter.

Budge was not yet finished with the game by any means but he
had now been removed irrevocably from his perch. In 1949, he
reached the US Pro final and lost to Riggs, and four years later
in the same event he succumbed in the final to Pancho Gonzales.
Ironically, in his last year on the professional tour in 1954, Budge
enjoyed an Indian summer by defeating Gonzales, who was then
the leading player in the world.

The record of Don Budge demonstrates that he was a heavyweight champion. He won the Grand Slam. He won other majors.
He won the status of top player in the world. However, these facts
do not of themselves tell us why Budge was great or indeed how
great he was. For the beginning of an answer to those questions, we
need to consult other authorities. One such was Ellsworth Vines,
who preceded Budge as the world's top player, competed against
him dozens of times and saw him play other prominent players of
the era. Vines was clearly an admirer, believing him to be exceptional
in terms of technical competence, power and consistency. Vines was
glowingly complimentary on so many fronts. He insisted that Budge's
backhand was unmatched for power and freedom of motion. The
forehand, he judged, was 'more mechanical but equally consistent'.
Very importantly, Vines contended that Budge was 'universally
acknowledged as having the best service return', with the capacity
to take the ball on the rise. This enabled him either to destroy a

net-rusher by producing a return that passed or troubled him, or to put such a player out of his comfort zone by forcing him to stay back and therefore cede to Budge the potential to control the point, which, by virtue of his own formidable groundstrokes, he was generally able to do. Vines noted approvingly that Budge relied on 'controlled power and depth backed by amazing steadiness'. Interestingly, the steadiness, the consistency – the unwavering performance – was not just within a match but lasted a tournament, a tour, a season, or more. Again, Vines was a major authority on this point. He declared, 'I played fifty-nine matches against Budge on two Pro tours, and never saw him when he was off.' The same themes of power, supremacy and consistency feature in the assessment of Budge by others. Tennis analyst Julius Heldman, who observed Budge at his peak, said that 'untouchable was the right word to describe Don'. He added, 'He never allowed an opponent to get his teeth in the match, and his overwhelming power was not subject to bad streaks.'

It is striking that Vines went out of his way to highlight the excellence of the Budge forehand, which he admiringly described as 'the most underrated shot in the history of tennis'. He believes that it was 'overshadowed by his legendary backhand' and few players then, or indeed now, could boast a superior backhand to forehand. Vines thought it needed to be given its proper weight as a shot whose technique as practised by Budge was flawless. Moreover, he judged it to be a 'magnificent, forceful weapon' and a 'relentless bludgeon'. In his prime, between 1937 and 1942, Budge is thought to have imparted to the ball an average miles per hour speed that had not been equalled up to that time.

If Vines waxed lyrical about Budge's groundstrokes and service returns, Julius Heldman was mightily impressed by his service. As he put it, 'It was a great serve ... because the ball was so heavy, deep and well-placed.' Uncommonly, his second serve, according to Vines, was hit almost as hard as the first, and Budge was not prone to double faults.

Formidable service though Budge possessed, it was not his usual practice to serve and volley. Rather, he would be content to gain an advantage with the serve to be exploited from the back of the court with groundstrokes which either won the point for him or which he used to come to the net on very favourable terms. Indeed, Jack Kramer concluded that what made Budge so tough was that he usually did not serve and volley. Although the latter tactic can be highly effective, a player approaching the net immediately after his serve does offer a target for an effective return. Budge offered no such target. As Kramer put it, 'a baseliner with a strong serve and great groundstrokes poses a special problem. You cannot attack off his serve and yet he can get to the net with his groundstrokes.' An opponent of Budge did not even enjoy the compensation of being able to win points readily through net-rushing on his own delivery. Again, Kramer explains the problem simply. 'Budge returned service so surely and powerfully. It simply wasn't possible to follow serve to the net with any hope of winning.'

Kramer is a considerable authority on great players, not merely because he was one himself but because, over the course of forty years playing and watching the sport, he observed champions from Vines to Connors. In his memoir, Kramer suggests that in his day Vines was unplayable and surpassed everyone. However, he is quick to add that on the measure of overall performance – week in, week out; month in, month out; year in, year out – Budge was superior. Indeed, as late as 1979, Kramer said, 'Don is still the best player I ever saw.' His explanation of his thinking was that Budge 'owned the most perfect set of mechanics and he was the most consistent'. Expressing himself with characteristic bluntness, Kramer declared, 'I am not sure of much in this world, but I know it has been almost forty years since Don Budge reached his peak, and I know damn well we haven't seen his equal yet.' Kramer was emphatic that Budge had strong groundstrokes – including the best backhand of any player he had competed against or seen – good volleys, an excellent temperament and no obvious weakness. Although it is by no means conclusive as to the extent of his greatness, it is noteworthy that Budge split sets with Rod Laver as late as 1962. Budge was then forty-seven, seven years past retirement and nearer to twenty years since he had been at his peak. Laver was twenty-four and already a Grand Slam champion, though arguably he reached the height of his powers in the mid- to late 1960s. The significance of the encounter was that Budge could hold his own against the man widely regarded as the biggest star of the 1960s and, by some, as the greatest player of the Open era.

So, Kramer thought that Budge was the greatest player. On one level, Kramer's verdict is important as he was a contemporary witness. On the other hand, Kramer did not place Laver in the very first rank (i.e. top six) of champions and, writing at the time, he was unusual in reaching that conclusion. Moreover, even if Kramer was right about Budge in 1979 – a proposition open, as with almost everything in sport, to dispute – that does not tell us how he should be compared with champions from the 1980s onwards.

Writing in 1994, E. Digby Baltzell judged that Budge marginally edged Rod Laver at the top of the list of champions. More than two decades earlier, in 1971, Will Grimsby noted that Budge was considered by many 'to be foremost among the all-time greats'. Paul Metzler, who analysed ten of the all-time greats in 1969, concluded that Budge was the greatest player before 1945 and believed him to be surpassed only by Jack Kramer. In 1986, an American magazine, *Inside Tennis*, invited thirty-seven experts to pronounce on the top ten of all time. Twenty-five players in total were named and Budge ranked third behind Rod Laver and John McEnroe. In 1999, an Associated Press poll ranked Budge fifth behind Laver, Sampras, Tilden and Borg. In 2006, a group of experts was asked to seed the all-time greats and Budge was placed sixth behind Federer, Laver, Sampras, Borg and Tilden, but ahead of Kramer and McEnroe. As ever, then, there is no consensus as to Budge's overall ranking. Yet there is a consensus that he is amongst the greatest players ever to pick up a racket and he is regularly cited in the top ten, often in the top five. Almost sixty years after he retired, and nearly fifteen years since he passed away, it is a testament to the weapons he had and the success he attained that Budge is recognised as a towering figure in the sport which he loved.

Chapter Four

Jack Kramer

IN MY EARLY teens, I confess, only slightly shamefacedly, that I was ignorant of Jack Kramer's past prowess. I was playing at the Queen's Club one day with some older folks, including a self-made Polish businessman who was a friend. After our match, the Pole and I chatted about great players. All of a sudden, he mentioned Jack Kramer. I exclaimed, 'Jack Kramer, oh yes, he is the man who made and sold the Wilson Jack Kramer Pro Staff racket.' 'My dear John,' my friend patiently replied, 'sure, Kramer later sold rackets, promoted tennis and became a pundit but in the first place he was a great champion himself.' I had had no idea.

Of all the champions described in these pages, Jack Kramer enjoyed, as my friend had hinted, by far the most wide-ranging and multifaceted career. Put simply, he was a player, coach, official, promoter, director, players' representative and television commentator, but that bald little list of roles does not begin to describe the intensity, scale or significance of his involvement with and impact on the sport over four decades. As a champion player who performed differently to any predecessor and pioneered a new approach to the men's game, he was not only highly successful himself but of seminal importance to the development of the game. As an entrepreneurial promoter of professional tennis and a formidable advocate of Open tennis, and an end to the amateurist philosophy that had undermined the sport, he was arguably still more important. However, this book is not about the achievements of players off the court. It is specifically and exclusively about prowess and success on the court – tournaments won, rankings held and records set. These are the yardsticks by which, in common with every other player in this book, Jack Kramer must be assessed.

Born on 1 August 1921 in Las Vegas, Kramer played from childhood, competed from the 1930s to the early 1950s, became the number one player in the world and won a total of five major titles: three Grand Slams as an amateur, namely the US Open in 1946 and 1947 and Wimbledon in 1947, and two professional majors, the US Pro Championship in 1948 and the Wembley Pro Championship in 1949.

Where did it all begin? Kramer's father was a railroad worker, eventually an engineer, for Union Pacific. Kramer senior worked hard but also had a good many hours off duty, hours that he devoted to playing games with his son, a luxury he had not himself enjoyed as a child but from which he wanted young Jack to benefit. Already the future tennis champion was running, playing ping-pong, pole-vaulting, trying football and excelling at basketball and baseball. Union Pacific had a makeshift tennis court, makeshift in that it had been designed as a basketball court but tennis lines had been painted on it and a net erected so it was just about fit for purpose. Kramer senior acquired rackets and Jack got his first taste. Retracing his steps in his 1979 autobiography, Kramer describes the turn of events almost nonchalantly, doubtless reflecting his attitude at the time. As he puts it, 'We went out there together and batted the ball around. It was just another way to spend time with my father. I didn't take it seriously.'

At that stage, in the early 1930s, Kramer was merely an accomplished all-round athlete but he had no aspiration to tennis supremacy. One event stirred Kramer and caused him to focus intently as he had never done before on tennis. The family had gone to San Bernardino (again), as work took Kramer senior there in 1935, and young Jack went to see the reigning Pro Champion, Ellsworth Vines, play an exhibition match on a clay court at nearby Pomona. A visual image can be incredibly powerful, especially to an impressionable young man, and this was a case in point. Previously, in San Bernardino, Kramer had for the first time seen a good player – a young man by name of Robin Hippenstiel. Now he saw, close up, the country's and the world's finest player up against Les Stoefen. To Kramer, Vines was strikingly impressive in every way. Tall, slim, magnificently attired in long, white flannels, serving phenomenally, hitting ferocious shots from and to all parts of the court. It was this experience of watching and admiring Vines that made Kramer decide, there and then, to dedicate himself to one sport, namely tennis. In due course, Kramer senior was due to return to his job in Las Vegas but he judged that Jack's opportunity to improve his tennis would be greater if he remained near Los Angeles, which he duly did. Kramer embarked on tournament play and he honestly recounts in his memoirs that his first competitive efforts were not successful. He lost in the first round of an event in Santa Monica, using a comparatively dated Tilden Top Flight racket.

The family soon moved to Montebello, east of Los Angeles, and Kramer promptly began taking lessons from a seasoned pro named Dick Skeen whom he describes as 'a tremendous help to me'. Paid $5 per month, Skeen provided the balls, tuition and practice sets. This help had an early impact on his competence and confidence because, although Kramer was shortly to part company with Skeen, he participated in ten tournaments in 1936, winning seven of them and losing the other three in the finals.

Growing stronger physically, gripping his racket better and learning to hit the ball with spin, Kramer was progressing rapidly, though he acknowledges that with that progress came a cockiness and explosive temper that irked his modest, strait-laced father. In one match, Kramer rowed with the umpire and hurled his racket. Acting decisively, Kramer senior promptly defaulted Jack from the match, brusquely telling his son, 'Cocky, you ever do that again, you'll never go back on a tennis court as long as you live in my house.' Kramer, duly rebuked, reveals that he never lost his temper again in that way.

Perhaps most significantly around this time, Kramer enjoyed the transformative benefit of advice from a club player in Los Angeles called Cliff Roche. No champion himself, Roche was nevertheless a keen and shrewd observer of the game who had thought deeply about the best approach to match play, about how to win. He was an advocate of percentage tennis. This was an approach Kramer came to adopt and apply throughout his career and it is worth spelling out in some detail what it meant. The first imperative, according to Roche, was to hold your own serve. This may seem obvious and, as advice, unremarkable, but its significance was deep. This was the pre-tie-break era. Matches were played exhaustively to a conclusion. If you did not lose your serve, you literally could not lose a match. Therefore, maximum attention, effort and energy should be devoted to winning the games on one's own delivery. Success on that front would then free up a player to consider how to approach games in which the opponent was serving. Roche advised Kramer not to bust a gut in the first few such games. If the server fell behind love–30, and certainly if he faced love–40, it was worth making the effort to break his serve. Otherwise, he advised, Kramer should relax, stay calm and preserve his energy until the set reached four games all. Then, and only then, it made sense to launch an all-out effort to break serve, though even then Roche judged that if the server reached 30–0 or 40–0, it was not worth going all-out to reverse that deficit with all the reserves of energy that would need to be expended before embarking on Kramer's own service game.

Kramer found the advice invaluable. He dedicated himself single-mindedly to the further development of his own service, both the powerful first delivery and the deep, heavily spun, well-placed second serve as his back-up. He thereby had the ammunition to close out game after game after game on his serve, often without any notable challenge or difficulty. Of course, this immediately put pressure on his opponent, who would often offer up errors that conceded the necessary break for Kramer. Even when it did not do so, Kramer had the freedom to take a swing at his service returns, enabling him now and again to break, through the delivery of winning shots, always with the comfort in his mind that even without a break he could be confident of holding on to his own delivery. In one sense, Roche's advice seems counterintuitive in that I and, perhaps, the reader will tend to think that giving 100 per cent to a match means striving mightily to win every point. Casually letting points go seems almost sacrilegious. Yet there was a method to his approach. Hold serve. Attack the other guy's. Conserve energy and win the points that matter most.

As a teenager at the Los Angeles Tennis Club, Kramer refined his skills, sharpened his competitive claws and raised his sights by practising against Ellsworth Vines, Bill Tilden, Bobby Riggs and others. These were masters of the game whose weaponry showed him what was possible and necessary if he was to reach the highest level. Kramer's first major opportunity arose in the autumn of 1937, aged just sixteen, when he was able to play regularly with Vines over a sustained period of four months, twice a week. He credits his matches with 'Elly' as being responsible for him becoming a forehand player and said that, on an afternoon in October in 1947 whilst watching Vines, 'it all came together'.

Kramer was hugely impressed and he clearly set out to emulate the best of what he witnessed. Moreover, he has no doubt that the experience of playing with Vines and other leading players dramatically hastened his progress. This is no real surprise. In most sports, a player will not improve by competing against lesser mortals. Jousting with equals is of some value. Pitting oneself against those a level or more above will result either in demoralisation or improvement, the former the fate only of a suspiciously weak person, the latter more likely, especially for a focused, ambitious, self-confident individual, which Jack Kramer assuredly was.

The dividend from intensive practice with the giants of the game was not long in coming. In 1938, Kramer reached the semi-final of the major men's grass-court championships in Rye,

New York. En route, he notched up a morale-boosting win over Elwood Cooke, then ranked seventh in the United States. Victory, and the decisive manner of it, prompted a laudatory and prescient tribute from Allison Danzig in the *New York Times*. Portentously announcing the arrival on the tennis scene of a prodigious talent, Danzig intoned: 'The lad's name is John (Jackie) Kramer, and it is well to remember it, for it may be mentioned in the same breath with Don Budge and Ellsworth Vines by 1940.'

Part of the Roche philosophy of percentage tennis stipulated that Kramer should minimise the length of points on the opponent's serve by forcing the issue – in other words, by all-out attack whenever possible. He urged Kramer to attack every second serve he could to produce winners or extract errors. When the strength of the second serve did not allow an immediate attack, Kramer should attack the first short ball he received and come in to the net. Kramer reveals that to pursue this tactic, he learned 'to slice a ball to get in, hitting it halfway between a dink and a drive'. The sliced shot skids off the court, stays low, and makes it tough for an opponent to produce an effective passing shot or lob. Put simply, if the approach shot is well executed and usually hit deep, it is a high percentage play.

Yet, invaluable though it was as a way of treating a short ball, Kramer clearly judged it to be a necessary but not a sufficient part of his arsenal of weapons. He developed the capacity to go straight from the back of the court to the net. As he puts it, 'What set me apart, what couldn't be taught, was that I could follow a ball in from the baseline with my forehand ... I learned to slice it going forward and with that I busted up all the usual percentages.' Roche imparted two further pearls of wisdom which stood Kramer in good stead for the rest of his career. First, he advised, hit with your strength, even if it means going into that of your opponent. The advice was similar to that proffered by Bill Tilden, whose rationale was that you should attack your opponent's strength to open up his weakness. Second, Roche counselled, on each and every key point in a match, get to the net, thereby placing the onus on the opponent to go for a passing shot.

1941 was a poor year for Kramer but on his own admission he was helped when Bobby Riggs and Frankie Kovacs turned professional, and 1942 opened altogether more auspiciously. In the spring, he took the southern California title, defeating Frank Parker in the final, but the year turned sour when Kramer contracted appendicitis. On recovery, Kramer was promptly sent off to join the Coast Guard in 1942 and, infuriatingly, a dramatic albeit temporary block was placed on his hitherto promising ascent to the top of the amateur game. Kramer declares in his autobiography that he is 'fairly confident' that, but for his appendicitis in 1942, he would have won the US Open at Forest Hills. Similarly, he believes that he would have won Wimbledon in 1943, 1944 and 1945, but none of those results was to be. After the war, Kramer played at Wimbledon in 1946 and was widely expected to win. However, he was suffering from severe blisters and, somewhat unexpectedly, he succumbed in the last sixteen in five sets to the rising Czech Jaroslav Drobný.

Following advice, Kramer abandoned the practice of applying any medicament to his hands and instead put a protective tape on the racket handle, thereby eliminating the source of the blisters. Restored to full fitness, Kramer went on to take the US Open singles title, overcoming Tom Brown in straight sets 9–7, 6–3, 6–0. Following this victory, and the tape solution to his blister problem, Kramer observes, 'I never lost another meaningful singles match as an amateur.' He stresses that he was an attacking player who played all his key matches on grass and that he simply 'drove people off the court'. Attacking player though he was, and proponent of the 'big game' to boot, Kramer was irked by the implicit suggestion that he achieved success purely by the technique of serve-and-volley. This was by no means the total picture. He was quick to point out that he could hit groundstrokes, claiming, 'Except for Segura I had the best forehand in the game at that time, pro or amateur. So you could say that I had the best one-handed forehand in the game. I could hit a forehand down the line as well as anyone I ever saw.'

The victory that had eluded Kramer at Wimbledon in 1946 became his in 1947. He required only forty-seven minutes to dispose of Tom Brown in the final, sacrificing a paltry six games. He made his mark both by the emphatic character of his victory in such quick time and also by defying the convention that gentlemen played in long, white flannel trousers. Instead, Kramer donned a pair of white shorts. At this stage in his career, Kramer felt that no one in the amateur game could give him a testing match if he performed to par, although this did have the advantage of forcing him to perform consistently to the high standard that was his norm or par. Indeed, Kramer speculates that the discipline of needing constantly to reproduce that high-level form to stay well clear of the pack might help to explain why he was then so successful as a pro, having to perform night in, night out.

Buoyed by his success at Wimbledon, Kramer triumphed at the US Open in Forest Hills for the second time. Now clearly the leader of the pack of players, he conquered Drobný in the semi-final and, in the final, he defeated Frank Parker in a five-set encounter of a topsy-turvy kind. Parker played with inspiration from the outset and took the first two sets but Kramer went up a gear and ran away with the next three for the loss of only four games.

Perhaps because I am British, and the sport began in England, I have always, almost subconsciously, regarded a Wimbledon title as the ultimate prize. Indeed, many great players of all nationalities have felt and expressed that sentiment themselves. In this regard, it is interesting to note the different perspective of Jack Kramer. He observes:

When I was an amateur I knew damn well that it was more important for me to win Forest Hills than to win Wimbledon. And Forest Hills was much harder to win. For one thing, the US Open is always played at the end of the summer, when players tend to be played out.

He adds, 'It is sure to be muggy and hot. When the tournament was on grass at Forest Hills, the grass was plain lousy. This made for upsets and kept everybody on edge.' Perhaps the fact that Kramer was American gave him a particular incentive to lift the US Open title, and to do so twice in succession was both gratifying and proof of his ascendancy.

Kramer never won the French Open. However, this is unsurprising given that he never played the event! The reason for this was that in 1947 the tournament was played after Wimbledon and Kramer wanted to continue playing on grass courts until after the US Championship, then also played on grass. Indeed, in those days, all the US summer tournaments were played on grass. By 1948, when the French Championship had moved to a pre-Wimbledon date, Kramer had turned professional and was ineligible to play. Conceding that a modern champion proves himself by winning on different surfaces – ideally, on the three major types, namely grass, hard and clay – Kramer makes two points in response to the possible criticism that the absence of a French crown is a blot on his record. First, he reminds us that Gonzales, Riggs, Sedgman and Vines never won the French. From the list of more recent champions, he would have been able to add the names of Connors, McEnroe, Becker, Edberg and Sampras. Secondly, and perhaps more tellingly, he stresses that in his day 'no one really cared for anything but Davis Cup, Wimbledon and Forest Hills'. In an impressively candid statement, further revealing his motivation for skipping the event, he observes, 'If I won the French, nobody noticed; if I lost it, it made headlines and my value diminished.'

Kramer admits that he learned to play tennis on a fast court and, early in his career, he disliked intensely playing on 'the dirt' (a synonym for clay) and feared defeat at the hands of lesser players. In fact, Kramer reckons that it should be 'easier for a fast-court player to adapt to a slow surface than the other way around'. The truth is, as Kramer has acknowledged, that he did not make the adjustment because he did not have to do so. There was no pressure on him to play in the French Open and, on turn-ing professional, matches were rarely if ever played on clay, so, again, he could stick to surfaces on which he excelled.

Kramer had signed with Jack Harris on 3 September 1947, two months after his Wimbledon victory and days before he held aloft his second US Open title. He did so because, as he puts it bluntly, no one in the amateurs 'could give me a match'. When Kramer turned professional, the reigning champion was Bobby Riggs. Billed to take him on, the contest was dubbed the 'Duel of the Decade'. The champion and the pretender took to the court on 26 December 1947. The occasion is as remarkable for the circumstances surrounding it as for the quality of the match. New York, where the match took place, had just suffered the biggest snowstorm in the history of the city. Many roads were impassable. The transport network was hugely disrupted, the weather was appalling, and there was surely a risk of a huge no-show. Yet it is testament to confirmed fans' real interest in seeing the giants of the game compete that a near-capacity crowd of 15,114 turned up. Riggs won the match in four sets 6–2, 10–8, 4–6, 6–4.

Kramer was unsparing in his self-assessment. 'I overhit, I missed lots of approach shots, and I couldn't pass Bobby at the net. I knew then that I was in for a tough go.' Tough the combat doubt-less was, but Kramer was determined to become top dog. He had done it as an amateur and quickly found that he was so obviously the best that no one could stretch him. Those below him had had a target in him to aim at – however unavailingly – but he had none at which to aim. Hence the wisdom, almost the neces-sity, of turning professional. Now he had in Riggs a superior, and Kramer had an incentive to improve in order to defeat him. This he duly did. Kramer decided that he needed to target and attack Riggs's backhand and he developed a high-kicking serve to direct to that wing, giving Kramer more time to close in on the net and win points from there. Ultimately, Kramer rode out the winner of the series 69–20 and thereby became the professional champion of the world in 1948. This was on top of his success in the Davis Cup, where, in the 1947 challenge round, Kramer had defeated both John Bromwich and Dinny Pails, enabling the Americans to retain the trophy over their Australian challengers.

As we have seen, Kramer was dominant in the amateur game in 1946 and 1947 and the overwhelming likelihood must be that he would have won further Grand Slams if he had remained an amateur. However, whereas Gonzales turned professional at twenty to twenty-one – a decision that soon seemed rash and precipitate – Kramer was twenty-six, had lost some time unavoidably because of the Second World War and was understandably keen, having proved himself the top dog at Wimbledon and the US Open, to make the best possible living on the professional circuit. In the US Pro Championships in 1948, Kramer won an excruciatingly tight five-set match in the quarters and then faced the toughest of tests in the semi-finals, where he met the legendary Don Budge, an American great who had won the first calendar Grand Slam of the Australian, French, Wimbledon and US titles in 1938. Budge was by then over thirty and not completely match-fit but still a superb player with an outstanding all-round game. Kramer trailed by two sets to one and was 4–3 down in the fourth with Budge serving, but he managed to pull the match out of the fire, triumphing 6–4, 8–10, 3–6, 6–4, 6–0. In the final, Kramer beat Riggs in four sets to win the title and to confirm his undisputed status as the best player in the world. Thereafter he remained the leading player in the world as, in his words, he 'clobbered' Pancho Gonzales to maintain the title. The year after his success over Budge and Riggs to take the US Pro title, Kramer won the Wembley Pro by beating Riggs in the final in four sets 2–6, 6–4, 6–3, 6–4. That was to be his last Pro Slam singles title, for he was beaten in five sets in the Wembley Pro three years later by Pancho Gonzales, who prevailed 3–6, 3–6, 6–2, 6–4, 7–5.

By any standards, Kramer's record was remarkable. He became the unquestioned giant of the game as an amateur, seeing off all challengers, often with consummate ease. He won all six singles matches he played for the US in the Davis Cup, leading his country to victory in 1946 and 1947. He snatched from Bobby Riggs the mantle of professional champion, won two professional majors in 1948 and 1949 and was thought to be the dominant player on the professional tour from 1948 to 1953. He beat Pancho Segura, Frank Sedgman and, satisfyingly for him, Gonzales, even scoring a late win over him in 1957 when Kramer was beyond his prime. Kramer is wonderfully outspoken. In his autobiography, although he stresses that he and Gonzales did not get on well – a point made abundantly clear twenty years earlier in Gonzales's own early memoir – it is emphasised that he judges Gonzales to be in the very top drawer of champions, though behind Budge, Vines and, perhaps, Riggs. Yet Kramer is keen to stress that he was superior to Gonzales, insisting, 'I don't believe he ever could have beaten me on a tour, because he didn't develop his ground-strokes sufficiently until I was out of serious play.' The respective merits of Kramer and Gonzales, enormous in both cases, must wait for a later chapter, but it is undeniable that Kramer in his prime enjoyed supremacy over his rivals.

Interestingly, Kramer, who was justifiably confident of his own abilities and showed little self-doubt, did question whether he could have played the unremitting back-court game that predominated in the Connors–Borg era and has become the overwhelming norm now. It would, he thought, have been 'too gruelling'.

Ultimately, his career as a player was shorter in years on account of the war in the early to mid-1940s and of injury at the end of the decade. As he said in retirement, 'I had reached the point in 1949 that I couldn't lift my arm. It was so bad that one doctor advised me to quit professional tennis and find another occupation. But cortisone and later derivatives fixed me up so well that I kept going for a number of years.' A brilliant performer, a strategist and tactician, and a never-say-die competitor, Kramer won big prizes and was defeated in the end not by a better player but by arthritis. For his record as a match player and a champion, he should always be remembered as one of the greats of the game.

Chapter Five

Pancho Gonzales

RICARDO ALONSO GONZALES, known also as Richard Gonzales but far more commonly called Pancho Gonzales, was a titan of top-flight tennis from the late 1940s to the start of the 1960s. He was the world number one professional player for a record eight years, won two major titles, namely the US Open in 1948 and 1949, and no fewer than fifteen professional Grand Slam titles albeit that they did not constitute an official category, including eight US Pro crowns, four Wembley pro tournaments and, in three successive years, the Tournament of Champions. Although Gonzales never won the French title, he was twice a semi-finalist as an amateur and twice a losing finalist when he turned professional. He was inducted into the International Tennis Hall of Fame in 1968.

An estimated 6ft 2in. tall, weighing approximately 180lb, he played right-handed with a single-handed backhand. Gonzales played competitively for a quarter of a century until he retired in 1974. Few would dispute that Gonzales was a huge figure in the sport – brilliant, entertaining, controversial and as ferocious a competitor as there is to be found. In common with every other judgement in this book, the extent of Gonzales's greatness is and will doubtless remain a matter of argument, but that he was an exceptional performer is not in question.

Born in a small apartment near Wrigley Field, Los Angeles, on 9 May 1928, Gonzales was a child of the Depression years. There were few luxuries in the home. According to his own account, food was not abundant but he never went hungry. He enjoyed the company of his siblings and had loving, supportive parents. In an era when tennis was as much a 'country club' pursuit in the United States as it was a favoured diversion of the upper classes in the United Kingdom, Gonzales hailed from a rugged working-class background. He came to play tennis almost by accident. I well remember as a young child asking for and being bought a bicycle. More than three decades earlier, Gonzales had made a similar request but, even though he was twelve years old, his mother was convinced that it was a dangerous contraption and refused to countenance the idea. Instead, at a cost of fifty-one cents, she bought him a tennis racket. Initially, Gonzales stubbornly refused to handle it at all but, eventually, he relented and opted to experiment. He recounts his experience in his autobiography in almost mystical terms, describing the feeling of triumph that he savoured when he successfully managed to bounce the ball up and down on the racket's surface. 'Such', he concluded, 'is the strange hand of destiny.'

Through the modest gesture used to offer her son an alternative to riding a bike, Gonzales's mother had given him the most important device of his life. Moreover, although she had initially urged him to use it, he had resisted and, as was to be a recurring feature of his life, Gonzales alone decided when to practise and to play. This is significant. He was not pushed. He decided for himself, motivated himself and ultimately drove himself.

It did not take long for him not merely to gain a taste for, but to become gripped, almost consumed, by tennis and by the time he was thirteen he described himself as 'madly in love' with the game.

At first, Gonzales had no dream of global greatness. His horizons were not so wide. He simply loved and was captivated by the game. Unlike millions of children of even moderately affluent parents who benefit from regular group or individual coaching, Gonzales was self-taught. He observed the play of others, committed it to memory and sought to develop it himself. In the process, he wanted to devote ever greater time to building his game. He did not loathe school and, though he makes no claim to academic distinction, he does maintain that he was 'good at mechanical drawing' and 'outstanding at draftmanship'. Nevertheless, those activities could not compete with the attraction of tennis which took over the young Gonzales. Playing mattered and, before long, winning – and, when losing, figuring out why, and how to win instead – mattered above all. Gonzales traces the thirst for winning to his early court encounters with his brother Manuel. The first time they played, Pancho lost and resolved to reverse that result. Thereafter, he said, 'It's been the same with anyone who ever beat me.' As he put it, 'I wanted to know why.' To that end, he says,

> I went over the matches carefully in my mind, mentally replaying every point remembered. I reconstructed. If opponents had a stroke I didn't have, and it was effective, I copied it to perfection, even tried to execute it better than they had. I borrowed Jack Kramer's rise-hitting, tried Ted Schroeder's looped cross-court shot, Pancho Segura's volley and many others. I borrowed them and tried to improve them.

Gonzales had such an appetite for the game that he regularly played truant in order to play tennis, feeling an inner and constant urge to get to a court and 'run, run, run'. His father made repeated efforts to persuade him to quit. It was not that he disapproved of sport in general or of tennis in particular. Rather, he believed in the value of education, of learning, of qualifications as the passport to a successful career. Tennis was a damaging distraction from what Gonzales senior saw as the pressing prior-ity of study, especially as his son was so hopelessly hooked on the game. In exasperation at the failure of his repeated exhortations to young Pancho to quit, one day he took his son's racket and broke it. Unfazed by this, young Gonzales indicated that he could easily acquire another racket and that he would not be deterred.

At the same time, Frank Poulain, who ran the Exposition Park Tennis Shop and was something of a mentor to Gonzales, told his incredulous father that Pancho could make a fortune from the sport by the age of thirty. Gradually, but perceptibly, Gonzales senior began to relent and to reconcile himself to the prospect of his son applying himself remorselessly to the search for serious success at tennis.

Paternal opposition was not the only hurdle Gonzales had to mount. The tennis establishment was discernibly snobbish, conventional, traditional, almost priggish, and its leading lights held huge sway over the fortunes of aspiring future champions. Despite learning of the prowess of Gonzales, the boss of the Southern California Tennis Association in the early 1940s, Perry T. Jones, learned of the young man's truancy and for a time banned him from participation in tennis tournaments. Ultimately, when Gonzales turned nineteen, Jones lifted the ban.

Shortly afterwards, there was a defining moment in his career. Hitherto Gonzales had been passionate about the game but he had not consciously aspired to be its dominant figure. He then played a second-round match against a youngster called Herbie Flam whom Gonzales had almost invariably beaten in the past but had not competed against since 1943. Gonzales was a practitioner of the big game, a serve-and-volley specialist, whereas Flam was an all-court player schooled in the art of rugged defence. If Gonzales had expected a comfortable win, that expectation was quickly confounded. He lost the opening set 10–8 and faced three match points on his own serve in the second. Gonzales aced his way out of trouble and eventually took the second set 8–6 and the third 6–4. It had been a Herculean struggle but Gonzales had come back from the brink and, through skill, nerve, and sheer unadulterated will, he had prevailed. It was seminal. As victory became his, Gonzales says, 'I took a solemn oath. I was going to be the best tennis player this game has seen, I told myself. Nothing would stop me now. I didn't care how long it would take, or how bumpy the path would be. I would make it. Damned right I would.'

Sure enough, many a youngster has an ambition that is in itself admirable but that exceeds his or her ability. Either the ambition is replaced by something else or it is simply not realised. In the case of Gonzales, the ambition was neither reckless nor ill-founded. He was no fanciful daydreamer but a talented guy with real weapons and an insatiable appetite for deploying and adding to them. In his late teens, he was developing a blistering serve (clocked at 112 mph), excellent volleys, a ferocious forehand, superb footwork, great anticipation and an immersion in strategy and tactics that availed him constantly over the next twenty-five years. In terms of stroke learning and the rigour with which Gonzales approached the mental side of the game, the great battle of wits, he was perhaps not dissimilar to Bill Tilden. He was, he reveals, seared by a desire or what he describes as something akin to an inextinguishable pilot light guiding him to seek victory. Reading about Gonzales's career reminds me of the former American President Lyndon B. Johnson, a man twenty years senior to Gonzales who also came from humble origins and who was utterly focused on the pursuit of power. Johnson could not stand losing and was determined to do everything, absolutely everything, to win. That was Gonzales.

At the age of fifteen, Gonzales had been arrested for burglary and he spent a year in detention. Subsequently, he had served in the navy during World War Two for two years and received a bad conduct discharge in 1947. Notwithstanding these setbacks and losses of precious play and practice time, Gonzales competed on the west coast in 1947 and made modest progress at the US National Championship and Forest Hills before succumbing to the hugely experienced Gardnar Mulloy in five sets. Perhaps more significantly, the season ended on a high when, in the Pacific Southwest tournament, Gonzales beat three big beasts of the game, namely Jaroslav Drobný, Bob Falkenburg and Frank Parker, losing in the final to Ted Schroeder. Aged nineteen, Gonzales finished 1947 ranked number seventeen in the United States.

Buoyed by these successes, Gonzales must have approached 1948 suitably emboldened and optimistic. That said, he would have been judged at best only to have an outside shot at winning the United States Championships. Seeded eight, a quarter-final appearance was anticipated and would have been more than respectable. He did a whole lot better than that, defeating Drobný in four sets 8–10, 11–9, 6–0, 6–3 and the South African Eric Sturgess in the final, 6–2, 6–3, 14–12.

Having won the Championship, Gonzales promptly came down with a bump. This may seem counterintuitive but it is not really so. Backing up a major victory with other major victories can be one of the most difficult feats in sport. Rarely does the first-time winner of a Slam immediately proceed to win the next, and sometimes winning even smaller titles can be unachievable for a period. Whether a winner takes his or her foot off the pedal or, alternatively, feels that the weight of expectations is burdensome, poor form after a great triumph is not uncommon. Gonzales went on to lose to Schroeder in the Pacific Southwest event and to Sturgess in Mexico City, but he had achieved a headlong advance reflected in his end-year ranking in 1948 as the number one player in the United States.

Gonzales began 1949 with a clear agenda. He aimed to win the most treasured prize in tennis, the Wimbledon title, and to retain his US title at Forest Hills. As we have learned, Gonzales had anticipated that his path to supremacy could be rocky, and so it proved. He started well enough, winning the National Indoor Championships in New York, beating Bill Talbert. He then proceeded to lose at the River Oaks tournament in Texas, to Sam Match in less than half an hour. In the French Championships he was worsted by Budge Patty and he fell in the third round at Wimbledon. He managed to hold onto the National Clay Court Championship against Frank Parker but suffered painful losses to Bill Talbert in New Jersey and at Long Island. Victory over Vic Seixas gave him the Pennsylvania Grass Court tournament and at Newport, Rhode Island he overcame Gardnar Mulloy in four sets.

So the record was very mixed and Gonzales's performance at Wimbledon in particular had been derided. He had put on weight and appeared bloated, spawning the unflattering description of him as the 'cheese champion'. Gonzales was never a prodigious drinker but neither was he a healthy eater. He loved beans but was essentially a hot dog and coke man – consuming the latter enthusiastically throughout matches – and a pretty heavy smoker. Allied to these debits on the balance sheet, he had evidently not been training quite as hard and was simply not in peak condition.

Nevertheless, he had resolved to retain his US title and he worked hard to get to the final and to avenge a string of defeats at the hands of Ted Schroeder. Encouraged by mentor Frank Shields to have a quiet, calm evening before the final, Gonzales was typically contrary, opting to go to the cinema to see a double horror show which did not lose him a wink of sleep. He knew Schroeder would be tough and he was. The marathon first set went to Schroeder 18–16 and Gonzales dropped the second set. In his autobiography, Gonzales concedes that his morale was now 'cracked' and he simply resolved to produce a 'good match' for the packed gallery who had paid 'good money' to see such a spectacle. He would battle as tenaciously as he could, 'even though my cause was almost hopeless'. Gonzales took the third and fourth sets 6–1, 6–2. Despite the fact that Schroeder had a 'superb' record over five sets, Gonzales took the final set 6–4 and he remembers 'the look of astonishment on Ted's face'.

At this time, Bobby Riggs, a former champion himself and now a tournament promoter, had envisaged signing Schroeder to take on the world professional champion, Jack Kramer, in an extensive tour of matches. Instead, he signed Gonzales. Whether Gonzales was wise to turn professional so soon after his second triumph in the majors is questionable. There was a gulf between the top amateur and the leading pro in favour of the latter. Consolidating his success in the amateur ranks might have been the more prudent, conservative course. Of course, Gonzales was many things but no one would have called him either prudent or conservative. He was a man who played the big game, took big decisions and risked big setbacks.

The contract with Riggs required Gonzales to play 123 matches against Kramer. He did and was heavily beaten ninety-six matches to twenty-seven. Later, he came to beat Kramer, but at the time this heavy defeat was damaging to Gonzales. The sheer remorselessness of a nationwide tour involving several dozen matches placed a premium on looking after oneself and Kramer was struck by Gonzales's poor eating habits, reckless approach to sleep and general lack of conditioning. Gonzales would happily have taken on Kramer again but, naturally, Riggs saw the situation very differently. Attracting punters at the box office demanded that they be offered an exciting contest. Riggs concluded from the evidence that they would not get it from Gonzales, bluntly informing him that he was 'dead meat'. Riggs explained the situation to Gonzales: 'Professional tennis is a funny sport. All the public really cares about is the champ and the challenger. Mainly the challenger. The stamp of amateurism hasn't fully dried on him yet, so he's a knight in shining armor, the people's choice, a fresh new personality.' Gonzales, he said, had been in that position but he was no longer. 'You're past tense now,' he told Gonzales. 'Your name's worth nothing. You came, you saw – and Jack Kramer conquered.'

Gonzales had earned $75,000 from the tour but, vanquished, his own prospects looked poor. Moreover, those who observed him traced a dramatic change for the worse in his attitude and demeanour. Previously, he had been regarded as a positive, upbeat, engaging personality. Apparently this ceased to be the case. Kramer, writing in 2002, claims that Gonzales's heavy defeat in his professional debut, and the damage done to his standing, had the effect that 'his nature had changed completely'. The commentator S. L. Price elaborated: 'He became difficult and arrogant. Losing had changed him. When he got his next chance, he understood that you either win or you're out of a job.' Ted Schroeder described him now as a 'loner', saying that he was 'always the unhappiest man in town'. Gonzales, utterly devastated, was less than reassured when Bobby Riggs suggested, 'Perhaps one day we can build you up again,' urging him to 'keep playing, keep in condition, keep your weight down, save your money, and stand by'.

Gonzales was in limbo. He could not return to the amateur game and would obviously not have wished to do so. Yet defeat by Kramer meant that the prime challenger status that he had briefly enjoyed was swiftly denied to him. Forced into a kind of semi-retirement between 1951 and 1953, Gonzales had to adjust to his new situation. He purchased the tennis shop at Exposition Park where he had hung around as a teenager and, in addition to cobbling together a living from that source, he featured in a number of professional events around the world. The downsides were twofold. First, they were not intense playing commitments but modest and spasmodic. Secondly, he was not the headline attraction and his remuneration reflected the fact. Nevertheless, he played, and appeared at the very least to maintain his playing level.

In 1950 to 1951 he toured Australia and New Zealand with Dinny Pails, Frank Parker and Don Budge, winning the Australian tour. He also won the Wembley Professional tournament in 1951, and the following year he was apparently the most successful pro. He played five tournaments and won four, notching up important wins over Kramer, Budge and Pancho Segura. Interestingly, in 1951, Gonzales's forehand was electronically measured and was recorded at 112.88 mph, faster than Kramer's, itself a searing shot of 107.8 mph.

Much of 1953 was very unfavourable for Gonzales. Between Wembley 1952 and Wembley 1953, he did not compete against a comparable player. Kramer, with whom Gonzales had never been bosom pals, was now a promoter and was given initially to playing in the tour matches that he promoted. In short, Gonzales was squeezed out and, lacking top-class match practice, he lost heavily to Frank Sedgman both at Wembley and in Paris. Fine player though Sedgman was, measured over a career, Gonzales was unquestionably his superior.

Towards the end of 1953, Kramer was suffering from back problems and for a period was unable to play. There was an opening for a top pro and Kramer signed Gonzales on a remarkable seven-year contract to tour the United States in 1954, though Gonzales complained bitterly about the terms of the contract, not only at the time but for a long time afterwards. Gonzales beat both Pancho Segura and Frank Sedgman and then crowned that achievement with victory over Sedgman in the final of the US Pro Championships, taking the match in four sets 6–3, 9–7, 3–6, 6–2. Later in the year, Gonzales performed creditably against Segura and Kramer in a Far East tour and finished the year in style in his Australian tour, decisively overcoming Sedgman and trouncing Ken McGregor no fewer than fifteen times without losing to him once.

From then on, until the beginning of the 1960s, Gonzales was the leading player in the world. He jousted regularly with Sedgman, Tony Trabert, Ken Rosewall, Lew Hoad and others and generally got the better of all of them. Trabert is on record as arguing that the decisive factor in Gonzales's advantage over him and the others was his ferocious service, which won him innumerable cheap points either because it was not returned or because it put him in a dominant position to win the point quickly. Not only did Gonzales possess a great serve but, phenomenal big-match player that he was, he could produce it under pressure, for example in the fifth set of a match. Indeed, such were the tales of his prowess, not to mention his indomitable will to win, that one commentator said that he had never seen Gonzales lose serve when serving for a set or a match. That service, combined with exceptional volleys and overhead, tremendous stamina and a competitive streak, a stubborn insistence on winning that was equal to that of any modern player, explained how Gonzales reached and stayed at the peak of the mountain of professional tennis for so long.

Part of the purpose of this book is to assess just how great the great tennis players have been. Unsurprisingly, there is no unanimous view. There are plenty who rank many above Gonzales but there are those who argue a case that he was in the very highest echelon. Vincent X. Flaherty of the *Los Angeles Examiner*, writing in the 1950s, declared that 'Gonzales unquestionably is the greatest tennis player in the world today and, undoubtedly, is one of the greatest performers the game has ever had.'

It is instructive to look at the record Gonzales notched up against some of his leading competitors and consider what some of them made of him. Trabert went head to head in a lengthy tour with Gonzales in 1955 and was comprehensively beaten 74–27. To say that he was not warmly disposed to the abrasive, grumpy, disputatious Gonzales would be a notable understatement. Yet Trabert is unstinting in tribute to his tormentor. He told Ned Cronin of the *Los Angeles Times*, 'Gonzales is the greatest natural athlete tennis has ever known ... He instinctively does the right thing at the right time. Doesn't even have to stop to think.'

Ken Rosewall, six and a half years junior to Gonzales, was signed by Kramer by the close of 1956 to take on Gonzales in 1957. Despite a painful cyst on his right hand, Gonzales won their ten-match Australian tour. Subsequently, they went to play in the US and Gonzales won the tour overall by 50–26. Kramer was briefly anxious that Gonzales so outgunned Rosewall that the match-up would cease to be of interest and that gate receipts would suffer. Later, however, Rosewall's performance strengthened, though there is no doubt that Gonzales had decidedly the upper hand. Even though it is obvious from his public comments at the time, as well as from his 1959 autobiography, that Gonzales regarded himself as the better player, he is full of admiration for Rosewall.

Gonzales viewed Rosewall as a 'fencer' and a strategist. That said, Gonzales was convinced that strategy 'can be overcome by sheer power', and the evidence of their direct combat is that it generally was. The only caveat to insert here is that they were not precise contemporaries. If Gonzales was at his peak in the late 1950s, Rosewall's pre-eminence was in the early to mid-1960s and, arguably, a little longer. For our purpose here, however, it is Rosewall's verdict on Gonzales that concerns us. Speaking to a newspaper in Princeton, New Jersey, Rosewall said: 'Pancho just doesn't seem to have any bad nights. It's not human. He's not human.'

Tennis is a game of match-ups. In other words, players often particularly like competing against some opponents and do so more successfully than against others. For all the quite outstanding qualities that Ken Rosewall possessed, Gonzales felt comfortable pitting his game against him and he built an ascendancy over him. Lew Hoad was a different and, for Gonzales, a more difficult proposition. Hoad was an attacking player with a big game not dissimilar to that of Gonzales. He had a powerful serve, strong volleys, very penetrating groundstrokes and a capacity to hit winners from and to all parts of the court. In researching this book, two words have frequently recurred in relation to Hoad – 'on' and 'hot'. When he was 'on' or when he was 'hot', he was unplayable. Early in their combat in 1958, Gonzales clearly found him so, as he won only nine of their first twenty-seven encounters. Gonzales realised that he was being pummelled on the backhand side and he remodelled the drive off that wing, developing it into a more offensive stroke, winning more than two-thirds of their remaining matches, leaving a final tally of 51–36 in favour of Gonzales.

Perhaps the most significant of the assessments of Gonzales comes from Kramer. They didn't get on, they didn't like each other, and they argued constantly – perhaps it would be more accurate to say that Gonzales argued constantly – about money. Nonetheless, writing in 1979, Kramer ranked Gonzales in an elite group led by Don Budge, followed by Ellsworth Vines, Bill Tilden, Fred Perry and Bobby Riggs. Perhaps surprisingly to the mind of some commentators who have tended to rank Rod Laver at or very close to the top of the tree, Kramer was 'positive', having viewed both at close quarters, that Gonzales would have beaten Laver regularly. In support of that proposition, he probably had in mind the fact that in January 1970, when Gonzales was forty-one and Laver was thirty-one and still ranked number one, Gonzales won their $10,000 winner-takes-all five-set match in Madison Square Garden. In fact, this one result scarcely seems conclusive and Laver subsequently won the tournament, defeating Gonzales in the process.

Whether Kramer's view on the relative strength of Gonzales and Laver was correct or not is not altogether material here. What counts is that one of the great players and authorities in the history of the game, who disliked Gonzales and was disliked by him and was fought in legal actions (unsuccessfully) by him, is nevertheless explicit that Gonzales was one of the half a dozen greatest players he had seen. Allowing for the fact that Bjorg and Connors still had successes ahead of them and that Kramer cannot in his autobiography have contemplated the careers of McEnroe, Lendl, Edberg, Becker, Sampras, Agassi, Federer, Nadal or Djokovic, the respect he pays Gonzales is still striking. Just to complete the tribute, for all that Gonzales was sour, argumentative, unclubbable and sometimes unpleasant to others, Kramer stresses his professionalism, comparing it favourably with the conduct of some later champions. As he tells it, although Gonzales may have been screaming at him in the changing room up until the point at which he was required to be on court, once he was there, 'Gorgo' would be the very soul of professionalism and 'play his guts out' for the public who bought the tickets, and therefore paid the bills. These priorities, Kramer noted sadly, are less important to 'modern hot-shots'.

Kramer was telling it as he had seen it. Gonzales, more than two decades earlier, had complained that he was treated like a 'slave' by Kramer, preposterously likening him to a dictator. Moreover, as Trabert had come to observe, Gonzales had behaved badly to many people but, on the court, almost without exception, he went about his business professionally. That fact, together with a hugely exciting brand of tennis, and the infectious enthusiasm that he displayed for his chosen art, made him a major crowd-puller as well as a great champion.

One match in the career of Gonzales which tells us much about him was his marathon contest against Charlie Pasarell at Wimbledon in 1969. Lasting five hours and twelve minutes, it was then the longest match in the history of that tournament, and its duration is widely credited for the introduction of the tie-break at the All England Club. Gonzales was forty-one, Pasarell twenty-five. Pasarell took the first set 24–22 and, with relatively poor light, Gonzales contended that the match should be suspended until the following day. The tournament referee insisted that they continue, whereupon a furious Gonzales effectively chucked the second set, sacrificing it 6–1. The match was then suspended, Gonzales suffering the indignity of being booed as he left the court.

Returning the next day, Gonzales fought back, winning the third set 16–14, and the fourth set 6–3. In the fifth set, Gonzales faced further adversity in the form of seven match points in total, including twice having to recover from 0–40 down on his serve. Gonzales eventually prevailed 11–9 in the final set. Legend has it that someone afterwards said to him, 'That was some comeback, Pancho. But surely when you were two sets down and when you faced all those match points against you in the final set, you must have thought Charlie had you beaten?' Gonzales is said to have replied, 'Hell no, I just thought that Charlie was being stubborn. Well, I'm stubborn too.'

Interestingly, when Gonzales was twenty-eight, Ted Schroeder had suggested to him, 'I'll give you one more year.' Gonzales had retorted, 'One? Hell! I'm good for at least five.' In fact, although Gonzales was not at his peak in the Open era and he did not win any of the four majors in it, he was still competing at the highest level and scoring notable victories. Reference has already been made to his win over Laver in 1970 in New York, but that is far from being the only example. A case in point is the 1968 French Open. Played on clay, the least favourable surface for the serve-and-volley tennis at which he excelled, forty-year-old Gonzales, who was in semi-retirement, nevertheless beat 1967 defending champion Roy Emerson. He went on to defeat him a further eleven times before he retired. Similarly, at the US Open in the same year, Gonzales knocked out the second seed, Tony Roche, in the fourth round. So his longevity at the top was remarkable.

In summary, then, a number of conclusions can be drawn. First, Gonzales was an exceptional tennis player in terms of gifts, guts and track record. As an amateur, he is reckoned to have won no fewer than seventeen singles titles, including two Grand Slam tournaments. Having turned professional, he has been estimated to have won eighty-five singles titles, of which we know fifteen to have been Pro Slam events. For eighteen successive years, from 1950 to 1967, he was barred from participation in the four major tournaments of Wimbledon, the US Open, the French Open and the Australian Open. Of the gaps in his career CV, the most notable is the absence of a Wimbledon title. Given, however, that as a professional he was the number one ranked player in the world for eight years, it is reasonable to think that he probably would have won Wimbledon if he had been eligible at his peak to compete. At the very least, the absence of such a title should not lead observers to downgrade his status as a great champion, given that he did not lose but simply could not compete.

Second, the performance of Gonzales up against his direct contemporaries was first-rate. He beat most of his principal competitors, Sedgman, Trabert, Rosewall and Hoad, more often than he lost to them.

Third, it is a commentary on his endurance and passion for the game that Gonzales stayed at the very top of the game for almost ten years and was able to compete at the highest level for twenty years, sometimes beating younger, higher-ranked players after he had turned forty. In the modern era, only Ken Rosewall can make a similar boast. There are commentators who believe Gonzales to have been the greatest player of all time. Others believe that there are players past, present or both who should be judged superior. What is certain, what is proven, what is undisputed is that Gonzales was not only a superb player and a great champion but one of the toughest, most indefatigable competitors ever to pick up a tennis racket.

Chapter Six

Ken Rosewall

THE CAREER OF Ken Rosewall, the Australian maestro and one of the most remarkable competitors ever to grace a tennis court, lasted more than twenty-five years, from his participation in Grand Slam events in the early 1950s to his eventual retirement in 1980. In that period, Rosewall, 5ft 7in. tall and, at 145lb, a slight figure alongside most of his taller, often brawnier, contemporaries, racked up an impressive array of major victories. He won eight Grand Slam titles, including four Australian Championships (1953, 1955, 1971 and 1972), two French Championships (1953, 1968) and two US Championships, one in 1956 and the other after the advent of the Open era in 1968. Although Rosewall never won the Wimbledon title, he was four times a losing finalist. Astonishing to the uninitiated observer as it may seem, the first and last of those finals were twenty years apart. In 1954, Rosewall lost at the All England Club to Jaroslav Drobný and in 1974 he was defeated by Jimmy Connors. In between, he succumbed to Hoad in the 1956 final and to another fellow Australian, John Newcombe, in 1970.

In addition, Rosewall acquired no fewer than fifteen professional majors, winning the US Professional title in 1963 and 1965, the Wembley Professional Championships in 1957, 1960, 1961, 1962 and 1963 and the French Professional Championships in 1958, 1960, 1961, 1962, 1963, 1964, 1965 and 1966. The reader will note that in 1963 he won the US, Wembley and French Professional titles. Importantly, Rosewall also won the WCT finals in successive years, 1971 and 1972, overcoming Rod Laver on both occasions to do so. Rosewall was ranked number one in the world in 1960, though it can certainly be argued that he was the top player in the world for the first half of the 1960s, and he was ranked in the top twenty of the world for a staggering twenty-six years, from 1952 to 1977. He is estimated to have won 133 titles in his career, though only twenty-eight of those are recognised by the ATP.

Born in Sydney on 2 November 1934, Rosewall was the son of parents who played tennis enthusiastically and themselves owned courts. A natural left-hander, Rosewall had his father, Robert, to thank for teaching him to play right-handed and his tennis journey began at a very early age. From three years old, at the behest of his dad, Rosewall played with a shortened racket, hitting two-handed strokes on both forehand and backhand sides. This was probably simply to encourage him to develop initial contact with the ball, some control of it and the boost to self-confidence that that aptitude must have generated. At five, Rosewall shifted to one hand.

Robert Rosewall told Ken's 1976 biographer, Peter Rowley, of his approach to the game with his young son. In his words: 'From books I taught him Fred Perry's forehand and Don Budge's backhand. The volley, overhead and lob he developed naturally. We would get up at four and five in the morning.' Revealingly, he adds, 'We would spend weeks hitting only one stroke at a time. I would drop a handkerchief on the ground, and he would hit to it.' Most of the great players will have practised assiduously from an early age, spending long hours on the court, honing their skills and hitting thousands of balls. However, the evidence here is that it was not just the hitting of balls, but the focused intent of the practice sessions that was uppermost in Rosewall senior's mind. He wanted Ken to develop a skill so thoroughly and comprehensively that, playing by instinct, he could repeatedly produce shots, including placements, of the highest quality as a matter of course. There can be no doubt that this approach paid dividends, as Rosewall came to be renowned for the accuracy and consistency of his ball-striking throughout his illustrious career.

Rosewall senior goes on to state: 'I didn't worry much about the service, as he had a natural overhead and tennis in those days emphasised groundstrokes.' In retrospect, that might have been a mistake, because for many years Rosewall was judged to possess a relatively weak serve and although in later years it improved markedly, coming to be very well-placed and consistent, it lacked real force and thereby denied Rosewall the many cheap points on which competitors with more powerful deliveries came to depend. Doubtless, at 5ft 7in., Rosewall would never have developed the powerful serve that Gonzales or later John Newcombe enjoyed, but more attention to the shot at an earlier stage in his career might have helped. Rosewall senior goes on: 'I taught him footwork, the right forward on the backhand, left on the forehand – that's very important – but he invented himself these very fast little steps for getting into position.'

It is worth emphasising that in his early years, Ken played almost exclusively on clay courts. Although people often have an image of Australian tennis being characterised by grass-court players – and, of course, most of the great Australian champions came to be supreme exponents of the game on that surface – the reality was that grass courts were very much a country club phenomenon in Australia. If you played tennis at an expensive club, it might, probably would, be on grass. Otherwise, clay, often referred to as dirt, was the typical surface. Hence it is no surprise that Rosewall senior concentrated so heavily on furnishing young Ken with first-class groundstrokes, the rudiments of the back-court game that would stand him in such good stead, especially on clay but in practice on all surfaces in the decades ahead.

On the back of Ken's dedicated cultivation of his art as a tennis player, his name appeared in July 1949 in the first issue of *Australian Tennis*. He had just won the New South Wales fifteen-and-under schools singles. The report described him as 'the best tennis prospect for many years', noting in particular his terrific ball control and his court craft, features of the Rosewall make-up that were to be pre-eminent throughout his career.

Aged fifteen, still competing at junior level, Rosewall nevertheless entered the adult New South Wales Metropolitan Championships and was defeated in the semi-finals by the top-flight Australian player Ken McGregor, more than five years Rosewall's senior. However, in 1951, Rosewall won his first men's tournament in Manly and this was the start of his swift rise through the ranks to the top of the game. At the US National Championships in 1952, Rosewall, still only seventeen, beat the number one seed, Vic Seixas – over whom he was to establish a long-standing dominance – in the last sixteen, prevailing in five sets 3–6, 6–2, 7–5, 5–7, 6–3. Writing in the *New York Herald Tribune*, Red Smith described Rosewall's victory as, 'A spectacle that occurs only once in a generation of big league tennis.' He adds that Rosewall played with the 'guile of a veteran twice his age and took a tyrannical control of tactics'.

In 1953, Rosewall, aged eighteen, won the Australian Championships, trouncing his fellow countryman Mervyn Rose 6–0, 6–3, 6–4. Distance and travelling time to Australia were such that most top-flight players in those days skipped the tournament, causing it to be slightly lesser regarded as a Slam title than other comparable events. Nevertheless, there was still substantial competition and it was a very big achievement for Rosewall to take the title and to do so in such comprehensive fashion. As if to underline his arrival in the big time, Rosewall then consolidated his triumph by becoming the first Australian to win the French Championships since Jack Crawford twenty years earlier. He achieved this distinction with a four-set victory over the American Vic Seixas 6–3, 6–4, 1–6, 6–2. That year, Rosewall also lifted the Pacific Southwest Championships. However, despite being seeded number one at Wimbledon on the strength of his success in Australia and France, he fell at the quarter-final hurdle at the All England Club to Kurt Nielsen. At the US Championships,

Rosewall reached the semi-finals but he was outplayed by Tony Trabert in straight sets and lost to him again in similar fashion in the Davis Cup challenge round on Rosewall's home turf in Melbourne. There is a sense, recorded in Rosewall's autobiography, that his season 'fell apart a little after Paris'. It was felt that a combination of too much play, stomach trouble and being pushed excessively hard by the Australian Davis Cup captain, Harry Hopman, caused him to burn out, finishing the season less well than he had started it. That said, he had advanced mightily in 1953, reflected in his world ranking at number two behind Tony Trabert.

1954 was one of four years – the others being 1956, 1970 and 1974 – when Rosewall made it to the Wimbledon singles final only to find that the most treasured title in tennis eluded him. Having beaten Rex Hartwig in five sets in the quarter-final, the score being 6–3, 3–6, 3–6, 6–3, 6–1, Rosewall triumphed in the semi-finals over his earlier nemesis, Trabert, winning 3–6, 6–3, 4–6, 6–1, 6–1. *The Times* was exultant and its praise for the young Australian unstinting. In its words, 'It was almost a perfect example of the infinite variety that can spring from the highest quality of modern lawn tennis. Every stroke known to the most critical was there – and there in plenty – as well as a dozen or more that had never been played before.' Warming to its theme of the young Australian's dazzling performance, the report went on, 'Indeed words must fail to describe some of Rosewall's half-volleys in the forecourt exchanges, his swift and sudden volleying of smashes, and his masterly change of direction in the very middle of a stroke of beauty – all these had to be seen to be believed.'

Rosewall had been taken the distance in both quarter- and semi-final encounters. Whether his exertions had taken their toll, we don't know. What we do know is that in his four-set final loss to Jaroslav Drobný, Rosewall appeared to lack a clear gameplan to tackle his Czech adversary. In his autobiography, Rosewall blames the Australian Davis Cup captain, Harry Hopman, insisting that the latter did not advise him how to play Drobný. Specifically, it appears that he was not advised, and he did not decide, to approach the net by driving or chipping the ball to Drobný's backhand wing, which was markedly his weaker side. Instead he camped on the baseline, did not take the initiative and thereby allowed the Czech to dictate the pattern of play. At the time, disappointed though he was about the outcome, Rosewall must have expected that other opportunities to win Wimbledon would arise and that, sooner or later, he would lift the trophy. As it transpired, Rosewall was right on the first point but wrong on the second.

In 1955, still only twenty, Rosewall won his second crown at the Australian Championships, handily thumping his friend and arch-rival Lew Hoad in straight sets 9–7, 6–4, 6–4. The tournament was played on grass. Hoad had a 'big game' characterised by a powerful service, rasping drives off both wings and a relentless tendency to take to the net and dispatch volleys with comparative ease. In this match, Rosewall was demonstrating at a very early stage in his career that, despite his lack of inches or muscle, he too could attack, keep his opponent pinned back, and exploit chances to conclude points economically.

Success at the Australian Championships was not repeated at Wimbledon. Rosewall progressed to the semi-finals but there he succumbed to Kurt Nielsen in four sets 11–9, 6–2, 2–6, 6–4. Once again, Rosewall appears in part to have blamed Harry Hopman, saying that he 'would have benefited from more advice for the Nielsen match'. At Forest Hills, in the US Championships, Rosewall dispatched Seixas in straight sets to reach the final but was thwarted there by Trabert 9–7, 6–3, 6–3. Although this defeat was a blow, Rosewall's victory over Seixas attracted fulsome praise from one of the great tennis journalists of all time. Allison Danzig was struck by Rosewall's recovery from 5–2 down in the third set. Maintaining that Seixas watched 'utterly baffled and bewildered' as Rosewall won the last five games, he described in the New York Times Rosewall and his performance: 'A stylist of the classical school in the production of his groundstrokes and a court tactician of unruffled composure and deliberation. The calm, unhurried manner in which Rosewall went about the job of defeating the energetic, fast-moving Seixas was an object lesson in conservation of energy.'

Seixas, more than once visibly exasperated by his losses to Rosewall, must have felt jinxed against the man from Sydney. At Wimbledon in 1956 in the semi-finals, Rosewall and Seixas fought a pulsating five-set match in which Seixas led 5–2 in the fifth set. Rosewall then reeled off the last five games, taking the match 6–3, 3–6, 6–8, 6–3, 7–5. *The Times* pithily summarised the outcome with the observation 'genius does what it must, talent what it can'. In the final, Rosewall was out-gunned by Lew Hoad in four sets as he was in the final of the Australian Championships. The general pattern was that Rosewall prevailed in longer rallies, Hoad in the shorter exchanges. Taking advantage of the grass, Hoad wisely attacked and strove to finish points quickly, doing so to deadly effect. 1956 had been a great year for Hoad but the Grand Slam was denied to him when the two friends and rivals met in the US Championships final and Rosewall prevailed in four sets 4–6, 6–2, 6–3, 6–3.

Richard Naughton, who co-authored Rosewall's autobiography, describes his performance as 'sublime'. In terms of range, versatility and all-round skill, Rosewall had provided a masterclass. Touch, strategy, net play and quality of return were all of the highest order and Rosewall's adaptation to and exploitation of the windy conditions were simply superior to Hoad's on that occasion. Bill Talbert, quoted in *Sports Illustrated* in September 1956, encapsulated Rosewall's triumph graphically: 'He was the master – a craft tailor sewing a garment of defeat for his victim.' The veteran American player, Gardnar Mulloy, himself a formidable competitor, writing in *World Tennis* in October 1956, declared, 'The new champion is a true racquet artist. He has the quickest reflexes and best groundstrokes in the game today and he is unbelievably fast at the net.' The point is well made and it serves to underline the fact that although the original and continuing foundation of Rosewall's playing style was strength off the ground, characterised by an exquisite backhand in particular, he fast became a superb volleyer – agile, blessed with superb touch, the capacity to use the angles of the court and impressive consistency.

In addition to his prodigious success in tournament play as an amateur, Rosewall performed to great effect for Australia, helping his country win three Davis Cup challenge rounds in 1953, 1955 and 1956. In those three years, Rosewall played seventeen singles rubbers, winning fifteen of them, including the last fourteen. It was a fitting conclusion to the amateur chapter in his career.

Unsurprisingly, given the huge impact Rosewall and Hoad had made in their opening years on the senior circuit, Jack Kramer, himself a former champion and now a swashbuckling, controversial and entrepreneurial promoter, had sought to entice both men to turn professional in 1955. At the time, the attempt failed, but a year later, Rosewall, though at that stage not Hoad, accepted Kramer's offer. He was contracted initially for twelve months for a sum of $65,000 plus 20 per cent of gate receipts in excess of $350,000. Kramer had arranged for Rosewall, the new young star, to emerge from the amateur game to take on 28-year-old Pancho Gonzales, the reigning world number one in the professional game, and holder of the US Pro title, the Wembley Pro title and the Tournament of Champions. Agreeing to the match-up, Gonzales vowed to 'blow Rosewall off the court'.

There seems little doubt, as Rosewall later argued, that there was a big gulf between the calibre of the top amateurs and the top professionals in favour of the latter. Some who turned pro did not make the grade. Others did, Rosewall obviously amongst their number. At first, however, it was an uphill struggle for Rosewall. He toured Australia and the US with Gonzales from January to May 1957 and was decisively beaten by fifty matches to twenty-six. As if to underline the fact of the quality gulf, Rosewall also played Pro tournaments in Sydney and Ohio in February and April respectively. In the first event, he lost comprehensively to Frank Sedgman – who was judged to be the second best pro in 1956 – and in the second he suffered a similar fate at the hands of Pancho Segura, the third best pro in 1956. Typically, however, Rosewall did not stand still. He set out to improve his game, for example by strengthening his service, and as 1957 went on, he achieved real results. In September, he won the Wembley title, defeating Segura, and at the end of the year he triumphed in an Australian tour which included Hoad, Sedgman and Segura.

1958 was a good year for Rosewall as he won the French Professional Championships on clay, beating Kramer, Sedgman and Hoad to do so. At the Forest Hills Pro tournament, Rosewall was runner-up and he tied for second place with Gonzales and Sedgman in the Masters Round Robin Pro in the United States.

In 1959, the Queensland Pro Championships were staged twice, in January and in December. Rosewall won both, beating Trabert in five sets in the first event and Gonzales 1–6, 7–5, 8–6, 8–6 in the second. That year, for the first time, Rosewall had the edge over Gonzales, prevailing 6–4 in their head-to-head encounters.

The feeling of triumph in relation to Gonzales was short-lived. In 1960, normal service was resumed and in a four-man tour involving Gonzales, Alex Olmedo and Segura, Rosewall was second below, but well below, Gonzales – of their twenty-one contests, Gonzales won sixteen. When Gonzales retired in the middle of the year – temporarily, as it transpired – Rosewall pushed forward, claiming six titles, the most prestigious of which were the French Pro at Roland Garros and the Wembley Pro. His victims were, respectively, Lew Hoad and Pancho Segura, both of whom fell in four sets.

1961 was a year divided between not playing at all and winning big when it mattered to him most. For the first half of the year, breaking the pattern of remorseless touring that had been standard fare for a decade, Rosewall took a time-out. From the summer onwards he competed and was successful in two major events. He won the French Professional Championship by beating Gonzales, now thirty-three but still competing at the highest level, in four sets 2–6, 6–4, 6–3, 8–6. He went on to take the Wembley Professional title by overcoming Lew Hoad in four sets. The French Championship, of course, was played on clay and the Wembley tournament indoors on wood – a fast surface – and it was a fitting commentary on his success as an all-court player in the second half of the year that Rosewall went on to win the New South Wales Championship in Sydney.

If 1961 had been a mixture for Rosewall, 1962 represented an unalloyed triumph. He retained his French Pro Championship title with a four-set victory over Andrés Gimeno and likewise held onto his Wembley crown, beating Lew Hoad 6–4, 5–7, 15–13, 7–5. The latter victory was described by the tennis historian Jo McCauley as 'one of the all-time great finals'. These were big wins but they were supplemented by a further five titles across Australia and Europe and two further titles in New Zealand.

In 1963, Rosewall worsted Laver in their tour of Australia and New Zealand, taking eleven of their thirteen matches. Thereafter Rosewall toured the US with Laver and others, Rosewall again winning more than he lost to Laver and emerging ahead of the pack. Of greater significance, perhaps, than the tours was the fact that Rosewall won the three big professional tournaments of the year, namely the US Pro – destroying Laver – on grass, the French Pro on wood – again triumphing over Laver – and the Wembley Pro on wood – defeating Hoad in four sets. Objectively, the evidence in 1963, measured by tournament victories and success in the key head-to-head rivalries, is that Rosewall was the number one player in the world.

Probably the highlight of the year for Rosewall, on account both of the quality of his performance and of the fact that it was against Laver, by then his closest rival, was that victory in the

US Professional tournament on grass. The two men had many very tight matches against each other. Frankly, this was not one of them. For much of it, the encounter was one-way traffic as Rosewall took control of proceedings to win 6–4, 6–2, 6–2. As Allison Danzig observed in the *New York Times*, it was 'an unforgettable exposition of the art, science, and vigor of lawn tennis at its finest'. *The Times* newspaper dubbed Rosewall 'the supreme surgeon'.

In 1964, Rosewall won the French Pro, defeating Laver on wood. However, he lost the Wembley Pro final to the Rocket in a marathon five-set encounter, succumbing 7–5, 5–7, 4–6, 8–6, 8–6. 1965 was characterised by regular tit-for-tat between Rosewall and Laver but in 1966 Rosewall fell to Laver again at the Wembley Pro, thrashed in straight sets 6–2, 6–2, 6–3, and thereafter it would appear that Laver established his ascendancy over Rosewall both in terms of the head-to-head results and in the world rankings.

From 1967 onwards, Rosewall is thought to have been in decline but that decline was neither rapid nor uninterrupted by great success. In 1968, for example, the world's first Open tournament was held at West Hants Club, Bournemouth – the British Hard Court Championships. Rosewall won the tournament, defeating Laver in the final in four sets. Similarly, at the French Open that year, Rosewall claimed the title with a four-set final defeat of Laver, causing the veteran tennis commentator Rex Bellamy to claim that Rosewall 'mesmerised Laver with his immaculate length and tactical nous'. Crashing out of Wimbledon to Tony Roche in the fourth round, however, prompted speculation that Rosewall was approaching the end of his career, but that verdict was still heavily premature. Rosewall clearly no longer enjoyed pre-eminence – just as forty years later Roger Federer would cease to be pre-eminent from 2008 but continue to perform strongly at the highest level – but he made it to the final of the French Open in 1969, where he was beaten in straight sets by Laver.

In January 1970, *World Tennis* described Rosewall as 'one of the fallen heroes of the game'. Even though Rosewall was by then clearly no longer the dominant or leading player in the world, the description seems dramatic and overstated. First, Rosewall was by then thirty-five and still competing at the highest level. Secondly, although the critics were not at that point to know it, Rosewall still had some phenomenal match wins in him. For example, at Wimbledon in 1970, Rosewall defeated Tony Roche in the quarter-finals 10–8, 6–1, 4–6, 6–2 and his performance was judged to be quite spectacular. One observer noted breathlessly in *World Tennis* in September 1970: 'His anticipation was uncanny for he supported his brilliant reading of Roche's intentions with a turn of speed that was amazing for a man his age.'

For the third time, Rosewall reached the final at Wimbledon, fourteen years after his second appearance and sixteen years since his first. He was outgunned over five sets by the big-serving John Newcombe, his fellow Australian and a man nearly ten years his junior. Yet at Forest Hills that year, at the US Open, Rosewall beat both Newcombe and Roche and won the title. To do so at any age would be a great achievement; to do so at the age of thirty-five was a magnificent feat. To be fair, both victories prompted lavish plaudits from the commentators. Referring to the defeat of Newcombe, Neil Amdur, writing in the *New York Times*, declared: 'Rosewall's service return is the finest in the game. His angled return, particularly down the line, forced Newcombe to stretch for the first volley rather than punch it for a winner.'

Commenting upon Rosewall's defeat of Roche, *World Tennis* in December 1970 observed: '[He] was all over the net, covering shots like a man with twice his reach and teasing his opponent with his feathery touch.'

In November 1970, on the back of some great victories and outstanding performances, a panel of tennis writers voted Rosewall Player of the Year. As has already been pointed out,

by the late 1960s, Laver had overtaken Rosewall in the rankings and established a modest ascendancy over him in their
matches. In this context, as well as for their own sakes as
exhilarating contests, the 1971 and 1972 WCT finals are of
particular interest. The 1971 final was worth $50,000 to the
winner and at least as much in prestige. Laver was thirty-three,
Rosewall thirty-seven and the former had won eight of their
nine most recent contests. They split the opening two sets and
Rosewall rode out the winner in four sets, taking the third
and fourth in tie-breaks. Rosewall's biographer, Peter Rowley,
highlights both the catlike movement of Rosewall and his
stunning backhand passing shots. For Richard Evans, both the
passing shots – 'sharp, deft' – and his superb backhand volleys
were striking testaments to the continuing quality of the old
master's game.

If the 1971 final was a fine match, the 1972 encounter was an
epic. Bud Collins, writing in *World Tennis* in 1975, speculated
that it may have been the best match ever played, and certainly
Mike Davies, the executive director of WCT, proclaimed it the
greatest he had ever seen. Watched by 23 million viewers, Peter
Rowley recalls that 'the tennis was absolutely beautiful', characterised by 'scores of perfectly placed shots, rifled at all angles'.
It was a remarkable see-saw encounter. Rosewall lost the first
set 6–4, blitzed through the second to win a bagel set, 6–0, took
the third 6–3 and lost the fourth in a tie-break. The final set was
very tight but fluctuating, Rosewall having an early break at 3–1
and 4–2, but Laver fought back. At 5–4 to Rosewall, with Laver
serving to stay in the match, Rosewall had a match point, but
it was promptly snatched from his grasp by an ace from Laver.
The match proceeded to a thrilling final-set tie-break. With
Laver serving at 5–4 up in that breaker, Rosewall was in trouble,
but he levelled the score at 5–5 with a scintillating cross-court
backhand service return which Laver could not control and
volleyed out. Rosewall followed that point with a backhand
return down the line past Laver to earn match point, and then

took the match with a well-placed service to Laver's backhand. This title was one of the greatest triumphs of Rosewall's career and the biggest disappointment of Laver's.

In 1974, Rosewall played relatively little and for the first time in twenty-two years he completed the year without winning a tournament. In one sense, therefore, it might be regarded as a year to be forgotten. In another, however, it was a year that spoke of the legend – the greatness – that is Ken Rosewall. At Wimbledon, he beat the number one seed John Newcombe in four sets, and progressed to the semi-finals to face Stan Smith, who had won the title two years previously when there had been a full complement of top class contenders, unlike the 1973 tournament, which most of the top players boycotted. Smith was twenty-seven, Rosewall was thirty-nine. Smith led by two sets to love and served for the match at 5–4 in the third. Later, he had a match point in the tie-break but could not take it. Try as he might, Smith simply could not finish the job and Rosewall eventually won in five sets. He had therefore reached his fourth Wimbledon final exactly twenty years after his first appearance against Jaroslav Drobný.

His legion of fans – I, then eleven years old, amongst them – all over the world must have been earnestly hoping that now, in what was surely the twilight of his career, Rosewall could finally win the one major title that had always eluded him. It was not to be. Sadly, it was not even close. Rosewall came up against the brash but brilliant 21-year-old from Illinois Jimmy Connors, who had been making his presence felt for a couple of years and was now visibly more formidable. Connors was frankly awesome. He provided a stunning display of power tennis, striking the ball with a ferocity, even brutality, with which no player at the time could have coped. Rosewall offered little resistance, perhaps understandably exhausted by his prodigious efforts in the previous fortnight. If he had been less weary – he declares that he was 'probably exhausted' – and had performed at his best, the match would doubtless have been closer but he would not have won.

The scoreline was 6–1, 6–1, 6–4 and it reflected the reality of a one-sided match.

Nevertheless, there can be precious few examples – I can identify none in the Open era – of a top player in a highly physical sport reaching finals two decades apart. Far from Rosewall's reputation being damaged – even though his pride may have been – it was enhanced. If proof were needed that Rosewall was still a force to be reckoned with in top-class tennis, he offered a repeat performance of his Wimbledon near-triumph when he competed at the US Open in Forest Hills two months later. Just as he had overcome Stan Smith at Wimbledon in the semi-finals, so at Forest Hills he dispatched John Newcombe in four sets to set up a contest again with Jimmy Connors in the final. This time the destruction was even more brutal than at the All England Club. Connors, striking the ball with staggering force, also placed it accurately and simply overpowered Rosewall 6–1, 6–0, 6–1. Again, the scale of the defeat will have hurt Rosewall but the real significance of his performance was, once again, the ability to reach the final when he was two months shy of his fortieth birthday. He had first reached the US Championships final in 1955, had won it in 1956 and 1970, and here he was, in 1974, a finalist again.

It was a tribute to his physical fitness and the fact that he had escaped serious injuries in his career. That was partly a matter of good fortune, but only partly. It was also attributable to his simple and first-rate technique and to the economic and nimble-footed character of his play. It was also a commentary upon his adaptability as a tennis player. He had long ago added exquisite volleys to his superb groundstrokes and for many years now Rosewall had cultivated the serve-and-volley technique which, though energetic, is less physically debilitating than playing constant long rallies from the back of the court. Jack Kramer puts this down as the secret to his success. 'Kenny wouldn't have lasted into his forties as a world-class player if he hadn't learned to serve and volley.'

Well, he had learned, and he did last.

Rosewall continued to play competitively, albeit not playing in as many tournaments, until he retired in 1980. He remained in the world's top ten until 1975 and the top twenty until 1977.

By any standard, Rosewall was a great champion. He possessed amongst the best groundstrokes of any player in any era and his backhand must rank as one of the finest. A great volleyer, superb mover around the court, strategically and tactically outstanding, he was one of the most formidable match players of all time. True, he lacked a great serve, but what he missed in terms of power, he partly compensated for with precision, variety and consistency. His tally of major titles as an amateur and a professional is immensely impressive. Moreover, though his failure to win Wimbledon is a debit on his balance sheet, no one could argue that Rosewall was unable to play on grass. He could and did, winning six of his eight Grand Slams on that surface and a further two Pro Slams on it. He was successful indoors as well as outdoors and performed exceptionally well on wood, the fastest surface, claiming no fewer than four of his fifteen professional titles on it.

Yet the one feature of Rosewall's career that stands out above all others is the sheer durability of his competitive success at top level. No other player has won or been a finalist in major tournaments over such a long period. Gonzales had a very long career, punctuated by periodic retirements, and some may judge him a better player, but he did not win major tournaments even as a pro, over as long a period. In the words of the former BBC tennis commentator, John Barrett, himself a former player and vastly experienced student of the game over six decades:

In every sport there are performers who for one shining moment, flash into memory like meteors across the night sky, and then quickly fade from view, and from meaning. Then there are the immortals, those legendary players who are recognised by the public, the media and their peers for the outstanding contribution they have made to the evolution of their chosen profession. Such a man is Ken Rosewall.

That is the reputation and legacy of the man.

Chapter Seven

Lew Hoad

LEW HOAD WAS a brilliant champion in the 1950s and, though he enjoyed modest and intermittent success as a professional, it is for his performances in the amateur game that he will chiefly be remembered. Born 23 November 1934, in Glebe, Australia – three weeks after his friend, rival and doubles partner Ken Rosewall – Lewis Alan Hoad was the son of a tramwayman. Standing at 5ft 10in. tall, Hoad was extremely strong, very quick and given from an early age to playing attacking tennis. He won four major singles titles, the Australian, French and Wimbledon crowns in 1956 and the Wimbledon title again in 1957 whereafter he promptly turned professional. As a professional, he won the Tournament of Champions in 1959 and was seven times the losing finalist in major events, twice in the US (1958 and 1959), three times at Wembley (1961, '62, and '63) and twice in France (1958 and 1960).

As a young boy, Hoad developed his renowned physical strength, most notably in his hands and arms, by training at a police boys' club. There he acquired a reputation as an accomplished boxer. Hoad's family life was both happy and encouraging. He had a strong father and a devoted mother. Also, aged ten, he was fortunate to have a skilled tennis coach, Joe Harris, thought to be the best player in or anywhere near the neighbourhood. At twelve, he rushed home to tell his father, 'Hey Dad, I can serve hard.' It is thought to be at around this time that Hoad first met Adrian Quist, a former Australian tennis champion and by then the general manager of the Dunlop Sports Goods Company. They played sets together and Quist was impressed by the natural ability Hoad demonstrated. Aged fourteen, Hoad, who was not interested in academic study, left school and joined Dunlop as a racket stringer and office boy. It is said that the job was offered by Adrian Quist on the back of Hoad's high-quality play in the Balmain District Championship. Part of the deal was that Hoad received free tennis gear and equipment and, very importantly, he was given two afternoons off per week in order to practise his tennis. Hoad received coaching from Quist and Dinny Pails and the chance to play exhibition matches with Jack Crawford, Jaroslav Drobný and Eric Sturgess.

How did Hoad approach the game? In a word: attacking. The retired British tennis commentator and noted authority on the sport John Barrett described Hoad as the 'dynamic Australian'. He was certainly that. He had a cracking first serve, thought by the former Wimbledon champion and world number one, Ellsworth Vines, to be the most severe delivery of any player under 6ft tall. The wrist snap in the stroke was especially acute and accounted for the sheer force of it. The second serve was also very effective. He had highly penetrating groundstrokes, of which his forehand was the more consistent, but he was well able to drive winners off both wings to all parts of the court. His volleys were of the highest quality, as was his overhead, and he was able not only to perform with power and accuracy but to do so throughout entire matches and tournaments. A brawny guy, Hoad was also extremely fleet of foot and could cover the net, the baseline and the area between the two with lightning speed.

However, whereas other champions highlighted in this book – from Tilden to Perry, from Kramer to Gonzales to Rosewall – were inclined to think tactically and, for the most part, to play the percentages, it was not Hoad's instinct to do so. As Jack Kramer was to note, Hoad would not 'temporise' even on key points. He would always seek to attack – and was never a great defender – though it is a commentary on just how good a player he was that

Hoad won the French championship in 1956 on the slow clay in Paris.

Vines describes Hoad as 'overwhelming' but adds the almost inevitable rider that he was erratic. The sheer steel-like strength of his wrist – perhaps analogous to the Perry wrist that Bill Tilden had perceptively identified – enabled him to hit shots that would have been beyond mere mortals. His speed, his acceleration and his awesome net game made him as formidable an opponent as you can conceive. Vines concedes that on his best days Hoad was 'invincible'. However, he did not, either as a youngster or later, vary his pace very much and he was given to lapses of concentration which could cost him dear.

Early in his career, competing at the New South Wales junior championships, an unseeded Hoad beat Ken Rosewall 6–3, 6–2, an enormous breakthrough, as he had lost to Rosewall in their previous matches. In 1950, at the age of sixteen, Hoad won the Australian junior title but lost in four sets in the National Hard Court men's tournament to Harry Hopman, who was later to become the Australian Davis Cup captain. Subsequently, he was to avenge the loss to Hopman with victory over him in the Victoria championship. The following year he beat Ham Richardson to take the national junior title of Australia.

In 1952 Hoad lost to Rosewall 10–8, 6–2 in the Australian junior championship but he was nevertheless chosen for the Australian team to go overseas that year. Thanks to his birthday falling three weeks after Rosewall's, he was the youngest Australian ever to represent his country abroad. At the National Hard Court event, Hoad beat Rosewall in a pulsating, topsy-turvy, five-set encounter, prevailing 2–6, 6–1, 1–6, 6–2, 11–9. At the Queen's Club tournament before Wimbledon, Hoad lost to Drobný in the semi-finals, though he did enjoy the consolation of acing the great Czech fourteen times.

Although this book focuses on singles, and attempts to rate champions on that basis, it is a fact that Hoad and Rosewall first caught the public's imagination outside Australia by their

performance in 1952 at Wimbledon in the doubles. The pair beat
Gardnar Mulloy – an outstanding American doubles player –
and Dick Savitt, who had won the singles in 1951. In the tenth
game of the fifth set, leading 5–4, the Americans had match
point. Rosewall then hit two superb backhand passing shots and
Mulloy lost his serve. Hoad held his own delivery and the young
Australians went on to take the match.

At the US Open, still only seventeen, Hoad beat the former
American champion Art Larsen in straight sets, before succumbing decisively to Frank Sedgman. There was no disgrace in that.
Sedgman was seven years Hoad's senior, performing at the peak
of his powers and the eventual winner of the tournament without
the loss of a set. When Hoad returned to Australia, he was still
not eighteen and had caused quite a stir by the audacity of his
on-court exploits. Adrian Quist, coach and counsellor, remarked
at the time, 'Hoad's innate shyness is almost an embarrassment to
him. At times, big crowds have mistaken this for superciliousness.'

At the back end of 1952, Hoad suffered a slump in form. The
early part of 1953 was not much better. Yet his best tournament at
this difficult time was the Australian Hard Court event, in which
Hoad recovered from 5–2 down in the fifth set to beat Rosewall.

In Rome in 1953, Hoad was beaten by Drobný in straight sets. In
Paris that year, having reached the semi-final of the French championship, he succumbed to Vic Seixas. Apparently Hoad felt jinxed
playing the man. Seixas mixed up his shots, varying the pace, direction and trajectory of the ball so much that there was no regular
pattern. Hoad could not get into a groove and was permanently
unsettled against the wily and experienced American.

At the Queen's Club event before Wimbledon in 1953, Hoad
beat Rosewall 8–6, 10–8 to take the title. At Wimbledon, he lost
in the quarter-finals 9–7 in the fifth set to Seixas. Then at the
Eastern Grass Court championships at South Orange, Hoad beat
Hartwig in the final. It was at this time that the back trouble
which would ultimately bring his career to a premature end
started to afflict him.

According to Ellsworth Vines, Forest Hills in 1953 resembled a furnace. Although Hoad was physically strong, he did not excel in extreme heat and he lost to Seixas on Centre Court, where the temperature was 118 Fahrenheit. In the Pacific Southwest event, Hoad, who was not accustomed to concrete, lost again to Seixas.

Vines maintains that around this time Hoad's groundstrokes, especially his backhand, were improving. At Melbourne in the Davis Cup, Hoad disposed of Seixas in straight sets. Rosewall, against expectations, lost his rubber to Trabert. Hoad and Hartwig then lost the doubles to Seixas and Trabert, meaning that the Australians had to win both of the reverse singles if they were to retain the Davis Cup. To his lasting credit and pride, Hoad fought and won a magnificent five-set contest against Trabert, triumphing 13–11, 6–3, 2–6, 3–6, 7–5 in front of a 17,000-strong crowd. Rosewall beat Seixus in four sets and the cup was kept in Australia.

Following a short spell of military service, Hoad went to Paris for the 1954 French championship. Although seeded one, Hoad lost to Gardnar Mulloy. At Queen's, Hoad played well and won the tournament, beating his fellow Australian Mervyn Rose in the final in straight sets. At Wimbledon, Hoad reversed his previous loss to Mulloy but he fell to Drobný in the quarter-finals.

In the US, Hoad retained his Eastern Grass Court title by defeating Mulloy and Rosewall in straight sets. Yet at Newport he lost to the seventeen-year-old Australian Roy Emerson, describing the defeat as 'one of the really bad matches I seem to get half a dozen times a year'.

At the US championship, Hoad lost to Ham Richardson in the quarter-final in five sets. Though generally an easygoing and good-natured character, Hoad could show annoyance, even exasperation, on the court. He won the Queensland tournament in 1954 but lost to John Bromwich – an Australian then beyond his prime – in the quarter-final of the New South Wales grass-court event in Sydney. When Hoad then lost to Seixas in the prestigious Victorian championship, he knocked the ball over the grandstand.

Challenged about his conduct by reporters, he said that he did it 'because I felt like it. I'm sick of everybody getting on my back.' Adrian Quist, who felt that young players were subject to huge pressure, not least from their own media, declared that Hoad 'is not a tennis automaton and I hope he never becomes one'. He acknowledged also that Hoad had trouble keeping concentration over long periods.

In 1955, Hoad married Jenny Staley, herself a quality tennis player. They had met aged seventeen and were to remain together throughout his career and beyond, later establishing a tennis school in Spain after his retirement from the sport. Their strong partnership endured until his tragic and untimely death from leukaemia in 1994.

In the quarter-final at Wimbledon that year, Hoad lost to Budge Patty. However, he performed strongly in the Davis Cup as Australia took it back 5–0 in the challenge round over the USA. Hoad beat Trabert and Seixus – each in four sets – and won his doubles rubber with Hartwig. At the US championship in Forest Hills, Hoad lost to Trabert in the semi-finals in straight sets. Trabert then turned professional. 1956 proved to be Hoad's big breakthrough year. Sure, he performed superbly, yet he also seemed steadier and more consistent. In a golden sequence, Hoad won the Australian, French and Wimbledon titles – defeating Rosewall, Sven Davidson and then Rosewall again. At the US, Hoad was bidding for the Grand Slam. After an auspicious start to the final in which Hoad took the first set 6–4 over Rosewall, the latter turned the tables. Changing tactics, Rosewall started to rush the net and effectively to hustle Hoad. It appears that Hoad did not respond with a mixture of drives, dinks and lobs, as might have been advisable, especially in the very windy conditions. Instead, he kept blasting attempted groundstroke passes but that day Rosewall had his number and won the title with a four-set victory. Ellsworth Vines observed that Hoad had 'all the talent in the world, but he was never a smart player as an amateur'. As an illustration, he makes the point that Hoad lost to

Budge Patty even though his serve, forehand, backhand and net game were all superior to those of his opponent. He simply did not think tactically.

In 1957, Hoad turned professional. In his big tour against Pancho Gonzales, Hoad got off to a strong start, winning eighteen of the first twenty-seven matches, but he could not sustain the lead. Gonzales had terrific staying power, the desire and capacity to slug it out for as long as necessary to win, and he emerged the tour victor by fifty-one matches to thirty-seven. Nevertheless, it is interesting that Gonzales, who was neither slow to blow his own trumpet nor overgenerous in singing the praises of his opponents, was laudatory in his verdict on Hoad. In an interview in the *New York Times* in 1995 shortly before his death, and not long after Hoad's premature passing, he acknowledged that, even when playing at his best, Hoad's game was 'better than mine'.

It is as well at this point to take a slightly closer look at the period of Hoad's true supremacy in the amateur game. This was in 1956 and, to a lesser but still considerable extent, in 1957. In 1956, seeded number one at Wimbledon, Hoad dropped only three sets in the entire fortnight. Playing with power, daring, fluency and accuracy, Hoad's tennis was an exquisite sight to behold. In the first four rounds, Hoad came through in straight sets. In the quarter-final, up against a fellow Australian, the Queenslander Mal Anderson, Hoad lost the first set and won the fourth 13–11. In the final against Rosewall, in the words of John Barrett, 'power conquered finesse'. Hoad beat Rosewall in four sets, 6–2, 4–6, 7–5, 6–4. From the first round to the last, Hoad had won twenty-one sets and sacrificed only two.

Ironically, although 1957 was a slightly less sparkling year for Hoad as he failed to hold on to his Australian and French titles, he was even more imperious at Wimbledon. He dropped just one set in the entire tournament, to Mervyn Rose, in the quarter-final. In the final, in a staggering display of attacking tennis, Hoad destroyed his fellow Australian Ashley Cooper, who was himself to lift the title the following year. Hoad blitzed Cooper aside 6–2,

6–1, 6–2 in fifty-seven minutes. The tennis commentator Lance Tingay observed of that performance: 'It was a display of genius and it is to be doubted if such dynamic shot-making was sustained with such accuracy before. If Cooper felt he had played badly, he had no choice to do anything else. Hoad was superhuman. It never began to be a contested match.' John Barrett has been similarly exultant about Hoad playing at that level. In his own words, 'When he was at his peak, as he was in beating Ashley Cooper to take his second Wimbledon singles in 1957, one could not resist the conclusion that no other man in the game, however great, could have lived against him.'

On the back of achieving supremacy as an amateur, Hoad followed Rosewall's example in turning professional. Twenty-four hours after his second Wimbledon triumph, he signed on the dotted line. Although, as mentioned earlier, he was ultimately worsted by Gonzales in their tour, Hoad could perform when he was motivated. Alongside his success in the Tournament of Champions in 1959 referenced earlier, he also won two-thirds of his matches against Rosewall. He got on well with Rosewall but there was a keen rivalry and observers had the sense that when they faced each other, Hoad, just as much as Rosewall, thirsted to win.

By contrast, in 1958, when Jack Kramer was thirty-seven, a part-time player and unquestionably past his prime, he beat Hoad in a series by thirteen matches to twelve. Kramer did not suffer from false modesty but he was under no illusion that at that stage he was a superior player. Rather, he said his victory 'was because he just didn't give a damn when he played me … It was the same thing with Segura, and Lew lost a majority of his matches to Segoo.' This is instructive as to Hoad's devil-may-care attitude. Pancho Segura was a world-class player but he was a rung below the level of great champions, Hoad included. A motivated Hoad would surely have got the better of Segura but whereas Rosewall and, say, Gonzales were spine-chillingly competitive, Hoad was not.

At twenty-five, Hoad developed a bad back but, for a period, he overcame it and was able to perform at a very high level. In 1963, for example, Hoad beat Laver in four sets in Sydney when the latter was a debut professional. Interestingly, he also beat Laver several more times until his back problem returned with a vengeance. Vines notes that at that stage Hoad handled Laver's serve better than Laver handled his. This run of victories might explain why Laver ranked Hoad the best of his contemporaries. It is inevitably in part a subjective judgement. Laver felt Hoad's heat and respected it.

I have read about and heard several witnesses who declare that when Hoad was 'on' or 'hot', he was unplayable. In terms of power, shot-making and speed, he was by all accounts awesome. Bud Collins highlights his 'remarkable weight of shot and free-wheeling attack'. However, there were weaknesses. First, he tended always to blast on his very first groundstroke even if it was not propitious to do so. In other words, unlike Kramer or Rosewall, Hoad was not a practitioner of percentage tennis. He took big risks and often paid the price in points lost which, with patience, could have been points won. Secondly, Hoad did not defend well. He seemed to care little for such an approach, but the capacity to retrieve effectively, to fend off another player's attack, even to opt for a more circumspect approach if Plan A is not working, are all part of the equipment of the greatest tennis play-ers. They formed no part of the Hoad method. Thirdly, for all his magnificent gifts, he did not always fight like a tiger as Gonzales, Rosewall, Connors, Borg and Nadal, to name but a few, have all done. Indeed, as a junior, Hoad was once accused of not trying and, although he and his coach thought the charge unfair, it is perhaps understandable that an observer could think so when he appeared distracted, impatient to finish, or simply nonchalant on the court. As John Barrett put it, 'He was an uneven player in that here and there he seemed bored and ready to lose to men below his class. That was a quirk of genius. When he was inspired to be at his most dynamic, he would have beaten anybody.'

Chapter Eight

Roy Emerson

ROY EMERSON WAS a multiple champion. Over and over again, this personable and popular Australian, with a demonstrated zest for life and love of tennis, proved himself to be top dog in the amateur game. He ended both 1964 and 1965 as the world number one amateur player, won twelve Grand Slam singles titles – a record for over thirty years until Pete Sampras surpassed it in 2000 – and sixteen Grand Slam doubles titles. His tally of twenty-eight remains an all-time male record and he was the first male player to win each major title at least twice. Moreover, only six other men in the history of the game have won all four majors in their careers. They are Fred Perry, Don Budge, Rod Laver, Andre Agassi, Roger Federer and Rafael Nadal. By any yardstick, Emerson boasts a quite outstanding record. The only caveat we should insert when extolling the virtues of this great champion and competitor is that most of his major titles were won in the closing years of the era in which participation in those events was confined to amateurs. In other words, ten of the twelve titles came between 1963 and 1967, when two of the maestros of the game, Rod Laver and Ken Rosewall, had turned professional. That said, Emerson built up an extraordinarily impressive record, displaying not merely prowess but consistency at the highest level of the game.

Born 3 November 1936, Roy Emerson began life on a farm in Blackbutt, Queensland. Subsequently, his family moved to Brisbane, where he attended grammar school and received regular tennis coaching. Some Grand Slam champions have won titles in their teens and it is commonplace for them to do so by the age of twenty-one. In that sense, Emerson did not make an auspicious early start to his title winning ways. His first major title came in doubles at Wimbledon in 1959 where, partnered by his fellow Australian Neale Fraser, he prevailed over another Australian combination of Rod Laver and Robert Mark 8–6, 6–3, 14–16, 9–7. Singles success followed in 1961 when Emerson defeated Rod Laver in the final of the Australian championship in four sets, 1–6, 6–3, 7–5, 6–4. As if to ram home his supremacy at that time, Emerson repeated his victory over Laver in claiming the US Open in 1961, on this occasion overcoming Laver in straight sets 7–5, 6–3, 6–2. At that time both tournaments were played on grass.

Six foot tall and playing right-handed, Emerson was regarded by his peers as supremely fit and well equipped to cope in the most demanding encounters occurring in gruelling conditions. 'Emmo', as he was dubbed by his many friends on the men's tour, was at heart a serve-and-volley specialist who naturally thrived on grass and carpet courts, i.e. fast surfaces. That said, in common with other great champions down the ages, he had the will and the ability to adapt to the testing conditions of clay courts and thereby won big tournaments on all surfaces.

It is often said that backing up a player's maiden Slam title success by winning the next such event is as challenging as anything in sport. Emerson did not do so but he did win the US Open only eight months after his first triumph. 1962 was less successful but Emerson still reached three Slam finals – in Australia, France and the US. On each occasion, his nemesis was his fellow countryman, friend and frequent doubles partner Rod Laver. In Australia, Laver beat him in four sets 8–6, 0–6, 6–4, 6–4. At the French, Emerson took the first two sets, only to be denied in five 3–6, 2–6, 6–3, 9–7, 6–2. At the US Open, Emerson was once again beaten in four sets 6–2, 6–4, 5–7, 6–4.

It was in 1963 that he returned to Grand Slam glory. Aged twenty-six, Emerson dropped only one set en route to the final of the Australian Open, defeating Bob Hewitt in the semi-final 8–6, 6–4, 3–6, 9–7. In the final, he mastered his fellow country-man Ken Fletcher, sweeping to victory for the loss of only seven games, 6–3, 6–3, 6–1. Building on that impressive win, Emerson proved his mettle and versatility in claiming his first French Open title, the only major tournament then – and now – played on clay courts. His final opponent was the first Frenchman to reach that stage since Marcel Bernard had won the title in 1946 – namely Pierre Darmon. He had beaten the 1961 champion, Manolo Santana, in a topsy-turvy semi-final over five sets, 6–3, 4–6, 2–6, 9–7, 6–2. Emerson had disposed of the big-serving British player Mike Sangster. In the final, after sacrificing the first set, Emerson took charge and rode out the winner in four sets 3–6, 6–1, 6–4, 6–4.

This represented a formidable start to the season – two majors contested, two majors won. Unsurprisingly, Emerson was expected to win Wimbledon. Rod Laver, who had won the crown at the All England Club in each of the previous two years, had now turned professional and Emerson certainly looked to be the strongest rider in the pack. Unfortunately for him, however, Emerson faced Germany's Wilhelm Bungert – who was to be a losing finalist at the tournament four years later – and lost a hard-fought tussle in five sets, Bungert prevailing 8–6, 3–6, 6–3, 4–6, 6–3.

Bungert was then defeated by Chuck McKinley, who in turn beat Fred Stolle in the final. Emerson fared no better at the US Open, where in the last sixteen he succumbed to the ferocious serving of the unseeded Floridian Frank Froehling III, 6–4, 4–6, 9–7, 6–2. He might have derived modest consolation from the fact that Froehling made his way to the final, where he was defeated by Rafael Osuna.

If 1963 was a great year for Emerson, tinged with disap-pointment at Wimbledon and the US Open, 1964 was still better. That year, Emerson won three of the four Slams, failing only at the French Open, where he was beaten comprehensively by the Italian Nicola Pietrangeli 6–1, 6–3, 6–3. Emerson dominated the season and he dominated his fellow Australian Fred Stolle, whom he beat in all three of those Slam finals. At the Australian Open, Emerson prevailed in straight sets 6–3, 6–4, 6–2. At Wimbledon, Stolle offered somewhat fiercer resistance, greatly prolonging one set and winning another, but still Emerson emerged victorious in four sets 6–4, 12–10, 4–6, 6–3. In the US Open final, Emerson again won very comfortably 6–4, 6–2, 6–4. In the course of these and other tournament triumphs in 1964, Emerson built a stretch of fifty-five straight singles victories and put together an overall winning record of 109–6 matches.

This remarkable run included two singles wins in the challenge round of the Davis Cup. In total, Emerson won seventeen tournaments that year, a supremacy reflected in his year-end number one ranking.

Alongside the personal prizes, Emerson was delighted to play his part in winning back the Davis Cup from the Americans. Emerson thumped Dennis Ralston 6–3, 6–4, 6–2. More particularly, however, Bud Collins described Emerson 'running like a greyhound and whacking piercing groundstrokes and volleys' as he beat Chuck McKinley 3–6, 6–2, 6–4, 6–4 to clinch the cup 3–2 for Australia.

1965 began auspiciously for Emerson as he won his fourth – and third successive – Australian Open title. Once again, Fred Stolle was the unfortunate victim of Emerson's superiority, though he made it the toughest of their Slam final encounters. Stolle shook Emerson by building a two-set lead before the latter fought back to win in five sets 7–9, 2–6, 6–4, 7–5, 6–1. At the French Open, Emerson was dumped out of the tournament in the quarter-final by an in-form Tony Roche 6–1, 6–4, 3–6, 6–0. At Wimbledon, however, Emerson successfully defended his title, conquering Stolle in the final 6–2, 6–4, 6–4.

At the US Open, Emerson was ambushed in the quarter-finals by the rising American, Arthur Ashe. Serving ferociously and hitting backhands with awesome power and accuracy, Ashe triumphed 13–11, 6–4, 10–12, 6–2. That setback notwithstanding, it had been another excellent year for Emerson. On top of his two Slam titles, he had won seven of the twenty-two tournaments he played and posted an 85–16 match record. As in 1964, Emerson was ranked the year-end world number one.

Amongst his many qualities, Emerson was an easygoing, clubbable character, popular with his peers. Competitive, to be sure, but never personally unpleasant, still less vengeful, he must nevertheless have been delighted to settle the score with Ashe, who had outplayed him in the US the previous autumn. At the Australian Open in 1966, Emerson won the title for the fourth successive year, delivering a tidy four-set victory over Ashe, 6–4, 6–8, 6–2, 6–3.

At Wimbledon, Emerson was well placed and widely expected to retain the title. As it transpired, he was thwarted by misfortune. In the quarter-final, up against his fellow Australian Owen Davidson, Emerson raced to a one-set-to-love lead in fourteen minutes, wrapping it up 6–1. In the third game of the second set, Emerson enthusiastically chased, perhaps overenthusiastically chased, a dropshot by his opponent and crashed into the umpire's chair, damaging his shoulder in the process. Emerson continued the match but appeared to be hampered thereafter for the remainder of the contest, as the tables were turned and Davidson took control to win 1–6, 6–3, 6–4, 6–4. Emerson was a great sportsman and made no complaint or excuse, but the overriding impression was that the crash had wrecked his competence and confidence alike.

In 1967, Emerson claimed his fifth successive – sixth in total – Australian Open title. Once again, he got the better of Arthur Ashe in the final, winning in three straightforward sets 6–4, 6–1, 6–4. Indeed, the semi-final had been an altogether more arduous and pulsating affair, as Emerson overcame Tony Roche in a thrilling five-setter, 6–3, 4–6, 15–13, 13–15, 6–2. In France, Emerson took his twelfth and last Slam singles title – and his second in Paris – with a four-set victory over Roche 6–1, 6–4, 2–6, 6–2.

Mention has already been made of success for Emerson in the Davis Cup, and 1967 was as fine an example as any. For the second time in three years, Spain took on Australia for the challenge round.

As usual, Emerson took care of business in his matches with typical skill and efficiency. He began by demolishing Santana in three clinical sets, 6–4, 6–1, 6–1. Now aged thirty-one, Emerson put up another formidable performance to defeat Manuel Orantes, more than twelve years his junior. Emerson won the encounter in four sets 6–1, 6–1, 2–6, 6–4. This ended a superb career in the Davis Cup in which Australia had won eight of nine challenge rounds, with Emerson posting an 11–1 singles record and 6–0 in doubles. Overall, his win–loss ratio was 21–2 in singles and 13–2 in doubles. Importantly, he had played the 'clincher' match for his country no fewer than five times, three times in doubles and twice in singles.

There is no denying that Emerson was an outstanding competitor. He won each of the majors and though he was naturally a fast-court player, his achievement in winning the French Open twice is proof of his adaptability. Statistically, his record, especially in the Slams, is superb. He won big tournaments, won them repeatedly and won them on different surfaces. That record places him firmly in the ranking list of all-time greats. Yet, in evaluating his accomplishments and comparing them with those of other maestros, it would be remiss or just plain coy not to recognise that Emerson is in a distinct category from everyone else in this book. He competed both before the advent of the Open era and after its inception, enjoying huge success in the first phase but not in the second. Put simply, he could not reproduce his triumphs when Rosewall, Laver and others competed in the majors from 1968. That he was a great

champion is a matter of fact. It is no discourtesy to Emerson
to conclude that others, including many who won fewer major
titles, were greater.

Chapter Nine

Rod Laver

IT WAS MY huge privilege to meet Rod Laver, albeit just once. In June 1977, the pre-Wimbledon so-called 'warm-up' tournament took place, as it still does today, at the Queen's Club in London. Today it is sponsored by Aegon. That year, the sponsor was Rawlings Drinks. The tournament director, Peter Bridge, was a family friend and he gave me, a fourteen-year-old tennis nut, a job for the week as a 'gofer', an errand boy for the players. From my mother, my coach and my television screen, I knew of the greatness of Rod Laver even though by then Laver was nearly thirty-nine and definitely beyond his prime. One day, I heard that he was practising his serve, alone, on one of the hard courts at Queen's. I went along to observe and saw that there was a steadily growing crowd watching the great man. Cheekily, I plucked up the courage to ask if he would let me stand at the other end of the court to pick up the balls and give them back to him so that he didn't have to change ends. He agreed and, after a few moments, he said, 'Come on, let's hit some balls.' Thereafter, he rallied with me for a quarter of an hour, running me around, playing a few dropshots, lobbing the ball over my head if I reached them, and giving me the most memorable tennis experience of my life before or since. I was an undistinguished fourteen-year-old junior player whom he did not know from Adam. He was Rod Laver, tennis legend. No media were present. He was not flanked by coach, trainer, agent or anyone else. It was incredibly kind and gracious of him to give me such an unforgettable experience. Arriving home that night, I recounted my good fortune to my mother, who had worshipped Rod Laver, and she could scarcely believe my luck.

In every discussion I have ever had with devotees of tennis – be they players, coaches, umpires or fans – about the greatest players of all time, Rod Laver always features, with many placing him at the very top of the tree.

Laver had a long (23-year) career which was split across the amateur and Open eras. He won forty-two singles titles after the advent of the Open era, when he was almost thirty, with many more as an amateur (up to 1962) and then on the professional tour (between 1962–3 and 1968). Across amateur and professional competitions, Laver is reckoned to have won at least 184 singles titles, including eleven Grand Slam singles titles. He is the only player to win the season Grand Slam twice, in 1962 as an amateur and in 1969, a month before he turned thirty-one, and he is the only male player in the Open era to have won the Grand Slam in a single season (Don Budge achieved the Grand Slam in 1938; Andre Agassi, Roger Federer and Rafael Nadal have all won a career Grand Slam, but none of them has ever taken all four majors in a single year). This achievement must be seen in the context of the era, and Laver himself has questioned whether he would have won the Slam in 1962 if some of the best players in the world at the time had not turned professional and thereby disqualified themselves from the then amateur Grand Slam championships.

On the flipside of the argument, Laver spent five of his prime years from 1963 to 1967 as a 'pro' unable to compete in most of the leading tournaments. He turned pro in 1962 just after his twenty-fourth birthday (and following his second Wimbledon singles crown), returning to the major tournaments in 1968 aged twenty-nine. Laver also won the pro Slam in 1967. He was ranked amongst the top ten twelve times, from 1959 to 1962 and from 1968 to 1975. In other words, he was still a top ten player at the age of thirty-seven, more than fifteen years after he first reached that level. Frequently introduced as 'the man with the

copper hair but the golden touch', his career record and statistics
and the manner of his triumphs – all-conquering in style, unfail-
ingly gracious in the way he conducted himself – have led many
tennis aficionados to rate him as one of the greatest or, indeed,
the greatest of all time.

Rod was the third of four children, with two older brothers,
Trevor and Bob, and a younger sister, Lois. His early life was
spent on the cattle ranch owned by his parents, Roy Stanley and
Melba Laver, and the family played on a home-made ant-bed
court in his parents' garden in Rockhampton. His father, Roy,
was instrumental in starting a tennis school in Rockhampton,
where young Rodney enrolled. A slight, sickly child, the man
who would later be known as 'Rocket', on account of the power
and speed of his play, grew strong and tough working on the
ranch and playing tennis. All three brothers won a number of
trophies in regional play in the early 1950s. Both Rod's mother
and his father were talented players, meeting for the first time at
a tennis tournament in Queensland. In every house they moved
to, a tennis court was a prerequisite. All the siblings played, but it
was Rod who showed the most talent.

Cultivating and nurturing that talent, there were two key
coaches in Laver's career – Charlie Hollis in the early years
and, later, Harry Hopman, the Australian Davis Cup captain.
Although toughened up in childhood, as we have seen, Laver
remained a relatively slight figure as an adult. He stood 5ft 8
in. tall and weighed 145–150lb. He played left-handed and, of
course, with a wooden racket. Charlie Hollis was keen to ensure
that Laver developed a sound technique and the capacity to play
every shot. A strong, flat serve, backed up by slice, topspin and
kick, and the ability to serve both down the 'T' and out wide were
crucial. Good groundstrokes, even in an age when most players
deployed a serve-and-volley approach to the game, were fundamental, as a player is receiving service fifty per cent of the time
and sound ball-striking off the ground is a vital building block in
any player's armoury. Hollis worked to develop in Laver a strong

forehand which he could hit to all parts of the court, either flat or
with topspin, together with the block or chop return.

On the backhand side, entertaining high hopes of his prodigy,
Hollis told Laver, 'You'll never win Wimbledon without a topspin
backhand.' In other words, a flat backhand can be useful but it
is more difficult to control than a shot with spin. Similarly, a
sliced backhand is an invaluable tool but it will not do the job
when a passing shot against an opponent at the net is required.
Hence Hollis drilled Laver repeatedly until he could confidently
hit over his backhand and it became one of his most outstanding
weapons. In 2012, Laver, with typical modesty, recounted that
for some time he would hit the lifted (topspin) backhand into
'the cheap seats' but gradually he acquired the control that made
it a winning shot for him. In today's game, much of the play is
from the back of the court – partly because the pace of the courts
is slower and because improved racket technology and slightly
fluffier balls are thought to favour the returner of serve – but
when young Laver was learning his craft, the volley was a vital
shot and, under the tutelage of Charlie Hollis, Laver learned to
volley well on forehand and backhand sides as well as to hit the
smash or overhead effectively to win points.

At every turn, Hollis emphasised the need to be positive. 'Go
for your shots,' he exhorted young Rod. 'You'll miss some, but
don't hold back.' The message was, 'Go for it – and with practice
you will develop the control, hit more winners and make fewer
errors.' The advice was sound. At junior level, players can win for
some time with a predominantly defensive game, but to achieve
success at the highest level, a player has to possess the weapons
to win points, rather than merely to wait for an opponent to lose
them. In any event, Hollis reasoned, it was more fun to attack
and attempt to win that way.

As the late tennis commentator Dan Maskell put it, Laver was
'technically faultless, from his richly varied serve to his feather-
light touch on drop volleys, plus a backhand drive carrying
destructive topspin where needed, or controlling slice when the

situation demanded it'. His left-handed serve was tough for an opponent to read, as Laver disguised his intentions effectively, and he could deliver it to any part of the service box with slice, topspin or kick. His wristy groundstrokes on both flanks were hit with heavy topspin, as was his attacking lob, which Laver developed into a weapon. His stroke technique was all the better for the fact that he turned his shoulders rapidly, hit through the ball and enjoyed superb timing. His backhand, often hit on the run, scored for him over and over again. When hit on the run it was a thing of beauty, had almost necessarily to be a point-ender and frequently proved to be so in his favour. Laver was fast, dextrous and blessed with an enormous left forearm, dramatically bigger than his right. As Rex Bellamy put it, 'The strength of that wrist and forearm gave him blazing power without loss of control, even when he was on the run and at full stretch. The combination of speed and strength, especially wrist strength, enabled him to hit ferocious winners when way out of court.' In the words of another commentator, Julius Heldman, 'He is competent on low balls, handling them with underspin for control, but he will cream any ball at waist level or higher.' Immense agility made him exceptionally difficult to lob against and he was a formidable counter-puncher.

Initially somewhat overambitious in his shot-making, Laver gradually developed percentage tennis as part of his play and in his heyday he was capable of adapting his playing style to all surfaces and conditions. Laver enjoyed an enviable record in five-set encounters, often coming back from the brink either by tactical adjustments or by supreme hitting.

After leaving school, Laver was hired as a clerk in Brisbane by the Dunlop Rubber Company and then, following a year in the Australian Army, in 1957 he went to England, where his first major victory was a defeat of American Barry Mackay at the Queen's Club in London.

In 1957, Laver was the Australian and US junior champion and clearly destined for a successful career. It was not the following year but in 1959, shortly before he turned twenty-one, that Laver reached all three finals at Wimbledon, winning the mixed doubles with Darlene Hard. He lost the singles final to Peruvian Alex Olmedo, following an 87-game semi-final victory – in the days before the introduction of the tie-break – over Barry Mackay. It was in 1960 that Laver won his first major singles title, the Australian championships – now the Australian Open – beating his fellow Australian and Davis Cup teammate Neale Fraser in five sets. Displaying the supreme fighting qualities and spirit of competitiveness which are the hallmarks of great champions in any sport, Laver came back from two sets down to prevail 5–7, 3–6, 6–3, 8–6, 8–6. The following year, he lost in the final in four sets to Roy Emerson. Building on that track record in Australia, Laver won his first Wimbledon singles title in 1961 – having lost in the final not only to Olmedo in 1959 but to Neale Fraser in 1960 – defeating Chuck McKinley in straight sets 6–3, 6–1, 6–4.

1962 was a stellar year for Rod Laver and a great year in the history of the game. Laver, buoyed by his successes of the previous three years, became only the second male player, after Don Budge in 1938, to win all four Grand Slam singles titles in the same year. In the Australian final he beat Roy Emerson in four sets 8–6, 0–6, 6–4, 6–4; in France he also beat Emerson, battling back from a two-set deficit to win 3–6, 2–6, 6–3, 9–7, 6–2; at Wimbledon, Laver scored a straightforward title victory over Marty Mulligan 6–2, 6–2, 6–1 and at the US Open at Forest Hills, he defeated Emerson again in four sets, 6–2, 6–4, 5–7, 6–4. Of course, it was a staggering achievement. Yet it is also striking that Laver won an additional seventeen titles in 1962, including the Italian and German championships (precursors to the Rome and Hamburg tournaments today). This 'clay-court triple' of Paris, Rome and Hamburg had been achieved previously only by Lew Hoad in 1956.

Thereafter, Laver departed the amateur game and competed on the professional circuit until the advent of the Open era in 1968. In his first full year as a pro, Laver won six tournament titles and became the number two professional player behind Ken Rosewall, nearly four years his senior, a fellow Australian, great career rival and the subject of another chapter in this book. In 1964, Laver captured the US Pro championship over Pancho Gonzales and the Wembley Pro (over Ken Rosewall who won the French Pro). 1965 was a glittering year for Laver as he picked up seventeen titles, won thirteen of his eighteen matches against Rosewall and eight of eight finals against Gonzales. The latter was by then thirty-seven but considered a major talent and still a threatening opponent to face. In 1966, Laver won sixteen events, including the US Pro championship, the Wembley Pro championship and eight other key tournaments. If anything, 1967 was even better, as Laver garnered nineteen titles, including the Wimbledon Pro (the only professional event ever staged at Wimbledon ahead of the Open era; Laver beat Rosewall 6–2, 6–2, 12–10 in the final), the US Pro championship, the Wembley Pro championship and the French Pro championship. This brought him a full house of the major Pro titles, a 'pro Grand Slam'.

The Open era started in 1968 at an event in Bournemouth and, for the first time, amateurs and professionals alike were eligible to play in the major tournaments. Laver reached the singles and men's doubles finals in Paris and, importantly, he took the inaugural 'Open' Wimbledon singles title, defeating Tony Roche in straight sets, and also winning a tournament in Los Angeles.

1969 was not only a phenomenal year for Laver but a landmark year in the history of the game. Laver won the Grand Slam for the second time, a feat unmatched before or since. In the Australian Open he beat Andrés Gimeno 6–3, 6–4, 7–5; in Paris he defeated Rosewall in straight sets, avenging a defeat at Rosewall's hands the previous year; at Wimbledon he beat rising fellow Australian John Newcombe 6–4, 5–7, 6–4, 6–4 and in the US Open final he beat Tony Roche 7–9, 6–1, 6–2, 6–2. In the course of his Grand Slam triumphs that year, Laver endured five five-set matches, twice coming back from two sets down in early rounds and winning a ninety-game semi-final against Tony Roche in the Australian

Open. In the four finals, however, Laver lost a total of only two sets, evidence of his clear supremacy as a big-match player. Laver proved his versatility by winning the Grand Slam tournaments on grass (US, Australia and Wimbledon) and clay (French) plus the two most important hard-court titles (South African Open at Ellis Park, Johannesburg and the US professional championship at Boston) and the leading indoor tournaments (Philadelphia, US Pro Indoor and Wembley British Indoor). With $124,000 in prize money, Laver was also the first player to break the $100,000 barrier in a year.

After 1969, Laver never won another Grand Slam title, but the trophy cupboard continued to be added to for years to come. In 1970, he won fifteen titles and $201,453 in prize money including the Tennis Champions Classic, Sydney Dunlop Open, Philadelphia WCT, Wembley, Los Angeles, South African Open, Saint Louis WCT, Montreal/Toronto, Louisville and Queen's in London.

The following year, Laver retained his title at the Tennis Champions Classic, winning thirteen consecutive winner-take-all matches against top players and banking $160,000 in the process. He also won seven tournaments, including the Italian Open in Rome on clay over Jan Kodeš, the reigning French Open champion, plus Bologna WCT, Berkley, Fort Worth WCT and London. For the year, Laver won a then record $292,717 in tournament prize money and became the first tennis player to exceed $1 million in career prize money.

In 1972, after wins in Denver WCT, Houston WCT, Toronto WCT, Richmond WCT and Philadelphia WCT, Laver finished as the points leader of the WCT tournament series, but he lost the play-off finals at Dallas to Rosewall in five sets. The match drew a TV audience of over 20 million and, as mentioned in Chapter Six, was described by the then executive director of the WCT, Mike Davies, as 'the greatest match I've ever seen'. Laver described this defeat – Rosewall won 4–6, 6–0, 6–3, 6–7, 7–6 (7–5) – as the biggest disappointment of his career. The pill was probably the more bitter to swallow as he had been defeated by Rosewall in the same final the previous year.

In 1973, Laver won seven tournaments, including four singles titles listed on the ATP website – the Sydney Indoor, Hong Kong, Toronto WCT and Miami WCT – and successfully participated in the semi-finals and finals of the Davis Cup, where he won all six of his rubbers for Australia.

The following year, Laver won six of thirteen tournaments and ended the year as world number four on the computer after singles titles wins at Bretton Woods, Las Vegas, Houston, Tokyo WCT, Palm Desert WCT and Philadelphia WCT. At thirty-six, Laver was the oldest player in the Open era to have been included in a year-ending top five.

In 1975, he won four singles titles – Orlando WCT, Caracas, Sao Paulo and La Costa WCT – and twenty-three consecutive matches. In 1976, Laver semi-retired from the main tour, competing only in a few events.

In the course of his long and illustrious career, Laver played in a number of truly great matches. One of the most outstanding was the occasion mentioned earlier of his victory against his fellow Australian Roy Emerson, in which Laver fought back from two sets down to win 3–6, 2–6, 6–3, 9–7, 6–2. Another was the four-hour thirty-five-minute, ninety-game match Laver played against Tony Roche in sizzling Brisbane heat in the semi-final of the 1969 Australian Open. Again, Laver emerged victorious, winning their marathon contest 7–5, 22–20, 9–11, 1–6, 6–3. The third example, referred to earlier in this chapter, was the mammoth struggle against Ken Rosewall in the WCT final. An epic encounter, Laver was eventually defeated in a fifth set tie-break but the quality of tennis was quite exceptional.

Inevitably, Laver won innumerable awards and set records which stand to this day. Inducted into the International Tennis Hall of Fame and the Australian Tennis Hall of Fame, Laver was voted BBC Overseas Sports Personality of the Year in 1969 and his record of twenty-eight consecutive match wins in Grand Slam tournaments in 1969 stands alone. Similarly, his eighteen titles in one season, 1969, has never been equalled. Likewise, his record of winning thirty-eight titles at the age of thirty-plus between 1968 and 1975 is unrivalled. In a poll by the Associated Press in 2000, Laver was voted 'The Male Tennis Player of the Century', ahead of Pete Sampras, Bill Tilden, Björn Borg, Don Budge, John McEnroe and Lew Hoad (tied), Ken Rosewall and Roy Emerson (tied) and Jack Kramer.

In an article in *Tennis Week* in 2007, the tennis historian Raymond Lee statistically analysed the all-time best players. Needless to say, this approach is not a conclusive guide, nor in any sense the final word – part of the fascination of the subject of 'the greats' is the impossibility of an agreed final verdict – but it is noteworthy that Laver topped his list ahead of Bill Tilden and Borg (tied), Roger Federer, Pancho Gonzales, Ken Rosewall, Don Budge, Ivan Lendl, Jimmy Connors, Pete Sampras, John McEnroe and Jack Kramer.

Laver himself always comes across as a strikingly modest man, which, if anything, adds to the appreciation of his greatness. He has lauded other great players past and present but does not seek to make a case for his own supremacy. Commenting on his achievement of the Grand Slam in 1962, he simply observed decades later, as reported in *ATP Deuce Magazine* in August 2008 that, if the rules had not, at that time, prohibited amateurs competing with professionals at places like Wimbledon and Forest Hills, he would have been unlikely to win against Rosewall, Hoad or Gonzales.

Reflecting on the respective satisfaction he derived from his two Grand Slam victories in 1962 and 1969, Laver said that although he found the first more difficult, the second was more satisfying for him because 'I had all the players in the world open and playing'.

On the differences between tennis in the past and the present, Laver says, 'The money's one thing. But today's game is much more physical than when we played. The ball is hit so much harder, the players generate so much speed and spin. I'd have to play differently if I was out there today.'

Let the last words in this chapter come from a recent champion and a past champion. Roger Federer reveres Laver, saying, 'He is one of the greatest legends we have in the game. What I see the most when I see video of Rod Laver is how easy he made it look.'

John Newcombe, the Australian holder of twenty-five Grand Slam titles, declares,

Rocket was the guy who had the respect of everyone. You can see it now in the respect he has from the Roger Federers and the Nadals and all those guys. They get the fact he was great and one of the greatest, but they can also sense that strength of humility that there is about him.

Chapter Ten

Jimmy Connors

JIMMY CONNORS WAS an outstanding American champion from the early 1970s to the early 1980s, building up one of the most impressive records of any player in any era. Connors won eight Grand Slam singles titles, including one Australian Open, two Wimbledon titles and five US Opens. In addition to those victories, he was the runner-up in a further seven Grand Slam tournaments and he won three year-end championship crowns, including two WCT finals and one Masters Grand Prix. The winner of seventeen Championship Series titles between 1973 and 1984, Connors claimed a record-breaking 109 ATP tournament titles – compared with ninety-four for Ivan Lendl, seventy-eight for Roger Federer, seventy-seven for John McEnroe and sixty-four for Pete Sampras. Amongst players no longer competing, his career win–loss record of 1,253–277 (81.79 per cent) appears in the modern era to have been bettered only by Björn Borg (82.7 per cent), and the number of his match victories exceeds that of any other male player. Connors held the number one world ranking for a then record 160 weeks from 1974 to 1977 and in total he occupied that pole position in the game for 268 weeks, a record surpassed in the Open era only by Ivan Lendl (270 weeks), Pete Sampras (286 weeks) and Roger Federer who occupied the number one slot in the rankings for 302 weeks. Armed with an insatiable appetite for tennis, and the thirst for competitive match play, Connors performed at the very highest level for the best part of a decade and subsequently proved himself capable of competing against later greats of the game up until the back end of the 1980s.

In the course of his remarkable career, Connors reached the quarter-finals or better of the major tournaments no fewer than forty-one times. That record has been matched only by Roger Federer.

James Scott Connors was born in East St Louis, Illinois, on 2 September 1952. His father, though supportive, had no interest in tennis, but his mother, Gloria, and grandmother, affectionately known as 'Two-Mom', were both passionate and relatively accomplished players keen to instil their love of the sport into young Jimmy. He first picked up a racket at the age of three and a half. In its full-size form, the racket was far too heavy. Hence his parents cut it down to approximately half the size. Still too heavy, Jimmy therefore began to grip the racket with two hands, a technique he was to continue to deploy on his backhand wing throughout his career. In his autobiography, Connors recalls that his mother encouraged but did not push him to play. As a kid, he was free to hit balls in the backyard if he wanted to do so, or not if he didn't. Practice sessions with mum were measured in quality, not quantity or length. His mother was keen to inspire him rather than to risk leaving him jaded or bored through excessively protracted play. Typically, a session would be forty-five minutes long and focused on a particular purpose.

Although Mrs Connors had not made it as a professional player, she had been a competent competitor, and a streak of defiance – an insistence on getting her own way, on coming out on top – was a prominent part of her character which trickled down to Jimmy. His elder brother, Johnny, had briefly played the game but lost interest. Jimmy loved the game and was intent on continuing.

Early childhood experiences can be formative and one incident in particular had a marked impact on Connors. Aged eight, playing on public courts in East St Louis, Jimmy saw two young thugs set upon and badly beat up his mum and granddad. His mum bled and lost her teeth. Jimmy watched in horror and was powerless to do anything. That incident filled Connors with an anger that he was determined to channel positively into his tennis. His attitude was in part shared or reinforced by his mum's own courage. A day after what must have been both a painful and a frightening experience,

Gloria Connors was back on the practice court. That gutsy, defiant response resonated with and inspired Connors. In his words, 'If she could hit balls the very next day after getting beat up, then I could play for one hour or five hours, no matter how bad my body ached.' He went on: 'I could always find something to drive me and most of the time it was those feelings of anger and rage that bubbled up from the past. My mother taught me how to harness those emotions. She called them Tiger Juices.'

When Jimmy was old enough to play matches with his mum, she did not go easy on him but played toughly. When Jimmy finally beat her, he was tearful and apologetic. Gloria, by contrast, said that she had waited and looked forward to it as a milestone of his progress. Just as play was competitive and hard fought, so was fitness training taken seriously. Pop, Jimmy's grandfather, was a great believer in what the Brits call skipping and Americans term 'jumping rope'. Connors recalls that his granddad always pushed him to jump rope for longer, knowing the wonders it would do for his endurance. Moreover, in addition to that endurance and general conditioning, footwork was recognised as fundamental to effective play. Jimmy had to be in the right position to play the right shot at the right time. Accordingly, he worked on that footwork every day.

At the age of eight, Connors took part for the second time in the Southern Illinois tournament and won the eleven-and-under event. From his first lessons onwards, Connors was taught to develop a strong groundstroke game, with an emphasis on taking the ball early and hitting it flat, one-handed on the forehand and two-handed on the backhand. At the age of sixteen, in what proved to be an inspired decision, Gloria took Jimmy to southern California to be coached by the former world-class player Pancho Segura. They developed a close bond that was to last nearly two decades. Together they developed not only Connors's shot-making, but his court craft, his tactics, his strategy. Segura had been the wiliest of competitors and appreciated more than most the need for his prodigy to have a gameplan, the imagination to revise it if necessary and the mental strength to see through his plan to fruition. Connors is refreshingly candid about what he did and did not achieve as a young player. In his words, 'By the end of my junior career, I made the US top ten for my age group, but I was far from being the best. Gottfried, Dick Stockton, and Eddie Dibbs were considered better than me, and they were.'

Even though Connors was not at that stage the best of the juniors, Segura claims that even then he was highly optimistic for his future, telling him years later that he had 'balls', was coachable and reminded Segura of a 'deer running around the court, chasing down every ball'. Segura had been impressed by Jimmy's character, his intensity, his drive, but also by the shots in his locker. He was convinced that Connors's service return would prove to be the best in the business and he judged that his double-handed backhand would be a potent weapon. As Segura admiringly recalled, 'It barely cleared the net with pace, and by the time the other guy had a chance to react, it was too late.' Concluding that the climate in California was more conducive to honing the skills and providing the practice opportunities of a future champion, Gloria Connors soon moved the family there and Connors was to strengthen his tie with his new coach.

The evidence was that Connors had developed a highly effective baseline game, marked by very penetrating groundstrokes that stayed low on the opponent's court and offered little scope for counterattack.

Segura shrewdly sought not to transform the Connors playing style but to build upon it. He had two notable priorities in developing Connors's approach. First, he wanted Connors to be more aggressive. Second, Segura was a strategist who had a keen sense of how different points should be played, depending upon the scoreline, the opponent and the conditions. Sitting with Connors, drawing diagrams on cocktail napkins, he sought to impress upon his man the merits of crafting points in particular ways. One other issue was important and Segura did not duck it – the issue of conduct. Connors was a fiery, almost explosive character. Some traditionalist observers would disapprove of displays of temper or other expostulations on grounds of etiquette or form, i.e. they were 'a jolly poor show'.

Segura was concerned only with substance, how conduct affected performance. Therefore, he advised his pupil: 'Jimbo, remember it's all about timing. Don't let anything get in the way of your tennis. Just make sure you act up, you get your concentration and your head back into the game.'

In 1970, just after the US Open, Connors won five qualifying matches to secure entry to the main draw of the Pacific Southwest Championships in Los Angeles. Roy Emerson, multiple Grand Slam winner, was his formidable opponent. Formidable but, at nearly thirty-four, both a little beyond his peak and yet highly rated. Emerson still had everything to lose, Connors nothing. The result could be of no significance or, alternatively, a revealing straw in the wind. Segura advised Connors to hit the ball low to Emerson's forehand, to attack, to prevent him settling and to try in particular to prevent Emerson coming to the net, where he was potentially dominant. Connors took the advice and won the first set on the tie-breaker. Emerson hit back, as great champions are wont to do, and took the second set, also on the tie-break. Connors recollects that, despite his disappointment at the loss of the second set, he stuck to his last – hustling, attacking, taking the ball early, hitting it hard, and the approach served him well. Connors broke serve early in the third set and went on to win the match.

In the latter part of 1971, Connors decided to turn professional and promptly competed on the hard indoor floors of Jacksonville, where he won the tournament. The following year, Connors opted to follow the route suggested by his agent, Bill Riordan, and to remain an independent player, alongside Ilie Năstase, Ion Ţiriac, Jan Kodeš, Roger Taylor and Vitas Gerulaitis. Specifically, unlike most of his fellow aspirants to world supremacy, Connors did not join the ATP.

At this time, and indeed throughout his career, Jimmy Connors carried in his socks notes from Two-Mom that he judged to be especially pertinent and shrewd. The notes contained the following simple instructions: 'Don't forget to take the ball early. Don't forget to keep your eye on the ball. Don't forget to reach up on your serve.'

As we have seen in other chapters in this book, in the pre-Open era the transition from supremacy as an amateur to success as a professional was by no means assured and almost invariably such success was not immediate. Therefore, the reader will appreciate that the transition not merely from amateur status but effectively from that of junior status to success as a touring professional was particularly tough. Connors, mentored and encouraged by Segura, had rightly made the leap up, but against the stars of the World Tour, it would take time for him to adjust to the demands of competing at top-flight level week after week.

For example, in 1972, aged nineteen, Connors travelled for what was then only the second time outside the US to play the French Open. Although he had just enjoyed some good wins in professional tournaments, Connors was fragile in the immediate aftermath of the passing of Two-Mom. With his concentration on the task in hand less than 100 per cent, his draw was perhaps the worst it could be. He met the indefatigable Maryland baseliner Harold Solomon in the second round and succumbed to him in straight sets. Solomon, like Eddie Dibbs, was a phenomenally consistent retriever who could and did fight for hours and hours to win matches and he was on this occasion – and indeed on a number of others – just too steady and too mentally strong for the unsettled Connors.

At Wimbledon in 1972, Connors fared better. In the opening round, he faced the seventh-seeded Bob Hewitt on Centre Court. Hewitt, in addition to being seeded to reach the quarter-finals, had arrived at the All England Club with valuable victories at the Bristol Open and the British Hard Court Championships behind him. Connors was watched and supported from the stands that day by his mum, by Pancho Segura, his coach, and by Bill Riordan, his agent. At one point in the match, Gloria Connors dared so much as to yell out, 'Come on, Jimmy!' and was vilified in the British press the following day in an orgy of snobbery and anti-Americanism to boot. In any event, the important point is that Connors – young, brash, raw but hugely talented and with the heart of a lion – defeated the 32-year-old Australian-turned-South African Hewitt. In the third round, Connors beat the Italian Adriano Panatta, and he made it to the quarter-finals where he was beaten in straight sets by the man who was to be the losing finalist that year, the Romanian tennis artist Ilie Năstase.

At the US Open, then played on grass, not yet a surface congenial to Connors, he was dumped out of the tournament by the American Tom Gorman in five sets, though he reminds us in his autobiography that he did notch up titles in Columbus, Cincinnati and Albany, bringing his total of winning tournaments to six. At Wimbledon and the US Open in 1973, Connors reached the quarter-finals, overcome respectively by Alex Metreveli – the Russian losing finalist that year – and John Newcombe. At Forest Hills, Connors had the additional fillip of beating the world top ten Dutch player Tom Okker in the fourth round. Connors was now making very solid, if not yet spectacular, progress in the big tournaments.

At the US Pro Championships in the autumn of 1973, Connors caused a major upset by beating Stan Smith, the 1972 Wimbledon champion and number one seed in the event, in straight sets in the first round. He then defeated the South African Raymond Moore and his fellow Americans Dick Stockton and Cliff Richey to reach the final and the enticing prospect of taking on the number two seed, the great Arthur Ashe. Advised by Segura to attack the Ashe serve with powerful, deep returns down the centre of the court, denying Ashe the angles on which he thrived, Connors dug in for their three-hour encounter, triumphing 6–3, 4–6, 6–4, 3–6, 6–2. Connors had a significant title under his belt and a major boost to his confidence in the process.

It now seemed that altogether bigger success could be in the offing and so it proved. 1974 was a stellar year for Connors. Statistically, it was the best of his career and amongst the best to be found on the circuit. The story really began at the Australian Open at the close of 1973. En route to the final, Connors defeated, amongst other players, no fewer than three Australians, lining himself up to take on a fourth, Phil Dent, in the final. Connors approached the match in a way that reflected his instinct and his strength: he played aggressively, stepping in to take the ball and hitting powerful groundstrokes to all parts of

the court, putting Dent on the defensive and leaving him little time
to choose and execute his own shots. The plan worked – the first
set went to a tie-break which Connors won by nine points to seven,
and he took the second set 6–4. Dent enjoyed vociferous support
from a highly partisan home crowd and he snatched the third set
6–4 but Connors quickly reasserted his control and took the fourth
set 6–3 to lift the title. Connors declared himself 'ecstatic' to win the
title, his first Grand Slam, even though at the time the tournament
did not attract the full cadre of top-flight players, partly because
of the journey time to Australia and on account of the fact that it
was scheduled as an end-of-season event when many players were
physically exhausted. Despite those factors, Connors was thrilled to
win his maiden Slam and, in particular, he believed it augured well
for his prospects in 1974, calling the victory a 'huge' one that would
set him up for the following year, which he identified as 'the most
extraordinary single year of my career'.

Sadly, tennis politics prevented Connors from taking part in the
French Open. He had signed for World Team Tennis, a lucrative
competition, and the International Lawn Tennis Federation, which
heartily disapproved of that commercial venture, therefore banned
Connors from competing in Paris. Yet Connors had enjoyed a real
'bounce' from his triumph in Australia. He won tournaments at
Rodnoke, Little Rock, Birmingham, Sansburg, Hampton (Virginia),
Salt Lake City and Tempe. In terms of his form and self-belief alike,
Connors seemed very well set indeed for Wimbledon.

The omens were encouraging. Connors had hit a rich vein of form
and he must have been quietly optimistic. Yet that optimism may
have been tempered by his own feeling that, at heart, he was not
a grass-court player. Sure, he hit the ball hard and played aggressively, but he did so predominantly from the back of the court.
Fundamentally, Connors felt that a grass court did not 'really suit my
game'. That game was oriented overwhelmingly around his groundstrokes. At this stage, Connors was starting to play more offensively.
He did this not by hitting groundstrokes harder or by aiming closer
to the lines. Rather, Connors opted for the tactic of mixing up his

game and making regular if unannounced excursions to the net, heeding the advice of Pancho Segura in the process. In the second round of Wimbledon, Connors thwarted Phil Dent 10–8 in the fifth set, whereafter he defeated Jan Kodeš, the defending champion, in five sets. That victory was followed by a four-set dispatch of Dick Stockton in the semi-finals. In the final, Connors met the in-form veteran Australian Ken Rosewall. As we saw in the earlier chapter on Ken Rosewall, the final was astonishingly one-sided as Connors simply imposed himself on his opponent and did not let up until victory was his. Connors describes the contest as 'a blur' but admits that he seemed to have 'all the time in the world'. The simple fact is that Rosewall, a supreme touch player, just could not cope with the unrelenting force of Connors's attacking style. The scoreline, 6–1, 6–1, 6–4, demonstrated starkly that awesome power consistently applied with accuracy was just too much for Rosewall, now thirty-nine, to handle.

If winning the Australian Open had been big for Connors, tasting victory at Wimbledon was gigantic. He now had a second Slam under his belt – and the history books show that backing up a first Slam with a second can be elusive for many players – and, perhaps even more satisfyingly, Connors achieved the world number one ranking on 29 July 1974, three weeks after his success at the All England Club. It was a key moment in Connors's career for two reasons. First, he had never before been ranked world number one. Secondly, although no one was to know it then, Connors proceeded to retain that ranking for 160 weeks. He enjoyed the year-end ranking as number one from 1974 to 1978. Following his success at Wimbledon, Connors beat Borg on clay in the Indianapolis final in August 1974 and began the build-up to the US Open title. There, Connors defeated all his competitors, taking on Rosewall in the final and producing another jaw-dropping performance which crushed his veteran opponent even more savagely than at Wimbledon. This time Connors won 6–1, 6–0, 6–1. This was an emphatic triumph and meant that Connors became only the second man at the time to have won three or more Grand Slams in a calendar year since Budge in 1938. Rod Laver had done it. Now Connors had performed a similar feat.

Stunning success in 1974 naturally fed the expectation that Connors would now become or remain the dominant player in the sport. In 1975, Connors did not play in the Australian or French Open. Wimbledon was his first opportunity to demonstrate that 1974 was no freak result but the harbinger of things to come. Predictably, Connors reached the final and was the heavy favourite over Arthur Ashe to take the title for the second successive year. It was not to be. Inevitably, a champion becomes a target. As he took the contest extremely seriously, Ashe worked out a gameplan. The essence of it was to slow the game down, deploy slice, cut off the angles on which Connors thrived, and prevent him establishing rhythm or becoming comfortable. Initially, Ashe was supreme and Connors all at sea, so the former won the first two sets by the same devastating margin that Connors had inflicted on Rosewall the previous year, namely 6–1, 6–1. Connors began to fight back and took the third set 7–5, but it proved to be but a lull in Ashe's onward march to victory, his first and only Wimbledon singles title.

By comparison with the heady triumph of 1974, the US Open in 1975 was also disappointing for Connors. He scored an impressive semi-final win over Björn Borg, defeating the Swedish clay-court maestro in three tight sets, 7–5, 7–5, 7–5. Ironically, having mounted what many observers would have considered the highest hurdle, Connors fell short in the final, limply bowing out 6–4, 6–3, 6–3 to the Spaniard Manuel Orantes, himself a supreme practitioner on the clay court. From winning three Grand Slams in 1974, Connors won none in 1975, though he performed sufficiently strongly all year round to retain his number one world ranking.

In 1976, he made just one final at his favourite hunting ground of the US Open and beat Borg on the clay, 6–4, 3–6, 7–6 (11–9), 6–4. As the reader can see, the third-set tie-break was the key to that match and Connors now owned his fourth Grand Slam title, with the double bonus of it being won over his arch rival Borg and, perhaps even more strikingly, on a clay court.

In 1977, Connors reached his third Wimbledon final, but despite a huge effort he was outlasted 6–4 in the fifth set by Borg. Connors had thought he could win, but paid tribute to Borg's underrated volley. Specifically, he notes in his autobiography that Borg's short volley 'would land and die instantly', saying, 'That was tough to play against.' Yet, scarcely two months later, Connors succumbed in the US Open final to Guillermo Vilas in four sets, squandering the last set 6–0. The following year at Wimbledon, he made no impression on Borg as the latter trounced him 6–2, 6–2, 6–3, although two months later roles were reversed as Connors claimed his third US Open title, now played on his best surface, a hard court, with a very straightforward 6–4, 6–2, 6–2 victory over Borg.

So, from the age of twenty-one to twenty-six, Connors reached eleven Grand Slam singles finals, winning five of them. There then followed a period of nearly four years in which Connors failed to reach a Grand Slam final. During that relatively fallow period, Connors did in 1980 win the second of his two WCT Year End Championship finals, defeating John McEnroe on carpet in Dallas in four sets, 2–6, 7–6, 6–1, 6–2. He also won Grand Prix Championship Series finals in Philadelphia (three times, in 1978, 1979 and 1980), Tokyo in 1980 and London in 1981, the latter being a five-set victory over John McEnroe from two sets down. Indeed, in total, between his 1978 US Open title win over Borg and his next Slam victory at Wimbledon over McEnroe in 1982, Connors claimed no fewer than twenty-two singles titles. By the standards of most players, that would be considered a superb record. The point, however, is that Jimmy Connors was not most players. He was a champion. Champions are champions because they win major titles. If they go a significant period without winning any, it is inevitable that commentators and pundits start to write them out of the script.

Connors noticed the critics. They bugged him. He was determined to prove them wrong. As he explains at the start of his highly readable autobiography, it was the critics that made him realise that he needed tennis, and to win; it was they who drove him to work even harder.

Connors believed that a key turning point in his eventual come-back came in that Wembley Grand Prix championship final on 15 November 1981 against John McEnroe. After dropping the first two sets at a canter 3–6, 2–6, Connors dug deep and turned the match round, winning the next three 6–3, 6–4, 6–2. Connors observes, 'I walked off that court that night, knowing one thing for sure. I was back.' Thereafter, Connors accumulated three further Grand Slam titles. Almost eight months later, Connors won Wimbledon for the second time, eight years after his first triumph, and his victim was John McEnroe, who had won the title the previous year and would do so in each of the next two. By then, Connors was almost thirty, McEnroe only twenty-three, but Connors, playing catch-up for much of the contest, stayed with his opponent and eventually won 3–6, 6–3, 6–7 (2–7), 7–6 (7–5), 6–4. It was a triumph of skill, of match play and, above all, of sheer undiluted grit. Fired by that success, Connors went on to claim his fourth US Open title with a four-sets defeat of Ivan Lendl, 6–3, 6–2, 4–6, 6–4. Finally, Connors followed up that victory by winning his fifth US Open title in 1983, once again beating Lendl in four sets 6–3, 6–7 (2–7), 7–5, 6–0. His last Grand Slam final came at Wimbledon in 1984, when he was demolished by McEnroe in straight sets 6–1, 6–1, 6–2. Nevertheless, Connors had enjoyed two spells of enormous success, 1974–78 and 1982–83. Getting to the top and staying there was tough. Returning to the top against a new generation of superstars was at least as tough and Connors met the test.

Probably the greatest rivalries were with Björn Borg, John McEnroe and Ivan Lendl. Connors was nearly four years older than Borg, six and a half years older than McEnroe, and seven years older than Lendl, so they were not precise contemporaries but he played against each of them a great deal. In their head-to-head major championship finals, Connors won twice against Borg – namely the US Opens in 1976 and 1978, losing the other two contests in the Wimbledon finals of 1977 and 1978. Overall, his tour record against Borg was a deficit of eight wins to fifteen losses. Against McEnroe, Connors won one of their major finals, the 1982 Wimbledon encounter described above, but lost the 1984 final to him. Overall, Connors won fourteen of their matches to McEnroe's twenty. Against Lendl, Connors won both of their major finals contests, namely the 1982 and 1983 US Opens. In total, Connors beat Lendl on tour thirteen times and was beaten by him twenty-two times, though it is only fair to record that Connors lost the last seventeen of their encounters, all between 1984 and 1992 when Connors was past his prime.

The evidence of Jimmy Connors's greatness is compelling. He won more tournaments, albeit not more major titles, than any player in the Open era. His career win–loss record is second in the Open era only to that of Björn Borg. He spent sixteen years in the world's top ten, so if consistency of performance at the top level is judged to be a part of a player's greatness, Connors is right up there. He reached the semi-final or better of a major title thirty-one times, a record overtaken only recently by Roger Federer, and he made the quarter-finals or better forty-one times over just under twenty years.

Connors did have weaknesses. His serve, though solid and accurate, was not as potent as that of other champions. His forehand was more error-prone than the backhand, mainly because it was hit very flat, low over the net and with little if any margin for error. It may be doubted whether Connors had the range or variety of shot-making skills of, say, McEnroe or Federer, to give but two examples. On the other hand, the facts speak for themselves. Connors was a terrific match player. Far more often than not – on clay, on grass, on hard courts, on carpet, outdoors or indoors – Connors found a way to win, a way to get the job done. He was a supreme competitor, blessed with a superb return of service and showed himself to be as tenacious a scrapper on the court as the game has ever known, a man determined to extract every ounce of advantage from his combination of inspiration (talent) and perspiration (effort). He was a great player, the victor as well as the vanquished in great matches and a player with a fabulous overall record in a professional career characterised by fighting spirit, a big-match temperament, enviable self-belief and a passion for tennis as competitive combat unsurpassed by any player described in this book.

Chapter Eleven

Björn Borg

BJÖRN BORG WAS a truly phenomenal tennis player who opened
and came to define a new era in his sport. Playing the game differently to all of his predecessors, and in what, by contemporary
standards, was a relatively short career in the top flight, Borg won
eleven Grand Slam titles and was runner-up on five occasions. His
tally included five consecutive Wimbledon titles (a record which
stood alone until Roger Federer matched it) and six French Open
crowns. In addition, Borg twice won the Masters Grand Prix Year-
End Championships and was also the losing finalist twice. He won
the WCT Year-End Championship finals once and was runner-up
three times. He claimed fifteen Grand Prix Championship Series
titles – the precursor to today's Masters Series tournaments – and
was runner-up in four such tournaments. Between 1974 and 1981,
he amassed his collection of sixty-four ATP recognised singles titles
on no fewer than four different surfaces, namely clay, grass, hard
courts and carpet, triumphing forty-one times outdoors and twenty-
three times indoors. He was also runner-up in twenty-four ATP
recognised singles titles. In the title-winning stakes, Borg's record
puts him joint fifth with Pete Sampras, outdone in the numbers game
only by Jimmy Connors (109), Ivan Lendl (94), Roger Federer (78)
and John McEnroe (77). In 1979, Borg became the first professional
tennis player to earn more than $1 million in prize money in a single
season. He retired in 1983 having earned $3.6 million in career prize
money, a record at the time, and in 1987, aged thirty, he was inducted
into the International Tennis Hall of Fame. His was a superb record

of match-winning success (82.72 per cent or 608 victories to 127 defeats) and the only blots on his career copybook were the failure to win either the Australian Open or the US Open, though he was runner-up in the latter four times.

What is the story of the man who dominated tennis in the second half of the 1970s? Borg was born in Södertälje, a manufacturing town south-west of Stockholm, on 6 June 1956. The city was based around one industry, auto-parts, and one sport, ice hockey. When Borg was nine, his father won a table tennis tournament and the prize was a gold-coloured tennis racket which apparently inspired the young Borg. His father gave him the racket and by this route was the tennis career of Björn Borg launched. He spent hour after hour in front of the garage doors, 'with a grip borrowed from table tennis and a stroke reminiscent of a hockey shot'. Through assiduous, indeed almost fanatical, practice, Borg nurtured, according to Stephen Tignor in his exemplary book about Borg and McEnroe, what came to be an unrivalled ability to hit one more ball in the court of his opponent.

Borg agreed to play one-handed on his forehand but not his backhand. Today, a two-handed backhand is the norm but in the 1970s it was very much the exception, not taught and indeed actively discouraged by coaches. This was partly because, though not against any rule, it was thought to be 'not the done thing', and perhaps also because it was thought awkward in terms of reach when chasing down wide balls, not to mention difficult in requiring a player to shift from the one-handed approach to the forehand shot. Borg, however, was determined to stick to his preferred technique, revealing thereby a streak of stubbornness and self-confidence which can be identified in all of the great champions. As he put it, 'Even though I'd tell the guys that some day I'd change, I knew I never would … The members got angry with me because I wouldn't listen. In the end that's the reason I got so far.'

In one crucial respect Borg did change, possibly on advice from others but also because he became convinced of the need to do so. In his youth, Borg had been a screamer in the mould of his future rival John McEnroe, smashing dozens of rackets in temper tantrums when losing or playing below par. Two factors explain the transformation of Borg from ranting rebel to inscrutable competitor. First, his parents were aghast at his misconduct, which attracted widespread criticism. Secondly, Borg himself eventually decided that, leaving etiquette aside, getting upset on court only lessened his chance of winning. Therefore, he resolved to remain calm at all times, showing no emotion at all. This expressionless demeanour, and appearance of complete unflappability, earned Borg the nickname 'The Ice Man' or 'Ice-Borg'. Less complimentarily, perhaps, the Romanian star player Ilie Năstase described Borg as 'The Martian'. Millions of fans the world over adored Borg – including millions of teenage girls who regarded him as a gorgeous sex symbol – and admired his temperament, which contrasted as sharply as did his playing style with that of John McEnroe. Most importantly for the student of tennis history, it defined Borg in an age when more aggressive behaviour and simple raw emotion were starting to replace the stiff-upper-lip demeanour which had characterised the game for much of the previous hundred years. Interestingly, Borg himself said during his prime years, 'People think I'm so cool and nothing bothers me, but inside I'm seething.' The external persona, however, of grace under pressure and total imperturbability simply added to the aura of the man.

Borg fashioned a highly distinctive style of play. As Tignor notes,

> For thirty years the accepted style of play in men's tennis had been to follow the serve forward, to attack, to pressure the opponent and to create wining angles by hitting your shots from as close to the net as possible. It was known as the Big Game, and it seemed to be the final word in strategy. But Borg, legendary from a young age for his stubbornness, turned the textbook – and the sport's geometry – upside down.

He played from the baseline, with powerful groundstrokes and his double-handed backhand. Hitting the ball hard and high over the net from the back of the court, he brought his shots down with heavy topspin which made his groundstrokes very consistent. It was not that Borg was the first player to deploy topspin. Others had done so, notably Rod Laver and Arthur Ashe, who played with topspin on both forehand and backhand wings. The difference with Borg was in degree and intensity. Whereas Laver and Ashe had used topspin merely as a way to mix up their shots, keep opponents guessing and pass them more easily when they were at the net, Borg used heavy topspin as a staple part of his match-playing diet. In other words, it was done as a matter of course, constantly, remorselessly and, from the vantage point of opponents, in a way that wearied or debilitated them. Surely the current player who most closely parallels that technique is Rafael Nadal.

Alongside unrivalled groundstrokes was unmatched fitness. Of course, world-class players all train hard and, by comparison with non-sportsmen, are very fit. Yet there is a sense in which Borg took fitness to a new level. Time and again, he demonstrated that he could outlast his opponents under the most gruelling conditions, and the combination of his superb footwork, speed around the court and staggering powers of endurance was clearly a key factor in his success in general and on clay courts in particular. The fitness was especially to the fore on such courts which are markedly slower than grass or carpet and thereby conducive to very long rallies.

One of the most impressive features of his career was Borg's dominance at Wimbledon, where he won each year from 1976 to 1980 inclusive, before succumbing in the 1981 final to McEnroe. His feat at the All England Club was all the more impressive as, unlike many of the great Wimbledon champions, he had not been brought up playing on grass and had not initially learned to serve and volley. It is a tribute both to his single-minded determination and to his ability that he learned to do so. In the postwar period, baseliners did not thrive at Wimbledon and some high-ranking baseline players, including Eddie Dibbs and Harold Solomon, often chose not to play at Wimbledon at all as they knew that their efforts would be unavailing. Borg developed a first-class, albeit often underrated service and, up against the best players, he almost always served and volleyed on his first serves, though understandably he opted to play from the baseline after his second delivery. Having dominated matches for years from the back of the court, the volley was by no means a regular part of his game. Moreover, unlike McEnroe and other greats such as Laver, Rosewall and Hoad, Borg rarely played doubles and did not develop his facility at the net through that expedient. Rather, he trained and practised the volley, specifically for making it a core part of his grass-court game. This was a major transition by Borg and a key feature of his greatness.

In contrast to some of the greats of the game who did not excel as juniors, Borg was precociously good in those early years. Indeed, by the age of thirteen, he was beating the best of Sweden's under-eighteen players, and Sweden's Davis Cup captain, Lennart Bergelin, who became Borg's coach, advised that no one should try to change Borg's unconventional strokes, as they were highly effective.

Aged fourteen, Borg joined the professional circuit. In May 1972, just before his sixteenth birthday, Borg became the youngest player ever to win a Davis Cup match as he won his debut singles rubber in five sets against a well-established professional, Onny Parun, of New Zealand. Later that year, Borg won the Wimbledon junior singles title, fighting back from 5–2 down in the final set to defeat Britain's Buster Mottram. Struck by his supreme cool and evident mental toughness, the Swedish press said that Borg had 'ice in the stomach'.

In 1973, tennis was about to undergo a change. Since 1968, the International Tennis Federation (ITF) had allowed players to be awarded prize money but it had prohibited anyone under eighteen from accepting it. In the year Borg turned seventeen, however, that rule was scrapped, meaning that Borg and anyone else who played would get paid prize money. That same year, 1973, the newly formed players' union, the ATP, became embroiled in a dispute with the ITF over the Yugoslavian player, Niki Pilić. Wimbledon

had barred Pilić from competing in the tournament because he had
failed to play the Davis Cup for his country, citing as an excuse a
prior commitment to a professional tournament. Players threatened to boycott Wimbledon, regarded by them and by aficionados
of the game alike as their most important event, if Pilić was not
reinstated. However, the British press and apparently home fans
rallied behind the tournament officials, who did not relent. The
upshot of this impasse was that seventy-nine of the game's top
players – including the defending champion, Stan Smith – refused
to play. Ilie Năstase, Jimmy Connors, the British number one Roger
Taylor, and Borg broke the boycott in order to compete, though
it is worth pointing out, to be fair, that aged seventeen Borg was
too young to be a member of the ATP union. The depleted field
ensured that Borg and Connors reached the quarter-finals, with
Borg becoming the first idol of the new generation of tennis players. Talking of escaping into his room, Borg said that every evening
he looked forward to it as he had an 'intense feeling' that he had
become girls' 'legitimate prey, even on the streets of London'.

Shortly before his eighteenth birthday in 1974, Borg won
his first significant singles title at the Italian Open, becoming
the youngest winner of the tournament. A fortnight later, Borg
became the then youngest winner of the French Open, recovering
from a two-set deficit to overcome the Spanish clay-court specialist Manuel Orantes 2–6, 6–7, 6–0, 6–1, 6–1. Early in 1975, Borg
beat the eleven-time Grand Slam champion, Rod Laver, then
thirty-six, in a semi-final of the World Championship Tennis
finals in Dallas, Texas, 7–6, 3–6, 5–7, 7–6, 6–2. In the final, Borg
was defeated by Arthur Ashe. Sadly, although the encounter with
Laver is of interest, it is not especially significant. Borg had by
no means reached his peak but Laver, though still performing
remarkably well at, in tennis terms, the advanced age of thirty-
six, was more than five years beyond his prime.

In the summer of 1975, Borg retained his French Open title,
defeating the impressive Argentinean left-hander Guillermo Vilas
in straight sets, and then at Wimbledon he progressed to the

quarter-finals before succumbing to that year's champion, Arthur Ashe, in four sets. Alongside his French Open triumph, 1975 was a memorable year for Borg as Sweden, assisted by two singles and one doubles victory by him, beat Czechoslovakia 3–2 in the final of the Davis Cup. By then, since 1973, Borg had notched up nineteen successive singles wins in the competition and, never losing another singles rubber, his career winning streak in the Davis Cup was thirty-three – a record unsurpassed today.

In early 1976, Borg won the WCT Year End finals tournament in Dallas, Texas, prevailing over Vilas in four sets, but he suffered a reverse in the quarter-finals of the French Open. He was defeated in four sets by the Italian Adriano Panatta, who had beaten Borg in the same tournament three years earlier and was the only player to defeat Borg at the French Open. Bitterly disappointed though Borg must have been not to win his third successive French Open, he bounced back in style at the All England Club to win the first of his five successive Wimbledon singles crowns. Borg did not drop a set in the entire tournament and overcame the volatile Romanian Ilie Năstase in the final. Aged thirteen, I was present in the crowd that day, and though sad that Năstase, then nearing the end of his career, could not win, was struck by just how ruthlessly effective a machine Borg was. At the time, Borg was, at twenty years and one month, the youngest male Wimbledon champion of the modern era. Subsequently, the record was to be surpassed by a seventeen-year-old champion by the name of Boris Becker, who is the subject of a separate chapter in this book. Later in the year, Borg also reached the final of the US Open. Today, the tournament is played on hard courts but it was then staged on clay, which would normally be thought advantageous to Borg. Nevertheless, he succumbed in four sets to the world number one, Jimmy Connors.

These days the top players would miss playing one of the four Grand Slam tournaments only through illness or injury. In 1977, however, Borg was contracted to play with World Team Tennis at the time of the French Open in which, therefore, he did not play. In the summer of 1977, Borg successfully defended his

Wimbledon title, but it was a much more taxing task than it had been a year earlier. In the semi-finals, Borg conquered his pal, the dynamic American Vitas Gerulaitis, in a marathon five-setter, 8–6 in the final set. In the final, Borg had to go to five sets for the third time in the tournament, before overcoming the resistance of another great champion and one of the toughest fighters of that or any tennis era, Jimmy Connors. As a result of that triumph, Borg briefly held the world number one slot.

Both 1976 and 1977 were fine years for Borg, but it was from 1978 through 1980 that he was at the peak of his powers. In each of those years he won the back-to-back Grand Slam tournaments of the French Open and Wimbledon.

In 1978, Borg won the French Open for the third time, in this case beating Vilas in the final and without dropping a set over the entire tournament. During the Open era only two other players have accomplished this feat, Ilie Năstase in 1973 and Rafael Nadal in 2008 and 2010. At Wimbledon in 1978, Borg beat Connors in straight sets in the final, though roles were reversed in the US Open final, where Borg was vanquished by Connors in straight sets. In the latter part of 1978, Borg lost his first encounter with John McEnroe in Stockholm, and that defeat was repeated in the 1979 WCT finals. That said, Borg now held the number one slot in the rankings. His pre-eminence was underlined when he claimed his fourth French Open singles title and his fourth consecutive Wimbledon crown. In Paris, Borg defeated his friend Vitas Gerulaitis in straight sets in the semi-finals and beat Víctor Pecci in a four-set final. At Wimbledon, Borg's final opponent was the then heaviest server in the game, the American, Roscoe Tanner, whose thunderbolt first serve was delivered at 140 mph. Borg won in five sets but, as if to prove what a troublesome opponent he was, Tanner beat Borg in the quarter-finals of the US Open in four sets. The match was played under lights – never to Borg's taste – and the result continued the pattern of relative failure at the US Open – a title which Borg never won.

At the start of 1980, at the Masters tournament in New York,

Borg narrowly defeated Connors in a very tight semi-final, 6–7, 6–3, 7–6. Thereafter, he proceeded to overcome Ivan Lendl in straight sets to win his first Masters and first title in New York.

Later in 1980, Borg again beat Gerulaitis, again in straight sets, to win his fifth French Open title and, once again, he did not drop a set throughout the tournament. Buoyed by his success in Paris, Borg went to the All England Club and secured his fifth consecutive Wimbledon singles title. It was undoubtedly the toughest of his victories and the match still stands amongst the greatest of Wimbledon finals. A fascinating clash of different techniques and temperaments, it was also a topsy-turvy encounter. Borg dropped the first set 6–1 as McEnroe dazzled with his attacking serve and formidable net play. Borg clawed his way back into the match, taking the next two sets 7–5, 6–3, and in the fourth set he had two championship points at 5–4. McEnroe survived and the contest entered a tie-break at 6–all – the most outstanding and memorable tie-break in the history of the Wimbledon championship. Three decades later, that tie-break is still shown on the BBC during rain delays at Wimbledon. In the course of it, McEnroe saved five match points and eventually prevailed 18–16. Of course, at that stage, it was still anybody's match but, going into the fifth set, McEnroe would have been the narrow favourite. He had won the fourth set, he had saved a total of seven match points to do so and he had the momentum with him. It is a commentary on Borg's greatness, mental even more than physical, that the Swede stayed with McEnroe and, after three hours and fifty-three minutes, prevailed 8–6 in the fifth set. Subsequently, Borg admitted that he had been afraid of losing the match and had sensed that his reign was coming to an end.

Later that month, on 24 July, Borg married his fellow tennis pro and longstanding girlfriend, the Romanian Mariana Simionescu, in Bucharest. He went on to beat McEnroe in the final of the 1980 Stockholm Open and then again, this time in a final set tie-break, in the season-ending Masters in January 1981, before trouncing Ivan Lendl 6–4, 6–2, 6–2 to win his second Masters title.

In 1981, aged twenty-five, Borg won his eleventh and last Grand Slam title. Fittingly, it was won at the French Open, a monumentally happy hunting ground for the Swede. He overcame Lendl in five sets and his record of six French Open titles stood until Rafael Nadal broke it by claiming his seventh French Open title in 2012.

Thereafter, it was downhill for Borg, though by no means disastrously so. Sure enough, he reached the Wimbledon final but only after fighting back from two sets down against Connors to win 0–6, 4–6, 6–3, 6–0, 6–4. In the final, McEnroe was ready for him and after a slow start the American took control in a close-fought contest, winning 4–6, 7–6, 7–6, 6–4.

At the US Open, Borg was again worsted in a four-set final by McEnroe and that was the last Grand Slam final Borg would play. In a career of stunning success, there were two omissions: the big, glaring hole was a US Open title and the other was an Australian Open crown. A finalist in 1976, 1978, 1980 and 1981, Borg was always the runner-up in the United States. For years, Roger Federer had the same experience at the French Open, having to settle for the role of losing finalist before claiming the crown in 2009. Sadly for Borg, the sequence remained unbroken. He did not enjoy or thrive playing under lights and he never seemed to produce his best when it was most needed at this great event. As for Australia, Borg appeared only once at the Australian Open, at the age of seventeen, and lost early in the tournament.

In 1982, Borg competed only once, yielding to Yannick Noah in the quarter-finals in Monte Carlo in April. The following January, he announced that he was retiring from the game. Even though he had played scarcely at all for a year, he was only twenty-six and evidently in good health, so it was a shock. The truth was that Borg was burnt out, devoid of motivation and keen not only to depart the stage but to be free of the remorseless grind of training, practice and competition which is the lot of every professional sportsperson.

Some may criticise the decision to quit at such a comparatively young age. It could be argued that he was funking the fight, eschewing the hard road he needed to tread to return to the status of undisputed number one, but there lies the rub. Borg clearly felt that he 'needed' to do no such thing. Perhaps he could have met that test and reclaimed his supremacy, perhaps not. Yet he had already secured his place in the pantheon of all-time greats. He had eleven Grand Slam singles titles to his name, matching Rod Laver, and second only to Roy Emerson. His achievement has since been surpassed by Rafael Nadal (thirteen), Pete Sampras (fourteen) and Roger Federer (seventeen). Borg had competed on the professional tour since the age of fourteen and, after twelve years, his appetite had been more than amply satisfied.

What were the most outstanding traits in Borg's make-up? The sheer unadulterated consistency and accuracy of his ball-striking, off forehand and backhand wings alike, was exceptional. His foot-work was superb and his overall physical fitness awe-inspiring. Yet perhaps his most impressive characteristic was his remark-able mental toughness in the most taxing conditions. Confronted with opponents playing spectacularly, facing real adversity, Borg was incredibly resilient. Sure, he was determined to prevail but, having as a young teenager been temperamental and hot-headed, he had trained himself to be the Ice Man, showing no emotion. Some tennis fans liked this, others thought it inhuman or plain boring. That is a matter of taste or choice. What is a matter of undoubted fact is that his calm exterior, his utter inscrutability, was a strength. Whatever was going on inside his head, Borg's outward imperturbability offered not a jot of encouragement to opponents. Magnanimous in victory, gracious in defeat, Borg was a magnificent ambassador for his sport. For me, what makes Borg one of the greatest champions is his achievement, as someone brought up on slow courts, not only to dominate on clay but to adapt his approach so comprehensively that he could also triumph on the All England Club turf. He was the clay-court giant and the grass-court giant. A transformative figure whose reputation will be writ large for as long as people talk and write about tennis, Borg is unarguably one of the greatest of the greats.

Bill Tilden: The first great champion, a multiple title winner who dominated the game in the 1920s.

Fred Perry: A three-time Wimbledon champion, Britain's most successful player was the canniest of performers.

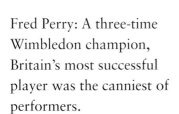

Right – Don Budge: The first and youngest ever winner of the Grand Slam, Budge remains a celebrated champion.

Below – Jack Kramer: A brilliant serve-and-volley player, he mastered the art of percentage tennis.

Right – Pancho Gonzales: World professional champion for eight years, he was the fighter of all 'fighters'.

Below – Ken Rosewall: Diminutive but exquisite player who featured at the top level for over two decades.

Top left – Lew Hoad: A brilliant shot-maker, unplayable in his day, but prone to inconsistency. *Top right* – Rod Laver: The only man to win the Grand Slam twice, regarded by many as the greatest ever. *Below* – Roy Emerson: A wonderful athlete, winner of twelve major titles, but fell short in the Open era.

Top left – Jimmy Connors: Renowned for power and endurance alike, he was amongst the most watchable of champions.

Top right – Björn Borg: Cool at all times, he was phenomenally successful on clay and grass courts alike.

Right – John McEnroe: Stunningly talented, he is renowned both for his shot-making and for his explosive temper.

Left – Ivan Lendl: Remorselessly powerful, hugely consistent and as fit as anyone in the game.

Below left – Boris Becker: The unseeded teenage Wimbledon winner, he was amongst the most flamboyant and exciting of champions.

Below right – Stefan Edberg: The most gracious of sportsmen, he was one of the finest volleyers ever.

Andre Agassi: Master of the serve return, exciting and brilliant, he won all the big prizes.

Pete Sampras: Seven-time Wimbledon champion, the serve-and-volley master dominated much of the 1990s.

Top left – Roger Federer: Arguably the most versatile champion, Federer has won more titles than anyone else.

Top right – Rafael Nadal: The king of clay and the most formidable competitor of the last five years.

Right – Novak Djokovic: His level of play in 2011, winning three major titles, compares with that of anyone.

Chapter Twelve

John McEnroe

JOHN McENROE IS one of the most outstanding, talked-about and controversial players of all time. A former world number one, McEnroe won seven Grand Slam singles titles (three at Wimbledon and four at the US Open) and a total of seventy-seven singles titles on the ATP circuit. In addition, he won a record eight Year End Championship titles, comprising three Masters Championships and an unmatched five WCT finals. In an era that predated the Masters 1000 series, McEnroe won nineteen Championship Series top-tier events of the Grand Prix tour. He achieved the best singles-season match record for a male player in the Open era in 1984 with a win–loss record of 82–3 (96.5 per cent) and his career singles match record was 875–198 (81.55 per cent). McEnroe will always be remembered both for his play and for his behaviour. A shot-maker par excellence, he displayed exquisite artistry on the court and is widely regarded as one of the finest volleyers ever. These attributes were to the fore in clashes with his great rivals Björn Borg, Jimmy Connors and Ivan Lendl. Yet he will also be remembered by friends, foes and dispassionate observers for his explosive temper, on-court tantrums and furious rows with umpires, linespersons and tennis authorities.

McEnroe was born in Wiesbaden, West Germany, to Kay (née Tresham) and John Patrick McEnroe senior. His father, whose family hail from Ireland, was then serving with the United States Air Force. In 1960 the family moved to the New York City area, where McEnroe senior worked daytime in the advertising industry whilst attending night classes at Fordham Law School. He went on to become a partner in one of the biggest law firms in New York. McEnroe's mother, Kay, is the daughter of a Long Island deputy sheriff and McEnroe is the eldest of three brothers.

Growing up in Douglaston, Queens, McEnroe began playing tennis when he was eight years old at the Douglaston Club with his brothers. At nine, his parents enrolled him in the Eastern Lawn Tennis Association, and he started playing regional tournaments. Thereafter, he went on to compete in national juniors tournaments, and at twelve – by now ranked seventh in his age group – he joined the Port Washington Tennis Academy, Long Island, New York.

Reflecting on the early years, McEnroe speaks of his love of sports from a young age. His father used to like to tell the story of the day when he and his son were playing in Central Park one day with a whiffle bat. The younger McEnroe – showing early promise – was demonstrating his ability at line drives. McEnroe recalls, 'An older lady walked up and said, "Excuse me, is that a little boy, or a midget in disguise?"'

Describing his family as 'upwardly mobile', McEnroe says that his parents 'expected achievement' and, seeing young John enjoying tennis and showing an aptitude for the game, they arranged for him to take lessons with the club pro, a high school teacher called Dan Dwyer who, according to McEnroe family legend, said when John was eight, 'I'm predicting we're going to see John at Forest Hills someday.'

Looking back on his formative years as a junior tennis player, McEnroe said, 'In a way I can't totally explain, I could feel the ball through the strings.'

When he started playing junior tournaments in the New York metropolitan area, McEnroe recalls that 'losing was the hardest thing to get used to. I was never very good at it.' Chuck McKinley – a professional acquaintance of McEnroe senior – was one of the best tennis players in the world in the amateur days of the 1950s and 1960s. His father asked McKinley to ask his friend Antonio

'Tony' Palafox (who hadn't admitted McEnroe junior to the top group of the Port Washington Tennis Academy) to take another look at him. Subsequently, Harry Hopman, a 'walking legend' of tennis, who had coached Rod Laver, Roy Emerson, Ken Rosewall and Lew Hoad inter alia, became director at the PWTA and was straightaway impressed by McEnroe. Interestingly, though McEnroe loathed losing and was sharply competitive from an early age, he exhibited one characteristic that Pete Sampras would later display – a concern to work on his game with a view to the medium and long term, rather than to be obsessed by a need for immediate supremacy, describing a conversation with his father in which he argued that he did not want to peak when he was young, but when it was right.

Just as the talent of McEnroe was evident from an early age, so was his explosive temper. He himself recalls that in his second summer of junior Davis Cup, he was playing in a clay-court event in St Louis where the grey-haired bespectacled umpire in his final match was a little slower with his decisions than McEnroe would have liked. Sure enough, the brash New Yorker remonstrated loudly, prompting his coach, Bill McGowan, to call him over to the fence and warn him to be quiet or be yanked off home. On that occasion, McEnroe buttoned his lip.

How did McEnroe play? In truth, as with many players, his approach evolved. Initially, he saw himself as a baseline player, although it would be a grave mistake to view him as defensive. He used a short backswing on both sides, hit the ball on the rise, constantly moving forward, and could more easily reach the net to end the point with a volley or smash. A left-hander, his forehand was of the Continental variety – now largely absent from the professional tour as it is particularly difficult to control when on the run – and he deployed a one-handed backhand, still common in the 1970s and 1980s but much less so now. His service was unmatched then or since. McEnroe would stand at least a metre or more from the centre of the court, with his back almost completely to his opponent, rendering it fiendishly difficult for an opponent to guess whether the delivery would be placed wide or down the T. The service was hit with extreme slice, which was tough for any opponent to handle and particularly effective against a right-hander in the advantage court. Skidding low on a grass court could make the shot virtually unplayable for an opponent. A superb volleyer, McEnroe believes that he was particularly adept at backing up to cover and execute successfully the smash. His fleetness of foot in this part of the court was a crucial element in his winning game because it allowed him to hug the net and thereby get the best possible angle for the volley. He was not worried about an opponent lobbing the ball over his head. He would usually reach a lobbed ball and dispose of it. In his words, 'I have always worked extensively on my smash. I see a lot of people in practice sessions – even a lot of professionals – go up and hit all of two or three overheads, thank you very much. It's not enough.'

McEnroe was never known for using huge power. Rather, he developed a mastery of serve-and-volley tennis, starting at Wimbledon in 1977. His athleticism, anticipation and 'feel' at the net were supreme assets and over the years he demonstrated an ability to use every type of volley, hit deep or dropped short, straight or angled.

1977 was a very significant year in McEnroe's development. As an eighteen-year-old amateur, he partnered fellow American Mary Carillo and won the mixed doubles at the French Open. That same month, McEnroe qualified for the main draw at Wimbledon and, as an unseeded debutante, he reached the semi-finals, where he lost to Jimmy Connors in four sets. This was an exceptional achievement, the best performance by a qualifier at a Grand Slam tournament and a record showing by an amateur in the Open era.

After that auspicious start at Wimbledon in 1977, McEnroe went to Stanford University and won college titles in 1978. Later that year, he joined the ATP Tour and won five titles in 1978, including his first Masters Grand Prix, overcoming veteran American former Wimbledon champion Arthur Ashe in straight sets.

If 1977 had established landmarks in his career, and 1978 was characterised by those title victories, 1979 was spectacular. After all, winning a major title is the pinnacle of success for a competitive tennis player. McEnroe achieved that goal at the age of twenty. He won the first of his seven Grand Slam singles titles at the US Open, defeating Vitas Gerulaitis in the final in straight sets. McEnroe thereby became the youngest male singles victor at the US Open since Pancho Gonzales, also aged twenty, in 1948. To cap this achievement, he won the season-ending WCT finals, defeating Björn Borg, by then a four-time Wimbledon champion, in four sets. McEnroe won ten singles and seventeen doubles titles that year, an Open era record.

In 1980, building on the progress made the previous year, McEnroe reached his first Wimbledon singles final. Although he lost in five sets, his defeat at the hands of Björn Borg was one of the most remarkable tussles ever witnessed on the Centre Court of the All England Club. In recent times, it has been matched in quality and excitement only perhaps by the Federer–Nadal final of 2008 and the Federer–Roddick clash in 2009. The tie-break in the fourth set of the match lasted twenty minutes and, as we saw in Chapter Eleven, after saving five match points, McEnroe prevailed 18–16. Try as he might – and did – McEnroe could not break the Borg serve in the final set and the Swede won it 8–6. Nevertheless, the new kid on the block had made real inroads and, two months later, he turned the tables by beating Borg in five sets in the final of the US Open to claim his second Grand Slam title.

Wimbledon in 1981 was a huge challenge and, as it transpired, a defining moment in the career of McEnroe. After all, he had beaten Borg to win his first major ten months earlier. On the other hand, he had in his mind, and on the record, the fact of defeat to Borg in the enthralling encounter of the previous year. Far from embarking on his 1981 campaign at the All England Club in a sea of tranquillity, the firework display began in round one. Up against fellow American Tom Gullikson, McEnroe fell behind

4–3 in the second set. On what he described as a 'miserable line call', he smashed his Wilson Pro Staff racket and received a warning from the umpire, Edward James. Later, when a service was to his mind wrongly called out, McEnroe threw his new racket and, in a phrase that subsequently became famous or infamous across the world, screamed, 'Man, you cannot be serious!' In arguing the toss with the umpire, McEnroe also gratuitously observed, 'You guys are the absolute pits of the world, you know that?'

Having demanded to see the tournament referee, Fred Hoyles, McEnroe concedes that he used a 'barnyard epithet to describe my opinion of the situation'. He goes on to volunteer that he pointed at the umpire and yelled, loud enough for the TV microphones and most of Court One to hear, 'We're not going to have a point taken away because this guy is an incompetent fool!' Not surprisingly, McEnroe was fined $7,550 for the obscenity, $750 for the comment about the umpire, and threatened with an additional $10,000 fine and possible suspension from the tournament if he indulged in further 'aggravating behaviour'. The incident was hugely controversial and McEnroe was slated in the media, but this potentially distracting background noise notwithstanding, McEnroe reached the final to face his most formidable adversary, Björn Borg, once again. This time McEnroe was victorious, serving and volleying exquisitely and overcoming Borg in four sets, thereby ending the Swede's run of forty-one consecutive singles wins at Wimbledon.

Sadly, despite his sweet victory, there was a hangover from his on-court outbursts. Customarily, the All England Club awards honorary club membership to its champions after their first victory. This honour was withheld from McEnroe because of his behaviour during the tournament. McEnroe played tit-for-tat by declining to attend the traditional champion's dinner that evening. He explained his actions in characteristically blunt terms to the media: 'I wanted to spend the evening with my family and friends and the people who had supported me, not a bunch of stiffs who are seventy to eighty years old, telling you you're acting like a jerk.' The honour of All England Club membership was subsequently conferred on McEnroe when he won the Wimbledon title for the second time.

The first Wimbledon victory was inevitably big for McEnroe and it could have presaged multiple encounters with Borg. In practice, it was not to be. Their final squaring-up took place two months later in the US Open final where McEnroe triumphed in four sets, thereby becoming the first male player since the 1920s to win three consecutive US Open singles titles. Thereafter, Borg did not play in another Grand Slam tournament and he retired from the main professional tour in 1982. McEnroe, however, won his second WCT final, defeating Johan Kriek.

In 1982, McEnroe was to fall at the last hurdle at Wimbledon, succumbing to the awesome determination of Jimmy Connors over five sets. However, he returned to winning ways in 1983, reaching his fourth successive singles final at Wimbledon for the loss of only one set and then positively trouncing the New Zealander Chris Lewis, 6–2, 6–2, 6–2, to lift the title. Trying his hand at the Australian Open for the first time, McEnroe reached the semi-finals before falling in four sets to Mats Wilander. In the same year, he reached the WCT final for the third time and beat Ivan Lendl in a thrilling five-set encounter. In addition, McEnroe won the Masters Grand Prix title for the second time, overcoming Lendl in straight sets. By his standards, 1983 was a good year. By almost anyone else's, it was outstanding.

Yet there can be no doubt that 1984 was the best year in McEnroe's career. In terms of the majors, other tournaments and win–loss record, it stands out supremely on his CV. At the French Open, McEnroe reached the final for the first and only time. Clay was not his preferred surface and it was a fine accomplishment but he will remember it for the disappointment of squandering a two-set lead over Lendl and losing 7–5 in the fifth set. Effective lobs and cross-court backhand passing shots were key to Lendl's victory, but in this match McEnroe exhibited both fatigue and temper tantrums, which must surely have weighed on the

American and given succour to his tenacious Czech adversary.
Significantly, the defeat ended a 42-match winning streak and,
in his autobiography, McEnroe describes the loss as his bitterest defeat. McEnroe was never much interested in the Australian
Open, but clearly he wanted to win the French and the narrow
failure to do so obviously rankled with him.

McEnroe was in full flight, however, only weeks later at
Wimbledon, conceding only one set – to Aussie Paul McNamee
– en route to the final and then putting on a phenomenal performance to sweep aside his old foe Jimmy Connors in only eighty
minutes for the loss of just four games 6–1, 6–1, 6–2. This was
his third and last Wimbledon singles crown and he backed up the
victory by lifting the US Open title, besting Connors over five sets
in the semi-final and dismissing Lendl 6–3, 6–4, 6–1 in the final.
On top of those huge wins, McEnroe took his fourth WCT final,
defeating Connors in three straight sets, and his third Masters
Grand Prix, beating Lendl in straight sets. In the course of the
year, McEnroe won thirteen singles tournaments and notched up
an 82–3 win–loss record, a 96.47 per cent success rate, which
currently stands alone. Roger Federer in 2005 stood at 81–3
before losing his last match of the year to David Nalbandian.
Aside from his individual supremacy in 1984, McEnroe was on
the winning US World Cup team and runner-up Davis Cup teams.
It is perhaps a poignant commentary on the career and image of
the New York maestro that this great season did not end free of
controversy. During the tournament in Stockholm that McEnroe
went on to win, he erupted. Having questioned a call by the chair
umpire and not elicited an answer, McEnroe snapped, 'Answer
the question, jerk!' He then slammed down his racket and was
suspended for twenty-one days for exceeding a $7,500 limit on
fines that had been created specifically because of his conduct.

In 1985, aged twenty-six, McEnroe reached the last of his
Grand Slam finals, at the US Open. There he was beaten comparatively comfortably by Ivan Lendl 7–6, 6–3, 6–4. McEnroe
had won seven Slams and had been runner-up four times, a

tremendous record, but the loss to Lendl was a chapter-ending experience for him.

In 1986, perhaps suffering burn-out from the mental and physical pressures of competing at the highest level, McEnroe took a six-month sabbatical from the professional tour. During this period he married the actress Tatum O'Neal, with whom he already had a son, Kevin. They went on to have two more children, Sean and, later, Emily, before divorcing in 1994. Later that year, McEnroe won three ATP tournaments but in 1987 he did not win a tournament, his first fallow year since turning professional. He took a further seven-month break from the game after the US Open. This decision was doubtless precipitated by the two-month suspension and $17,500 fine imposed on him at that event as a result of his misconduct and verbal abuse.

After that 1986 sabbatical, McEnroe struggled to regain the form that had produced his greatest triumphs. He lost three times in Grand Slam tournaments to Ivan Lendl and in 2000 admitted that he had used cocaine during his career. He periodically achieved notable victories but the heady heights of the early and mid-1980s were not to be scaled again. Disqualified at the 1990 Australian Open during an outburst in his fourth round match, McEnroe was fined $65,000 for bad language, intimidating a lineswoman and racket abuse. McEnroe ended the year ranked thirteenth in the singles and the following year he slipped to twenty-eighth before retiring at the end of 1992 ranked twentieth in the world. That decision brought down the curtain on a remarkable career. First ranked number one in the world on 3 March 1980, McEnroe occupied that perch no fewer than fourteen times between 1980 and 1985 and finished the year at number one in four successive years from 1981 to 1984. In total, he spent 170 weeks at the top of the rankings.

To me there are three features of McEnroe besides his pure playing ability that warrant attention – his temperament (touched on intermittently during this chapter), his fitness and his attitude to ethics in sport. First, let us focus on the temperament. Although it was a big problem, it is a matter of record that it did not always or even generally wreck his chances in a given match or tournament, although there is some evidence that it undermined the concentration and performance of opponents. McEnroe acknowledges that it was an issue, describing his fifteen years on the world tour as 'a pretty wild ride' and confessing, 'I was the bad boy in the public's eyes.' He is also on the record saying, 'I was a one-way street – mad, madder and maddest'; he regretted not being able to 'turn the other cheek' and that he put it down, ultimately, to his fear of losing.

This is sad but also a tad curious given the sheer enormity of his talent and the fact that he became a Grand Slam title holder at the age of twenty. Yet it did not quell the self-doubt or insecurity.

Interestingly, McEnroe claims that for the first few years he 'almost never spoke an obscenity to an umpire or a linesman' but then 'at a certain point I went over the line' and, referring to his rapid rise to the top, he observes that at such an age 'the oxygen doesn't always flow to your brain'. In September 1977, during a bad-tempered performance against fellow American Cliff Richey, the latter stopped play, put his hands on his hips and addressed the people in the stands. He declared, 'I've been a professional tennis player for ten years, I've been the number one player in the United States, and I refuse to sit back and not say anything about what this kid is doing out here.' McEnroe insists that he was 'incredibly embarrassed' by the ferocious dressing-down but says, 'It was a lesson I would periodically forget over the coming years, whenever fatigue got to me.'

McEnroe also concedes that for all his admiration for the Wimbledon tournament and its 'tremendous history', he found England to be 'stodgy and quaint'. What is more, he complained in retirement that people tended to forget 'the genuinely lousy level of officiating that was prevalent in professional tennis when I came along'. He accepts, importantly, that his father was right in thinking that he would probably have done better had he been able not to lose his temper. The conduct was often inexcusable but it is fair to say both that the quality of officiating has greatly improved – through training, professionalisation, and the use of Hawk-Eye technology – and that McEnroe was on the receiving end of a good deal of pomposity and sheer snobbery from some officials and fans. He should have risen above that, and he lost out by his inability to do so. Staggering success though he enjoyed and notwithstanding the greater talent than many other champions that he displayed, the absence of ruthless self-control cost him as it led to defaults, suspensions, fines and enforced absences, and probably caused him, not least through a cumulative toll, to win fewer titles than he otherwise would have done.

The second point, relating to fitness, is simply stated. McEnroe was not unfit but, as he himself notes, in matches longer than two hours – even though he won many – he became much more vulnerable because he 'wasn't in the amazing physical condition of a Borg or a Lendl'. So, ability, hunger, determination – yes. But temperament and outstanding physical condition? No.

Thirdly, and finally, if McEnroe is slated for his frequent misconduct, he deserves credit for refusing to play in Bohuptswana, South Africa at the height of the apartheid era. In September 1980, a South African businessman, Sol Kerzner, offered McEnroe and Borg $750,000 each to play a one-day exhibition in his casino. The winner would also receive $250,000. McEnroe refused to play because he would be giving cheer to the apartheid regime. As he put it, 'I was proud to look at myself in the mirror after that: for one of the first times in my life, I had actually taken a stand.'

Blessed with perhaps as much natural talent as anyone in the history of the game, much about John McEnroe was exceptional: his service, his groundstrokes, his volleys, his anticipation and, of course, his suspect temperament. He repelled many, but he also attracted huge support and interest to the game which he continues to love and be involved with to this day. His place in the gallery of great champions is secure. The only question, to which an attempted answer will be offered later in this book, is 'How great was McEnroe?'

Chapter Thirteen

Ivan Lendl

THE CZECHOSLOVAKIAN PLAYER Ivan Lendl was a pre-eminent star of the world tennis circuit in the 1980s whose performances were defined by power, relentless competitiveness and outstanding fitness. Lendl won eight Grand Slam singles titles, including three French Opens, three US Opens and two Australian Opens, and he was a losing finalist in a further eleven Grand Slam tournaments, including on two occasions at Wimbledon. For eleven years in succession, Lendl reached a major final, a record shared with Pete Sampras, and his achievement in making the final of the US Open in eight consecutive years has been matched only by the 1920s American maestro Bill Tilden. In addition, he won two WCT finals titles and five Masters Grand Prix titles, in the process racking up the record of appearing in nine consecutive finals. As if this were not outstanding enough, Lendl claimed a record twenty-two Championship Series titles over a nine-year period. In total, he won ninety-four singles titles, second only to Jimmy Connors, who won 109.

After earlier reverses, Lendl won his first Grand Slam title in 1984 in Paris and that triumph propelled him to number one in the world. He ended the year ranked number one in 1985, 1986, 1987 and 1989 and, in total, he occupied the top slot for 270 weeks. That distinction was exceeded only by Pete Sampras and by Roger Federer. This summary of his record suffices to demonstrate that Lendl was certainly amongst the most successful tennis champions of all time.

It was no accident that Ivan Lendl should take to the tennis court. Born in Ostrava, Czechoslovakia on 7 March 1960, Lendl was the son of highly accomplished players, his mother once reaching the number two ranking in Czechoslovakia. Reared in the sport, he practised intensively and played on the junior circuit as a teenager. Lendl was, despite his height, immensely agile, very fast around the court and a player with remarkable endurance. Aged eighteen, he tasted glory and laid down important markers for the future by winning the boys' singles titles at both the French Open and Wimbledon, and he was ranked the world number one junior player. After Lendl turned professional that year on the back of his triumphs at junior level, it is striking that he made his mark quickly. In 1979, he reached a singles final, suffering defeat in three sets at the hands of Balázs Taróczy. The following year he claimed no fewer than seven singles titles. Especially significant about these successes was the fact that Lendl won three of the tournaments in three consecutive weeks and on three different surfaces. Those victories were in Tokyo on clay over Eliot Teltscher, 3–6, 6–4, 6–0, in Hong Kong on a hard court over Brian Teacher 5–7, 7–6 (7–2), 6–3 and in Taiwan on carpet, again vanquishing Brian Teacher, this time in four sets 6–7, 6–3, 6–3, 7–6.

That run of success was no flash in the pan. In making the transition from the junior level to the professional tour, Lendl had started to build up a formidable armoury of weapons. His forehand was hit with controlling topspin, bringing great consistency, but he struck the shot hard and it was flatter than either Borg's strokes then or those of Nadal now. It therefore reached opponents quickly and with real weight behind it. He hit the shot effectively to all parts of the court and developed a particular flair for the running forehand, either hit down the line or cross-court. His backhand in the early years was predominantly a sliced shot, useful both defensively and as an approach on his rare sorties to the net. Later he developed a topspin backhand which was vital to his successes at the highest level.

Lendl had a powerful service and his physical conditioning was a priceless asset.

In 1981, fortified by his wins the previous year, Lendl did even better. He won no fewer than ten tournaments. The list makes impressive reading, not least because many of the finals were won in dominant fashion. In Germany, Lendl picked up the Stuttgart Indoor trophy, defeating New Zealand's Chris Lewis 6–3, 6–0, 6–7, 6–3. That victory was followed by a straightforward win in Las Vegas over the indefatigable American baseliner Harold Solomon, 6–4, 6–2. In Montreal, he prevailed over Eliot Teltscher again, disposing of him without difficulty in straight sets 6–3, 6–2. From there, Lendl took the clay-court title in Madrid, overcoming Pablo Arraya in straight sets 6–3, 6–2, 6–2. In Barcelona, Lendl scored a stunning victory over the top-flight Argentinean Guillermo Vilas 6–0, 6–3, 6–0 and in Basel he notched up another title win, beating José Louis Clerc with consummate ease 6–2, 6–3, 6–0. In Vienna, his victim was the highly experienced Brian Gottfried, beaten 1–6, 6–0, 6–1, 6–2 and in Cologne, Lendl thumped Sandy Mayer 6–3, 6–3. In Buenos Aires, Lendl defeated Vilas on home ground, by the glaring margin of 6–2, 6–2. Perhaps the sweetest and certainly the most remunerative of his 1981 victories was to capture his first season-ending Masters Grand Prix tour title in a Herculean struggle against the electrifying American Vitas Gerulaitis, whom Lendl conquered in five sets, winning 6–7 (5–7), 2–6, 7–6 (8–6), 6–2, 6–4. In addition to those ten triumphs, Lendl was the losing finalist in Richmond, United States, to Yannick Noah, to Jimmy Connors in La Quinta, to Björn Borg in four sets in Stuttgart, and to José Luis Clerc in Indianapolis. Perhaps most encouragingly, Lendl reached his first French Open final, where he took Björn Borg, clay-court master then without equal, to five sets before the Swede triumphed 6–1, 4–6, 6–2, 3–6, 6–1. Lendl ended the year ranked sixth in the world, unchanged from 1980, but his confidence will have been greatly enhanced by the many additions to his trophy cupboard.

In 1982, Lendl made further progress, both in winning titles and in improved ranking. He competed in twenty-three singles tournaments and won fifteen of them, scoring forty-four consecutive victories in the process. Reflecting the pattern of 1981, Lendl claimed numerous title victories on hard courts and clay, but he dramatically increased his success on carpet courts, winning nine titles on the surface compared with only the success over Gerulaitis on carpet the previous year. The fifteen titles were won over thirteen different opponents as Lendl triumphed in Delroy Beach, Italy (twice), West Germany (twice), France, Strasbourg, Dallas, Forest Hills, Washington DC, North Conway, Cincinnati, Los Angeles, Hertford and New York City.

Perhaps the most eye-catching victories were over Gerulaitis in four sets in Italy, coming through 6–7, 6–4, 6–4, 6–3 and, in particular, over John McEnroe, by then already a Grand Slam title winner and world number one. Lendl worsted McEnroe in the WCT finals in Dallas on carpet, defeating the New Yorker in four sets 6–2, 3–6, 6–3, 6–3 and in commanding fashion in New York City, home to the Volvo Masters, where Lendl won 6–4, 6–4, 6–2. This was Lendl's second victory in the year-ending championship.

By the close of 1982, Lendl was ranked number three in the world, up from six a mere twelve months earlier. Despite the cheering conclusion to the year, Lendl suffered disappointments in 1982. Defeats by Yannick Noah in La Quinta, by Vilas in straight sets in Monte Carlo, and over five sets, sacrificing a two-set lead, in Madrid were blows, as was his loss 6–3 in the third set to Gerulaitis in Toronto. Yet, without doubt, the biggest misery was inflicted by his loss to Connors in the US Open final. Connors won the contest 6–3, 6–2, 4–6, 6–4. First time round in the 1981 French Open final, Lendl had stretched Björn Borg to the very limit. Against Connors, however, in New York, Lendl was always playing catch-up and could not establish a grip on the match. This was the second Grand Slam final for Lendl and his second defeat. He was still a young man, only twenty-two, but a great many champions had won major titles at an earlier age and yet Lendl was unable to impose himself on his opponent.

1983 took a by now familiar course. Lendl won seven more
tournaments in the course of the year. He defeated Vilas to don
the crown at Detroit in a WCT final on carpet. He beat Kevin
Curren in Milan on carpet in three sets and on clay in Houston he
beat Paul McNamee in three straight sets. In another WCT final
event at Hilton Head on clay, Lendl trounced Vilas without mercy,
riding out the winner 6–2, 6–1, 6–0. Perhaps most satisfyingly
that year, Lendl edged McEnroe in a very tight final on carpet
in San Francisco. Coming from a set down, Lendl prevailed 3–6,
7–6 (7–4), 6–4.

Alongside those uplifting wins Lendl experienced a number of
near misses, losing in six finals. He played second fiddle to Peter
McNamara, falling in a final-set tie-break in Brussels to Jimmy
Connors in the US Open, to Mats Wilander at the Australian
Open and, painfully, to John McEnroe three times, of which the
losses at the Dallas and Masters finals must have been particularly irksome. However, to return to those major finals, Lendl
simply failed to perform in Australia, where Mats Wilander won
comprehensively 6–1, 6–4, 6–4. At the US Open, the loss was in
four sets but Lendl lost the fourth set 6–0. The nagging concern
at this stage of his career, for Lendl and his fans, was that for
all the power and doggedness of his performances, his physical
fitness and his consistently strong play in tournaments throughout the year, there was something missing when he appeared on
the biggest stages. He had now reached and lost four Grand Slam
finals and was intent on breaking the cycle. He had finished the
year ranked number two in the world, but he was a man with a
mission to win a major title.

1984 was the year of the breakthrough. Ironically, Lendl was a
less prolific tournament winner than in any of the previous three
years. He claimed three titles only and was the runner-up in no
fewer than seven – excluding the Rotterdam final with Connors,
which was abandoned because of a bomb threat – with Lendl
worsted again on five occasions by John McEnroe and once, in
three brutal sets, by Connors in Tokyo.

Yet in Paris in the final of the French Open, Lendl tasted victory for the first time. It was no crushing victory but amongst the tightest matches of his career to that point. What made it all the more rewarding was that Lendl had stared into the abyss at two sets down to John McEnroe and again when he trailed 4–2 in the fourth set. Showing not merely skill but grit and character, Lendl hung in there and clawed his way back into the contest, pipping McEnroe to the title 3–6, 2–6, 6–4, 7–5, 7–5. The match lasted four hours and eight minutes and Lendl became only the fourteenth man in 107 years to overcome a two-set deficit to win a Slam. Although Lendl subsequently lost the US Open final to McEnroe in straight sets and was defeated by him again in the 1984 Volvo Masters final (played in January 1985), Lendl will have derived enormous satisfaction and confidence from his first Slam victory. Despite it, he ended the year ranked number three in the world, a rung below 1983.

In 1985, Lendl, buoyed by his Slam success, won eleven titles over eight different opponents, including two victories against John McEnroe, Mats Wilander and the emerging star and 1985 Wimbledon champion, Boris Becker. Once more, Lendl achieved his successes on clay, hard courts and carpet, though he was unable to break through on grass. Alongside the victories he suffered two final losses to McEnroe, in Stratton Mountain and Montreal, and was unable to hold on to his French Open title, submitting in the final to Mats Wilander who won their contest 3–6, 6–4, 6–2, 6–2. However, for Lendl, the greatest significance of 1985 was that he backed up his first Slam victory of the previous year by winning the US Open with a commanding victory over John McEnroe 7–6, 6–3, 6–4. He had been 5–2 and break point down in the first set. He then hit a cross-court backhand winner to reach deuce, broke serve and later won the set in the tie-break by seven points to one. That joy was reinforced by success in the Masters Grand Prix title in New York City, Lendl's third such victory, this time at the expense of Boris Becker. Lendl had first been ranked world number one in February 1983 but he had not held the ranking at the end of a year. In 1985, he did.

1986 was another stellar year for Lendl as he won nine titles. Of these, the most significant were in Paris and New York. At the French Open, where he had opened his Grand Slam title account two years earlier, Lendl dominated his Swedish adversary, Mikael Pernfors, winning in straight sets 6–3, 6–2, 6–4. In New York, he trounced Miloslav Mečíř 6–4, 6–2, 6–0. Lendl had added Slam titles, bringing his tally to three, and those victories were reinforced by his success in the Masters Grand Prix title, in which Lendl brushed aside the challenge of Boris Becker with a 6–4, 6–4, 6–4 victory. Once again, Lendl ended 1986 as world number one. There had been one nagging disappointment in the year, namely his straight-sets defeat in the Wimbledon final by Boris Becker, but the balance sheet in tournament wins and prize money alike was hugely in surplus.

In 1987, Lendl won eight titles as he consolidated his position as the leading player in the world. John McEnroe was performing erratically at the time, Jimmy Connors remained a formidable competitor but was well into his thirties, Mats Wilander was superb but lacked the remorseless intensity of Lendl, and Boris Becker sparkled intermittently. What marked Lendl out from his peers was the sheer consistency of his performances throughout a season. The highlights of 1987 were Lendl's triumphs at the French Open and the US Open. In both finals the opponent was Mats Wilander. In Paris, Lendl prevailed in four sets 7–5, 6–2, 3–6, 7–6 (7–3) and he repeated the achievement in New York, coming from a set down to defeat Wilander 6–7 (7–9), 6–0, 7–6 (7–4), 6–4. Lendl rounded off a tremendous year with victory over Wilander in the Masters final in New York City for the loss of only seven games over three sets. For the third consecutive year, Lendl was ranked world number one.

Yet, for all that he had amassed six Grand Slam titles, including three successive wins at the US Open, he experienced not the disaster but the disappointment of defeat at Wimbledon. As in 1986, Lendl reached the final but he was thwarted by the Australian Pat Cash. Lendl had a powerful serve but it was inconsistent, some commentators believing this was attributable to an over-high ball toss, and he could not dominate with serve. Moreover, though Lendl could volley, it was not his strong suit and approaching the net was not his normal gameplan. Cash, a relatively traditional Australian performer, served and volleyed to great effect and was able to impose his game on Lendl, triumphing 7–6, 6–2, 7–5. As Bud Collins put it, 'For all his countless hours of practice, Lendl wasn't a natural. He was mechanical. And it showed as the 22-year-old Cash crushed his opponent's spirit.'

Measured by the exacting standards that Lendl had set for himself, 1988 was a relatively lean year. Lendl won titles in Monte Carlo, Rome and Toronto but he failed to secure a Slam title, having to content himself with a losing finalist appearance in New York at the US Open, where Mats Wilander beat him 6–4, 4–6, 6–3, 5–7, 6–4. In addition, Lendl made it to the final of the Nabisco Masters in New York City but was beaten in an awesome five-set thriller by Boris Becker, 5–7, 7–6, 3–6, 6–2, 7–6. At Wimbledon that year, Lendl made the semi-final, a feat he was to repeat for the next two years, but he could not better it. That year, Lendl was ranked number two in the world.

After the comparatively modest pickings of 1988, 1989 was altogether more successful for the Czech. Of the seventeen tournaments he played, Lendl won ten of them, notching up victories in Melbourne, Scottsdale, Miami, Forest Hills, Hamburg, London (Queen's), Montreal, Bordeaux, Sidney and Stockholm. Of those titles, the Australian Open was naturally the biggest prize. It was Lendl's seventh major title but his first Australian Open crown, won at the age of twenty-eight – nearly twenty-nine – at the expense of Miloslav Mečíř 6–2, 6–2, 6–2. Alongside his impressive wins, Lendl was also the runner-up in two tournaments in 1989, losing a three-set match to Stefan Edberg in Tokyo and the final of the US Open to Boris Becker in New York, his eighth consecutive final appearance in the event.

In 1990, Lendl retained his Australian Open title, defeating Stefan Edberg in the final, the latter retiring injured with a torn abdominal muscle when the match was squared at one set all and Lendl was leading 5–2 in the third set. It was the eighth Slam title for Lendl, and his last. Thereafter, he was to reach one further final, namely the Australian Open in 1991, where he was defeated in four sets by Boris Becker. Now approaching thirty-one, Lendl had peaked comparatively late for a modern top player, enjoying a magnificent run from 1985 to 1987 in particular, but the glory days were at an end.

Aside from the Australian Open title in 1990, Lendl was to win four more tournaments that year, in Milan and Toronto over Tim Mayotte and at the Queen's Club and Tokyo against Becker. His victory on the London grass over Becker was in straight sets but their duel in Tokyo on carpet was snatched by Lendl in a final-set tie-break in a three-set match. Lendl appeared in one other final that year, also against Boris Becker, but was thrashed by him 6–2, 6–2 in Stuttgart.

From 1991 to 1993, Lendl won six further titles – notching up a victory amongst others over a young Pete Sampras in 1991 – and was a losing tournament finalist on nine occasions, including to a more experienced Agassi in 1992 and a similarly improved Sampras in 1993. In 1989, Lendl had returned by the end of the year to world number one but had slipped back to number three the following year and to number five in 1991. Unsurprisingly, in 1992, Lendl fell slightly, aged thity-two, to number eight, to number nineteen in 1993 and to fifty-four in 1994. Lendl ceased competitive play after his second-round defeat at the US Open that year and, suffering from acute back pain, he retired from the game on 20 December 1994, aged thirty-four.

What, overall, are we to make of Ivan Lendl?

First, he was an exponent of the all court game, characterised by ferocious groundstrokes, extreme fitness and relentless application. He himself described his approach as 'hitting hot' and it is doubtful whether anyone hit the ball consistently as hard as he did at the time, for the most part with remarkable accuracy.

Secondly, he is perhaps as remarkable as anyone both for his work rate and for his methodical planning. Lendl was the ultimate professional in that he was not content to depend on talent, fitness and a decent practice schedule. He prepared meticulously, going to previously uncharted lengths to maximise his chances of success. Indeed, it is said that his run of eight consecutive US Open finals was substantially attributable to his decision to hire the same people who laid the courts at Flushing Meadows in order for them to install an exactly similar court on which he could practise at home in Connecticut.

Thirdly, his match play record is impressive by most relevant yardsticks. His career win–loss record was 81.8 per cent. He won eight Grand Slam titles over seven years and was runner-up eleven times. That record of nineteen Grand Slam final appearances stood unbeaten until Roger Federer exceeded it in 2009. Moreover, for Lendl to appear in the final of the Year End Championship tournament nine times was evidence of quite phenomenal consistency against his closest rivals. In five of those finals, he won. That consistency of performance is further proven by the capture over his career of ninety-four titles. Achieved over fourteen years from 1980 to 1993 inclusive, that is close to seven per year, not to mention the fifty-two occasions on which Lendl was a runner-up. The only player to boast a similar record in that respect is Jimmy Connors.

There can be no doubt that the ability and record of Ivan Lendl qualify him for inclusion in the top bracket of champions. In common with every other player – as in any field of human endeavour – there were weaknesses. Lendl had a fine service when it was 'on' but it could be erratic and though he strove mightily to improve his volleying it was never a great strength and certainly not on a par with that of some other champions. In addition, it is a gap in his record that Lendl did not win Wimbledon. He is not alone in the galaxy of greats covered in this book in that unwanted distinction; Gonzales and Rosewall sit alongside him. Gonzales is in a different category, however, as he was barred at his peak from playing in the tournament by virtue of his professional status. Rosewall spent twelve years as a professional but he did have several opportunities and could not realise them. Other champions failed to win one or other of the Australian, French and US titles. Failure to win Wimbledon does not mean that Lendl was not a great champion. He certainly was, yet he would have been even greater if, like others initially averse to grass, he had been able to adjust sufficiently to claim what is usually regarded as the biggest prize in the sport, as Björn Borg did to a spectacular degree and as Rafael Nadal has done. In recent decades, far fewer tournaments have been played on grass but the gulf between Lendl's success on other surfaces and the lack of it on turf is underlined by the fact that only two of his ninety-four career titles were won on grass, namely at the Queen's Club in 1989 and 1990.

There is one last consideration. Some observers believe that Lendl was a dour performer – hugely efficient and effective but not an inspiring or charismatic figure. I watched him play and entertain in the summer of 2013 at a charity event and was struck by the authority, humour, and quick wit of the man, albeit that these qualities were displayed almost two decades after he retired. It may be that Connors, Borg, McEnroe, for example, had a greater impact on audiences and, indeed, in motivating others to take up the sport. Yet if the test is to win, and win consistently at the highest level, there is no question about it. Ivan Lendl passed the test with flying colours and he warrants respect and admiration for his outstanding accomplishments over fourteen years.

Chapter Fourteen

Boris Becker

BORIS BECKER IS one of the most fascinating and talked-about champions of the modern era, and, indeed, probably of any period in the history of tennis. The fact and the manner of his winning his first Wimbledon singles title were as stunning, and made as great an immediate impact on tennis, as anything in my memory. Becker won six Grand Slam singles titles, consisting of three Wimbledon crowns, two Australian Opens and a US Open title. He was also a losing finalist on a further four occasions at Wimbledon. On top of those achievements, he won the ATP Year End Championship finals (now known as the ATP World Tour finals) three times and was the runner-up on a further five occasions. In addition, Becker won the WCT Year End Championship final in 1988, having been the runner-up in the event in 1986. He won five Masters 1000 Series titles and eight Championship Series titles. Over a period of fourteen years from 1985 to 1999, Becker won no fewer than forty-nine singles titles and was the losing finalist another twenty-eight times. In addition, he was a mainstay of the winning German Davis Cup team in 1988 and 1989. He is a former world number one and he was inducted into the International Tennis Hall of Fame in 2003. Of all his accomplishments, winning Wimbledon for the first time at the age of seventeen from an unseeded position in the draw, the first German man to win the title, is the most remarkable. He was the youngest man to lift the title, and that record stands to this day.

Born in Leiman, West Germany on 22 November 1967, Becker is the only son of Elvira, who was brought up in Czechoslovakia, and of Karl-Heinz Becker, an architect, who is said to have founded the tennis centre in Leiman, where Becker learned the game. His parents were Catholic and raised him in the faith.

In his autobiography, Becker recalls that he was three or four years old when he first lifted his father's tennis racket out of the boot of the car and started hitting balls against the wall of the tennis club or against the shutters of the family home. Assuming that it was a normal-sized adult racket, it is a wonder that young Boris could handle such an implement. Whether he held it by the grip or halfway up he does not tell us but, at any rate, he started the process of developing shots and, crucially, the hand–eye coordination required to produce them consistently. His first coach was Boris Breskvar, who taught him on the indoor court built near to his home, and this grounding doubtless explains why he was always comfortable playing indoors as well as outdoors.

One of the most thrilling features of Becker's play, which first came to the attention of a mass audience at Wimbledon, was his headlong lunges to play volleys at full stretch. To do so, retaining control of the ball in the process, is exceptionally difficult but Becker had trained for the purpose. Observers recall that his coach laid gym mats on both sides of the court towards the net to encourage Becker to leap for the ball, requiring a skill and an energy that was to captivate and enthral spectators throughout Becker's illustrious career. Later on, Günter Bosch became coach to Boris and the former Romanian tennis professional, Ion Ţiriac, became his manager. Becker acknowledges and Ţiriac confirms, however, that unlike some players who almost welcome relieving themselves of responsibility for decisions on practice, playing schedules, contract negotiations, exhibition events and other commitments, Boris had views, expounded them, often insisted on them and, when he felt strongly, simply followed his own instincts. He did it his way, though he valued guidance, interaction and testing his thoughts against those of his team of close advisors.

Becker turned professional in 1984, aged sixteen, and shortly after his seventeenth birthday, he had an early taste of success. No, it was not a title win at that point, but Becker, ranked only 200 in the world, played at the Australian Open in Melbourne and beat the American Tim Mayotte, a top twenty player, in four sets, winning 6–4, 7–6, 2–6, 6–4. It was no flash in the pan, for Becker progressed through a further two rounds to the quarter-finals. It was an auspicious debut, a confidence-booster and a trigger for further success within weeks. In January 1985 Becker won the Young Masters title in Birmingham against Stefan Edberg, then regarded as the leading young player and nearly two years older than Becker. In a foretaste of some of their epic battles to come, their final was a see-sawing five-set affair, the first such match Boris had played, and he won it 4–6, 6–3, 6–1, 4–6, 6–3.

By now, both Becker's physique and his playing style were set. Six foot three inches tall, Becker was a man of athletic build, who had enjoyed football and basketball in his youth, and he had advantages of reach and power that he was to deploy to the full. A right-hander with a single-handed backhand of real power, his play was built on a fast and accurate service, excellent volleys and striking athleticism which enabled him to cover the net effectively and to retain impressive control of his shots in doing so. If the powerful serve and the dive volley were the most striking features of his approach to the game, it should be noted that he boasted a penetrating forehand, impressive backhand and effective service return which caused all sorts of problems for opponents. Becker was far from being a one-trick pony – serve-and-volley only – as the extent of his talents allowed him to be versatile, but there is no doubt that his overriding preference was to attack, and such an approach equipped him to perform particularly well on fast surfaces such as grass and carpet courts. As he put it, 'My gameplan has always been to attack; that's in my nature.'

In 1984, on the Wimbledon grass, Becker had won two matches, before succumbing to the American Bill Scanlon in the third round. However, in 1985, Becker served notice of his intention to make a big impact very soon on the professional game when, just over a week before the start of the Wimbledon championships, he won the warm-up event on grass at the Queen's Club in London. His victim was the 27-year-old South African Johan Kriek, who had been ranked seventh in the world the previous year and who had twice won the Australian Open, albeit three and four years earlier. Becker came through the final very comfortably, 6–2, 6–3, prompting Kriek to observe prophetically, 'If Boris serves as well at Wimbledon as he did against me today, he will win the title.' Becker had won the first of the forty-nine titles of his career and the second was set to follow without delay.

No doubt buoyed by his success at Queen's and the encouraging prediction of his highly experienced adversary Kriek, Becker almost literally threw himself into his bid to take the Wimbledon title. From his opening-round defeat of the big-serving American Hank Pfister in four sets to his ultimate triumph, John Barrett notes that Becker 'served like a demon'. After defeating Pfister, Becker disposed of Matt Anger from the United States in straight sets, and in the third round he eventually outlasted the number seven seed, Sweden's Joakim Nyström, winning 9–7 in the fifth set, after saving three match points on Nyström's serve in the process. Becker himself volunteers that he took 'huge risks with each return'. Daring was rewarded and Becker thereby booked a last-sixteen clash with the American Tim Mayotte, whom he had beaten in Melbourne the previous year. This, however, was at Wimbledon, usually regarded as the world's premier tennis event, and it was a big proposition. Becker twisted an ankle in the later stages of a very tight match and had been thinking of quitting but Ion Țiriac yelled out to him to seek a three-minute break for examination by a doctor, and Becker resolved to continue, proceeding to win the contest 6–2 in the final set. He reveals in his autobiography that in the changing room he thanked Țiriac, saying, 'You won this match for me.' The victory over Mayotte was marked by frequent headlong dives for wide volleys and Becker demonstrated his prowess in the use of the technique.

By now, Becker had won four matches and was in the quarter-finals, where his opponent was the Frenchman Henri Leconte. The match was interrupted by rain and Becker came through in four sets. In the semi-final, he encountered the number eight seed from Sweden, Anders Järryd, who had progressed one round beyond the tournament organisers' expectations. Once again, Becker was the victor in four sets.

In the final, Becker was pitched against the experienced South African Kevin Curren, twenty-seven years old and the man who had defeated both the number one seed, John McEnroe, and the number three seed, Jimmy Connors. On the face of it, in light of those victories, the enormity of the occasion and the greater street wisdom acquired by several years on the professional tour, Curren would have seemed the favourite. Curren himself thought so. As he said afterwards, 'I should have had the advantage. Being older, being to the semi-finals, being on Centre Court. Maybe he was too young to know about all that stuff.'

Ironically, Becker went on court, he tells us, feeling no fear whereas Curren appeared nervous. Curren was a big server and delivered nineteen aces in the match but Becker dished up twenty-one. Becker always rallied strongly, frequently outdoing Curren off the ground and backing up a strong serving performance with a steadiness off both wings from the back of the court that hurt Curren. Becker won the first set, suffered the disappointment of losing the second in a tie-break in which he had led 4–2, but regained control by decisively winning the third set tie-break by seven points to three. With a break of serve he took the fourth set 6–4, winning the match and the tournament. Becker was seventeen years and 227 days old, the youngest man in history to win the Wimbledon singles title and the only German to do so. The youth of the victor was and remains the most stunning feature of Becker's triumph, together with the significant albeit lesser consideration that he was unseeded, i.e. expected not to progress beyond the third round. The only other unseeded player to win the men's singles at Wimbledon was Goran Ivanišević in 2001. Becker was reckoned beforehand to win a maximum of two matches but in fact he won seven.

Beyond his youth, there was another point of interest, at least to the tennis cognescenti. That was the sheer adventure, the closeness of matches, the combination of bare-knuckle ride and long waits entailed by his triumph. As Bud Collins has stressed, three of Becker's first six matches were suspended and held over for another day. This could have helped Becker but it could also have hindered him by reducing recovery time before the following match. Yet the bigger point about the matches Becker played at that Wimbledon was just how hard fought they were. En route to his triumph in the final, Becker lost eight sets and 126 of 292 games, a losing percentage of 43.15. This was a heavy toll of games lost. In 1949, the men's singles champion Ted Schroeder had lost eight sets – he was the only other man to do so – and he sacrificed 40.8 per cent of the games, a marginally smaller sacrifice than Becker sustained thirty-six years later. The credit to Becker is that he became accustomed to tight matches and was not psyched out by them. He withstood the pressure, served superbly, attacked remorselessly and triumphed unforgettably. Curren conceded to reporters that Becker was 'incredibly talented' though it was perhaps superfluous and surely gratuitous for him to add that Becker was 'not nearly as good as McEnroe'.

Becker celebrated with a hot soak, wryly observing in his autobiography, 'Back then a physiotherapist was beyond my means.' Becker's mother, Elvira, was delighted but not surprised by his victory. She said, 'I knew that if he didn't lose his nerve he'd make it. If he didn't work himself up into that frenzy of his, he'd be all right.' Ion Ţiriac had also been convinced that Becker would win, from the moment the Romanian manager witnessed his man's ready dismissal of Pat Cash in straight sets at Queen's. Becker, at the time, was elated. In his autobiography, with the benefit of nearly two decades' hindsight, Becker has a different take. In his own words, 'I would have preferred more time: time to develop my game of tennis, and to develop my own character. Had I won Wimbledon at the age of twenty-three or twenty-five, instead of seventeen, I would have become a better tennis player.'

After Wimbledon in 1985, the remainder of the year brought mixed fortunes for Becker. A month after his triumph at the All England Club, he played in the Davis Cup for West Germany against the USA

on clay, a surface with which he was not, and never became, altogether comfortable. The rubber took place in Hamburg, Germany
won and Becker played his part. That was a high. Lows came for
the newly crowned Wimbledon champion with an early defeat in a
tournament in Kitzbühel and, more crushingly, with a loss in the last
sixteen of the US Open to Joakim Nyström, whom he had beaten at
Wimbledon. This time, Becker offered up sixty-four unforced errors
to the Swede and paid the price for a sloppy performance.

On the back of the Wimbledon victory, Becker had automatically become big news. Expectations were high, pressure intense
and the chorus of criticism swift and biting when he faltered. Some
competitors can block off criticism by refusing to read newspaper
reports or by intense concentration on the next match or practice
session, or both. Becker was not able to do so at that stage of his
career. He noticed what was said and it could get to him. As he
put it, 'Whenever I lost, especially in the early rounds, I was seldom
shown mercy.' On the positive side, Becker won the Grand Prix
Championship Series tournament in Cincinnati in August on a hard
court, comprehensively beating the Swedish star Mats Wilander,
6–4, 6–2, and he reached the finals of both the indoor tournament
in Wembley, London, and the Year End Championship final in New
York, succumbing in both cases on carpet courts to Ivan Lendl. The
New York defeat was a straightforward loss, but the Wembley loss
went to five sets and Becker acquitted himself well against a fearsome and highly experienced opponent.

In March 1986, Becker won a tournament in Chicago on carpet,
beating Lendl 7–6, 6–3 and he was a losing finalist to Anders Järryd
in Dallas. Unfortunately, in the run-up to Wimbledon, Becker exhibited very indifferent form. In a string of tournaments in France, Italy
and the United States, Becker suffered quarter-final exits and the
same fate befell him at Queen's, where he had triumphed over Johan
Kriek a year earlier. This was not the ideal preparation for his bid to
defend his Wimbledon title, which he was utterly intent on doing. As
Becker put it, 'I was eighteen, and had to win at least one more time.'
He did not want it to be said that the 1985 triumph was somehow

a fluke, an oddity, a never-to-be-repeated upset of the natural order. He wanted to prove that he could fight and win on the biggest stage on an ongoing basis.

Sure enough, Becker reached the final and he was up against Lendl, now twenty-six, and equally focused on winning before it was too late. Becker is refreshingly candid in his autobiography about his self-belief. He says, 'I was convinced I'd win. It sounds strange, but the previous night I'd dreamt of victory just like the year before. Lendl, on the other hand, seemed frightened, almost transfixed.' Becker's premonition of victory was well founded. He won the match in straight sets, 6–4, 6–3, 7–5. Although there is unique significance to a maiden victory, especially as Becker was the youngest to notch it up, his successful defence of the title was more important for his status as a player of the highest rank. Becker said that the event had 'transformed [him] from a boy to an adult'.

Lendl was ranked number one in the world at the time, Becker number two, so the victory could not have been sweeter or more poignant. To detractors or simply sceptics who questioned whether Becker could pull off another Wimbledon title, he had provided the most emphatic answer, defeating the sport's top-ranked player for the purpose. After Wimbledon, the rest of the year went relatively well for Becker. In August, it is true, Lendl got his revenge, on a somewhat smaller stage, when the two met in the final of the Stratton Mountain tournament in the US on a hard court, Lendl emerging victorious 6–4, 7–6 (7–0). A week later, in Canada, Becker won the tournament over Stefan Edberg 6–4, 3–6, 6–3. Becker did not thrive at the US Open but in October he returned to winning ways, first clinching a title in Sydney on a hard court, overcoming Lendl in four sets 3–6, 7–6 (7–2), 6–2, 6–0 and, a week later, beating Edberg in the final of the tournament in Tokyo on a carpet court, prevailing 7–6 (7–5), 6–1. At the beginning of November, in Paris, on carpet, Becker won the title by defeating Sergio Casal 6–4, 6–3, 7–6 (7–3), and he ended the year with the disappointment of losing the Year End Championship final on carpet in New York, where Lendl mastered him in straight sets 6–4, 6–4, 6–4.

It had been a great year for Becker, though it is hard to overstate the pressure on the man after his initial stunning success. Expectations went through the roof. People seemed to think that Becker should win all the time and, almost inevitably, they were to be disappointed. As the *Observer* newspaper noted at the end of 1986, 'He needs extraordinary qualities of resilience and resolve to cope with the absurd expectations of his country.' Those expectations are never higher nor the audience more potentially unforgiving than when a player competes for his country in the Davis Cup. In March 1985, before his first Wimbledon triumph, Becker had competed in a match against Spain, winning one singles tie and losing the other. Later that year, when Germany played Sweden in the final of the competition in Munich, Becker won both his singles rubbers, overcoming Edberg – whom he dubs 'my eternal rival' – in four sets 6–3, 3–6, 7–5, 8–6 and Mats Wilander 6–3, 2–6, 6–3, 6–3. However, his teammate Michael Westphal was ranked only about fiftieth in the world and, unsurprisingly, he lost to Wilander in three sets and went on to lose to Edberg in four. Realistically, Westphal's defeats were predictable and the pressure on Becker to deliver three victories was intense. With the score tied at 1–1 after the opening singles, all eyes turned to the doubles, where Becker partnered Andreas Maurer, but they were beaten easily 6–4, 6–2, 6–1. Becker later noted, 'The first jeers. I began to be afraid of the coming matches. Expectations had got way out of hand.' The Swedes had won the final by three matches to two. The German crowds were upset. Becker, who had given his all, was deflated.

By the high standards Becker had now set for himself, 1987 was a relatively poor year. He did not win a major title or reach a final, making the semi-finals of just one of the four Grand Slam events, namely the French Open. At Wimbledon, when he was ranked world number two and seeded number one, and hunting for a third successive crown, he suffered a shock defeat by the world number seventy, Peter Doohan, in the second round in four sets.

In the Davis Cup that year, there was to be no ultimate triumph for Germany but Becker did play one of those exhilarating matches that can also prove to be fortifying and, in a real sense, life-enhancing. Against the US, Becker played McEnroe in the United States. He and his teammates were engaged in a group play-off against the Americans and took it very seriously. Becker revealed in his autobiography that he had been helped in preparation by the British professional, Stuart Bale, a player well known to me. Bale was ranked only about 200 in the world but he was a highly competent left-hander and will have given Becker invaluable practice, not least in facing a swinging left-handed serve which McEnroe could make into a nightmare for right-handers in the advantage court. That preparation came in handy as the match with McEnroe was a momentous marathon. Becker began inauspiciously by losing his serve for the first time and, with it, the opening set 6–4. The second set, the longest of Becker's career, lasted two hours and thirty-five minutes, Becker clinching it 15–13 to level the match. The contest lasted six hours and thirty-eight minutes before Becker won it 4–6, 15–13, 8–10, 6–2, 6–2. The Germans won the tie three matches to two, remained in the world group and saw the Americans relegated. Becker was the hero of the hour and the team had paved the way for greater success in years to come.

On the tournament front, Becker had modest rather than outstanding success. At Indian Wells in February, Becker won the title, beating Edberg in straight sets in the final, 6–4, 6–4, 7–5. In April, he won a tournament on carpet in Milan, defeating Miloslav Mečíř 6–4, 6–3 and he followed up that victory by regaining the Queen's Club title which he had first won two years earlier, this time out-doing Jimmy Connors on the west London grass, 6–7 (3–7), 6–3, 6–4. In August, he was runner-up to Stefan Edberg 6–4, 6–1 on the hard court of Cincinnati.

In 1988, a major title once again proved beyond the grasp of Becker but he reached the Wimbledon final, where he was worsted by Stefan Edberg in four sets 4–6, 7–6 (7–2), 6–4, 6–2. Importantly, Becker also added seven tournament victories to his tally. At Indian Wells, he retained his title, besting Spain's Emilio Sánchez in four sets 7–5, 6–4, 2–6, 6–4. From there, he claimed the WCT title in Dallas, beating Stefan Edberg 6–4, 1–6, 7–5, 6–2 on the American carpet court. At Queen's in June, he repeated his victory over Edberg in three sets 6–1, 3–6, 6–3 before losing the big encounter against the Swede in the Wimbledon final three weeks later. In August, on the hard court of Indianapolis, Becker won the tournament with a business-like conquest of John McEnroe 6–4, 6–2 and in Tokyo in October on carpet his final victim was the Australian John Fitzgerald, whom he defeated 7–6 (7–4), 6–4. The following month, in Stockholm, Becker won a hard-court title, beating the Swede Peter Lundgren 6–4, 6–1, 6–1. The culmination of this winning sequence, and probably the most satisfying victory of the lot, came in the final of the Year End Championships in New York City in December, where on the carpet court Becker was triumphant in a nail-biting, excruciatingly close five-set battle against Ivan Lendl, Becker winning 5–7, 7–6 (7–5), 3–6, 6–2, 7–6 (7–5). On top of these inspiring personal successes, Becker helped West Germany to win its first Davis Cup in 1988.

After a two-year drought in terms of major titles, Becker had a superb year in 1989. He suffered disappointment in Paris in losing in the semi-finals to Stefan Edberg, but a month later at Wimbledon, at the venue and on the surface he relished, Becker disposed of Edberg with a relatively uncomplicated 6–0, 7–6 (7–1), 6–4 victory. In previous years he had failed to make a breakthrough at the US Open but this time he made it to the final and came off better in a tough four-set encounter with Lendl, winning 7–6 (7–2), 1–6, 6–3, 7–6 (7–4). Becker's groundstrokes had markedly improved and Lendl generously said, 'He just has more power in his game than I do.' This was the first and only year in which Becker took two Grand Slam titles.

On the ATP circuit, aside from his majors, Becker won tournaments in Milan over Alexander Volkov 6–1, 6–2, in Philadelphia over Tim Mayotte 7–6, 6–1, 6–3 and in Paris over Stefan Edberg 6–4, 6–3, 6–3. In Monaco, on clay, he lost to Alberto Mancini in four sets and at the Year End Championships in New York City he lost in four sets to Edberg, who took the match 4–6, 7–6 (8–6), 6–3, 6–1. He posted very good results for the year but retention of the Davis Cup in 1989 for West Germany will have been special for Becker, whose performance was crucial. In the Munich Olympia Halle before West Germany reached the final, Becker came back from two sets down to beat Agassi. Combined with Becker's compatriot Carl-Uwe Steeb beating Agassi unexpectedly and the Germans winning the doubles, they had won the tie.

The harsher side of sport, and evidence of the unrelenting pressure on Becker, was provided when Becker, realising that he was 'running on empty' and that the remaining singles was a dead rubber, passed on it and enabled Patrick Kühnen to play against the American Brad Gilbert. Kühnen lost and 'the spectators booed, the press blew its top … that hurt. The state of my health clearly meant nothing to them.' He went on to complain that 'when, after eight hours of high performance in just two days – the equivalent of five football matches in a row – I couldn't go on any more, the buckets of manure got tipped up over my head. Such ingratitude,' he declared in his autobiography, 'especially towards Patrick' – his teammate, who had fought like a tiger. For all his frustration at the patent injustice of some of the criticism lobbed at him, Becker must have felt vindicated and proud to be part of the West German team that retained the Davis Cup in 1989 over Sweden. Becker's finest hour in that contest in Stuttgart was his routing of Mats Wilander for the loss of only four games, 6–2, 6–0, 6–2. Overall, indeed, his record in the Davis Cup was strong. He played sixty-five matches for his country and won fifty-three of them. Becker did not attain the number one ranking in 1989 but he had the consolation of being named Player of the Year by the ATP tour.

In 1990, Becker again reached the final at Wimbledon – his fifth appearance in six years and his third in succession against Stefan Edberg. A fourth title was the prize, but it was not to be for Becker. The match went to five sets thanks to a fight back from the German but Edberg prevailed 6–2, 6–2, 3–6, 3–6, 6–4. At the US Open, Becker fell to Andre Agassi in the semi-finals. He had enjoyed two Slam victories the previous year but in 1990 he was denied. Yet the trophy cupboard was not barren that year. Becker won titles in Brussels, Stuttgart (handsomely over Lendl), Indianapolis, Sydney and Stockholm (the latter two matches being wins in three straight sets over Edberg).

In 1991, Becker began the year on a high, winning the Australian Open for the first time. He was working with the Australian coach Bob Brett at the time and the link-up paid dividends. It was a swash-buckling start as Becker defeated Ivan Lendl in four sets, coming from a set down to romp home 1–6, 6–4, 6–4, 6–4. Becker achieved the coveted world number one ranking from his success in Melbourne but he was unable to back up his Australian triumph with victory at the French Open. There, he was beaten by Agassi. Becker was doubtless fed up to fail again in Paris, but in a sense, his loss in the Wimbledon final a month later to his fellow German Michael Stich will have been a more bitter blow. Becker could have been expected to lift this fourth Wimbledon title but he was strangely lacklustre. Stich performed more sharply and Becker paid the price. Aside from his success at the Australian Open and final defeat at the All England Club, Becker won a tournament in Stockholm over Edberg 3–6, 6–4, 1–6, 6–2, 6–2. He was also a losing finalist in Monaco on clay and on a hard court in Indianapolis, where his conqueror in a tight three-set match was Pete Sampras. In the course of 1991, Becker held the number one slot for twelve weeks but, once again, he was unable to hold that distinction at the end of the year. Unfortunately, that inability to be number one at the end of the year remained a constant throughout his career.

1992 was a year marked by the absence of a major title for Becker but he did win some worthwhile prizes. In February, on the carpet court in Brussels, Becker won the title by pipping Jim Courier to the finishing post in a Herculean five-set thriller, Becker coming from two sets down to win 6–7 (5–7), 2–6, 7–6 (12–10), 7–6 (7–5), 7–5. The following month he won the Rotterdam tournament, defeating Alexander Volkov 7–6 (11–9), 4–6, 6–2. In October in Basel, his final victim was Petr Korda, defeated 3–6, 6–3, 6–2, 6–4. In Paris in early November, Becker beat Guy Forget 6–7 (7–3), 6–3, 3–6, 6–3 and in the final of the Year End Championships in Frankfurt, Becker overcame Jim Courier again, this time in straight sets 6–4, 6–3, 7–5.

This was his second year-end title and it is a big positive in Becker's record for, although it is not equivalent to a Slam title, it is the year-end showdown between the world's top-ranked players, and thereby carries considerable cachet.

1993 was a poor year for Becker. Beset by marital problems and tax disputes, his form suffered. The year had started reasonably enough with victory in Doha over Goran Ivanišević 7–6 (7–4), 4–6, 7–5 in January and defeat of Sergi Bruguera in the Milan final, but Becker made no headway in the Grand Slam events that year and reached only one other final, losing in Indianapolis in August in straight sets to Jim Courier. Once again, in 1994, there was a dearth of big trophies. Becker failed to progress significantly in any of the four major events, though he had the modest consolation of tournament victories in Milan, Los Angeles, New Haven and Stockholm and losing finalist appearances in Rome, Sydney and at the Year End Championships in Frankfurt, where he was outdone in four sets by Pete Sampras 4–6, 6–3, 7–5, 6–4.

Champions naturally strive to go on being champions, and at the highest level. Anything less is a disappointment. By that yardstick, 1995 was again a disappointment. Becker had lost ground; others, most notably Pete Sampras, were firing on all cylinders and Becker was unable to recapture the consistent top-quality form that had brought him big titles in the 1980s and in Australia four years earlier. Nevertheless, Becker did receive a tonic from defeating Andre Agassi in the semi-final of Wimbledon to reach the final for the seventh time. There, he was decisively beaten by Pete Sampras 6–7 (7–5), 6–2, 6–4, 6–2, the American winning his third successive Wimbledon crown. Becker also notched up a tournament victory in Marseilles, as well as runner-up slots in Milan, Monte Carlo and Paris. Perhaps the highlight of the year was to score his third victory in the Year End Championships, a title staged in Frankfurt, where Becker mastered Michael Chang in straight sets 7–6 (7–3), 6–0, 7–6 (7–5).

In 1996, Becker steeled himself to make a pitch for a Slam title and he succeeded. Almost precisely five years after he had last won a major, the 1991 Australian Open title he won at the expense of Ivan Lendl, Becker secured his second Slam title in Melbourne. Carrying on where he had left off two months earlier at the Year End Championships in Frankfurt, Becker overcame Michael Chang on the Australian hard court in four sets 6–2, 6–4, 2–6, 6–2. It was his sixth and last major title success, though he added precious tournament victories to his tally by defeating Stefan Edberg to claim his fourth Queen's Club title in June, besting the Dutchman Jan Siemerink to win in Vienna and, sweetest of all, prevailing in five sets over Pete Sampras 3–6, 6–3, 3–6, 6–3, 6–4 to lift the trophy in Stuttgart. That performance caused Sampras to observe, 'Becker is the best indoor player I've ever played.' In December, he notched up one further victory of note, taking the Grand Slam Cup in Munich by defeating Goran Ivanšević 6–3, 6–4, 6–4.

Ironically, one of his best performances of the year and probably of his career left him the loser but in a spectacular contest. In the final of the Year End Championships in Hanover in 1996, Becker saved two match points in the fourth set but was eventually beaten in a humdinger of a scrap, Sampras riding out the winner of their five-set marathon 3–6, 7–6 (7–5), 7–6 (7–4), 6–7 (11–13), 6–4. Becker subsequently said that the encounter 'was amongst the best games I ever played'. In 1997, 1998 and 1999, Becker won no further titles, and he retired from the game, aged thirty-one, in June 1999, having clocked up a career record of 76.91 per cent, 713 wins to 214 loses and earned over $25 million in prize money, putting him seventh in the list of earnings winners.

What should be the overall assessment of Becker? He was unquestionably a great champion, as his six major titles testify. His special place in history is substantially attributable to the fact that he was and remains the youngest man to win the men's singles at Wimbledon, but that point should not be overdone. His distinction is not on that account alone but on two other crucial grounds – the manner of his play and his success, at least for a time, in claiming further big titles. The manner of his play was remarkable and exceptional. The big serve, the effective volleys were impressive, even remarkable. What was exceptional was the sheer combination of power, shot-making and breathtaking athleticism. Diving for volleys as Becker did was itself proof of energy and will. That he frequently did so with magnificent results rendered him exceptional. It also made him an exciting, alluring player to watch and he will be remembered and esteemed as a result long after other champions have been all but forgotten. So, winning early, winning several times and winning in such majestic style in the most important theatres of his sport sufficed to place Becker in the ranks of great champions. He won for himself, he won for his country; he won new followers and practitioners for the sport.

A downside of his career was inconsistency. Having scaled the heights, Becker could not stay there as long as he would have liked or win as frequently as he would have hoped. He was a professional for fifteen years, but five of his six major titles came in a six-year period from the ages of seventeen to twenty-three. It must have been a disappointment to Becker that, for all his talent and early success, he added only one major, the Australian Open of 1996, to his trophy cupboard in the last eight years of his career. True enough, other great players came along, most notably Pete Sampras and Andre Agassi, who took twenty-two Grand Slam titles between them. Yet one cannot resist the conclusion that the unrelenting pressure on Becker brought about by his early success, time spent fulfilling contractual duties of marketing etc., and the body-blow of ongoing personal troubles took their toll on the German. Without them, he could, and probably would, have won even more than he did.

For a time, Becker radiated and felt huge confidence. His self-belief was fundamental to his attacking play and the success it produced. As he put it, 'My strength was that I lost all fear as soon as I stepped onto the court, even though beforehand I'd have been really nervous.' For the most part, concentration and willpower made it possible for him to jump over walls he encountered in the course of a match. Moreover, Becker at his peak was much more than a great shot-maker. In common with all great champions, he understood the importance of tactics and, most importantly, of being able to recognise the key moment when his opponent was beginning to crumble under the pressure and become vulnerable.

Interestingly, John McEnroe, the subject of another chapter in this book, is glowing in his appraisal of Becker. He believes that history will assess him 'as one of the most charismatic players of all time'. He judges 'really impressive' what Becker achieved for the sport and reckons that his movement around the court was 'magical', 'beautiful' and 'breathtaking'. Describing Becker as one of 'the most interesting and impressive men of his generation' and 'a real personality', McEnroe notes that he had to cope with huge pressure and problems, attributing the fact of his survival over the years to 'self-belief'.

Yet, for all his talent and virtues, he did underperform. Ion Ţiriac, his manager, argues that 'he didn't realise his full potential', adding that he 'should have won three times as much as he did; he should have won more than Borg'. In truth, Becker was strong-willed and he often refused to heed advice. He would practise but often for much shorter periods than Ţiriac judged necessary. Perhaps the most glaring hole in his record is the absence not merely of a clay-court major – the French Open, where his best performance was to reach the semi-final three times – but of any clay-court title in fifteen years on the main professional tour. Becker had won a youth tournament on clay but he could not attain success thereafter on the surface. As he acknowledges, his unfailing mission was to attack. On clay, defence is vital and, in his words, 'the aim is to make fewer mistakes than your opponent. Paris is won by those who minimise risks and who hang on in there for four or more hours.' Becker could not do so.

Boris Becker won big prizes. He was a great champion. He left an indelible impression on his sport as one of the bravest, most exciting, most audacious players ever to bestride a tennis court. He could have won more, perhaps a lot more, and didn't. Up against others' records, that is on the debit side of his account. Yet the credit side was mighty impressive and for so long as people talk about great tennis champions, the name of Boris Becker will invariably feature.

Chapter Fifteen

Stefan Edberg

BORN ON 19 January 1966 in Västervik, Sweden, Stefan Edberg was one of the giants of the game from the mid-1980s until the early 1990s. From turning professional in 1983 to his retirement from the professional tour in 1996, Edberg won six Grand Slam singles titles, including two Australian Opens, two Wimbledon crowns, and two US Opens, and he was the runner-up in the 1989 French Open. In addition, he won the ATP Year End Championship final in 1989 and was the runner-up in that event the following year. 1988 saw him as the runner-up in the WCT Year End Championship final. The Swede amassed a total of forty-two singles titles in his career, including the major tournaments already mentioned, as well as four Masters Series titles and four Championship Series titles, and was ranked in the world's top ten for ten successive years, including no fewer than nine years in the top five. In two successive years, he ended the season as world number one and he occupied the top of the perch for a total of seventy-two weeks. Edberg played on four successful Swedish Davis Cup teams, namely in 1984, 1985, 1987 and 1994, and participated in no fewer than seven such finals, a record unmatched by any other Swedish player. A bronze medallist in the 1988 Olympic singles and doubles alike, his career singles record was 806–270 (74.9 per cent) and he won $20,630,941 in prize money.

Perhaps unsurprisingly, Edberg, always the most gracious gentleman on and off the court, won the ATP Sportsmanship

Award five times (1988–90, 1992 and 1995) and, as a result, in 1996, the year in which he retired from the tour, the ATP renamed the award 'The Stefan Edberg Sportsmanship Award'. In 2004, Edberg was inducted into the International Tennis Hall of Fame in Newport, Rhode Island in the United States. Amongst all of his extraordinary decorations and distinctions, Edberg is also said to have been the childhood hero of Roger Federer, to whom a separate chapter is devoted. On a personal note, I simply mention that I had the pleasure of meeting Edberg in June 2011 at the Aegon tournament at the Queen's Club and was struck by the courtesy, understatement and gentle charm of this outstanding competitor.

Six foot two inches tall, Edberg played right-handed with a Wilson racket. After early experimentation with a double-handed backhand, John Barrett tells us that his first coach, Percy Rosberg, persuaded young Stefan to convert to a single-handed stroke. These days the double-hander is the norm and often thought to be an advantage, not least in coping with heavy topspin strokes, jumping up to shoulder height. Yet the proof of the pudding was in the eating and Edberg's one-handed backhand was widely viewed as one of the finest of his, or any other, era. However, he was probably best known and will always be remembered for his supreme prowess as a serve-and-volley player. Many practitioners of that art, from Kramer and Gonzales to Newcombe, Becker and Sampras, to give but a few examples, were renowned for the power of their first serves. Interestingly, Edberg was not. His was no mean delivery, frequently well placed, and he could apply a variety of spins, but it was not a thunderbolt. Indeed, he would typically choose to spin the serve, knowing that the slower delivery would win him valuable time to get to the net, where he backed himself, in terms of athleticism and technical competence, to take control of points through the sheer quality of his volleying.

In common with most, though not all, of his fellow 'greats', Edberg's star shone brightly in the galaxy from his early playing days. Indeed, he was probably the most successful junior player ever, becoming the first to win a calendar year Grand Slam in 1983. In that same year, Edberg turned professional and won his first career doubles titles in Basel. Yet 1984 was the launch pad for his subsequent career. In March 1984, aged only eighteen, Edberg won his first singles tournament on the professional circuit in Milan, overcoming his fellow Swede, Mats Wilander, a man seventeen months his senior and by then already a winner of three Grand Slam titles. Edberg prevailed in straight sets 6–4, 6–2. Later that year, at the Summer Olympics in Los Angeles, when the tennis tournament was a demonstration event rather than the full medal sport it became four years later, Edberg won the event over the Mexican Francisco Maciel 6–1, 7–6 (8–6). These victories spoke of the potential of Edberg for stardom and will have given him a psychological fillip in what can ultimately be the loneliest of sports.

Yet good though the year was, the promise did not deceive for 1985 was to prove markedly better as Edberg won his first major title, took three other tournament trophies and was twice a runner-up. In February, in Memphis, on carpet, Edberg triumphed over the Frenchman Yannick Noah by the devastating margin of 6–1, 6–0, a rare scoreline at the top of the men's game in particular. Ironically, roles were reversed to Edberg's disadvantage in Bastad, Sweden, in July when, in the final on clay, Mats Wilander gained revenge for his Milan defeat, thumping Edberg 6–1, 6–0. In Los Angeles in September, on a hard court, Edberg was narrowly pipped at the post in an incredibly tight final, by the American Paul Annacone 7–6 (7–5), 6–7 (8–10), 7–6 (7–4). In more recent times, Annacone has been known as the successful coach who guided Pete Sampras and later helped Roger Federer to return to Grand Slam success and, for a few more months, to world number one. Yet it should not be forgotten that Annacone was himself an accomplished professional player to whom defeat was a disappointment but no disgrace for Edberg. Only a week later, Edberg was again a finalist, on carpet, this time in San Francisco, where he defeated the South African-born Johan

Kriek 6–4, 6–2 to claim his second title of the year. That victory was followed by another trophy in October when Edberg beat the Frenchman Yannick Noah on a hard court in the Basel final, emerging victorious after a much more taxing encounter than when the pair had squared up in February, Edberg winning 6–7, 6–4, 7–6, 6–1. Yet, good though these results were, better still was soon to come. In December 1985, at the Australian Open in Melbourne, Edberg, still almost six weeks shy of his twentieth birthday, won his first Grand Slam title. The tournament was then played on grass; Edberg thrived on fast courts, where his serve-and-volley game could be too hot to handle, and the Swede defeated his fellow countryman Mats Wilander in straight sets, 6–4, 6–3, 6–3. At Wimbledon, seeded fourteenth, Edberg had only reached the last sixteen before succumbing to Kevin Curren, but this was the most dramatic breakthrough of his career. He had won a major title, done so against an established Slam champion, and beaten a fellow countryman to boot. It augured well for the season to come.

In 1986, Edberg again reached the final in Memphis, where he had triumphed twelve months earlier, but this time he was outdone by the American Brad Gilbert, 7–5, 7–6 (7–3). At Wimbledon, seeded five, Edberg would have expected to improve on his fourth-round appearance in 1985, but it was not to be. In the third round, he was dumped out of the tournament by the Czech Miloslav Mečíř. Bouncing back in Gstaad in July on clay, Edberg took his first title of the year, winning a topsy-turvy five-set battle with the Swiss Roland Stadler, 7–5, 4–6, 6–1, 4–6, 6–2. In August, Edberg was outgunned in the Toronto final on a hard court by Boris Becker, who overcame him 6–4, 3–6, 6–3. Again, Edberg was vanquished not victor in the Los Angeles final in September, also on a hard court, where his conquerer was the multiple Grand Slam title champion and former world number one John McEnroe, who came through convincingly 6–2, 6–3. In October in Basel, once again on a hard court, Edberg enjoyed a confidence-boosting victory over Yannick Noah in a four-set tussle which featured three tight tie-breaks, Edberg prevailing 7–6 (7–5), 6–2, 6–7 (7–9), 7–6 (7–5). The following week in Tokyo, Edberg, now displaying an admirable consistency of top-flight performance, reached the final in the city's indoor event on carpet, only to be worsted again by Boris Becker 7–6 (7–5), 6–1. A fortnight later in Stockholm on a hard court, Edberg trounced his fellow Swede Mats Wilander by the stunning margin of 6–2, 6–1, 6–1. So, in 1986, Edberg reached seven tournament finals, six of them between July and November, winning three and losing four. He had by no means attained dominance but, on a regular basis and a variety of surfaces, Edberg was there or thereabouts.

He did not defend his Australian Open title in 1986 for the simple reason that it was not played in that calendar year. Instead, the event was staged, to general approval, in January 1987 – and has continued to this day to be the first Slam of the year. It fell to Edberg to defend his title, which he duly did. It was no easy task. Having reached the final, Edberg was pitted against the popular Australian Pat Cash, himself a formidable attacking player who was comfortable at the net. For the last time, the tournament was played on grass and the Edberg–Cash match was a humdinger of a contest. Edberg raced to a two-set lead, was pegged back by the gutsy Cash to two sets apiece, but the Swede held on to win in the fifth set, the result 6–3, 6–4, 3–6, 5–7, 6–3. As has so often been observed, including in these pages, if there is one challenge that can be as demanding as winning a first major title, it must be backing it up by winning a second, thereby proving that victory was not a one-off. Edberg faced the test and came through by defending the title which he had previously won, doing so against a home favourite and prevailing after being taken the distance. The icing on the cake was provided by his victory in the doubles title too, partnering Anders Järryd.

Success in Australia was the springboard for a stellar year for Edberg – a year in which the Swede competed in eleven singles finals, winning seven of them. Three weeks after the Australian Open, Edberg consolidated his progress with victory in Memphis.

It was a bittersweet occasion, for the final featured Jimmy Connors, seven times a champion at the event, the holder of eight Grand Slam titles, by then aged thirty-four, but still competing in the most outstanding fashion in main tour events, as he was to do for a few years to come. Sadly, however, Connors sustained a knee injury and was forced to default with Edberg leading 6–3, 2–1. That said, it was Edberg's second title of 1987, his second title in Memphis and the eleventh title of his increasingly illustrious career.

A week later, at Indian Wells, Edberg was again a finalist, only to be thwarted once more by his then nemesis, Boris Becker. This was the third successive final in which the German had got the better of the Swede, this time with Becker prevailing in a best-of-five-sets contest in three straight sets, 6–4, 6–4, 7–5. The following month, in Rotterdam, Edberg made his way to the final, on carpet, and came back from a set down to defeat John McEnroe 3–6, 6–3, 6–1. Success in the Netherlands was followed by success in the Tokyo outdoor event on a hard court a month later, as Edberg fended off the challenge of the American David Pate, 7–6 (7–2), 6–4. In August, in Bastad, on clay, it must have been a blow to Edberg to lose in the final for a second time. Two years earlier, he had been denied by Mats Wilander. This time, another fellow countryman, Joakim Nyström, fought back from a set down to beat him 4–6, 6–0, 6–3.

A fortnight later, in Montreal, on a hard court, Edberg had to play second fiddle to the formidable Czech Ivan Lendl, who won their encounter 6–4, 7–6 (7–2). Thankfully, however, victory was soon at hand – and over the man who had been gaining the upper hand regularly, Boris Becker. Meeting on a hard court in Cincinnati, Edberg won decisively, 6–4, 6–1, picking up his fifth title of 1987 and the fourteenth of his career. In September, he lost in the final in Los Angeles on a hard court to David Pate, the American whom he had beaten five months earlier on a hard court in Tokyo. This time the American prevailed 6–4, 6–4. It was a disappointment, but the season had gone remarkably well, with a clutch of trophies and a semi-final appearance at Wimbledon to add to the CV.

In October, Edberg enjoyed victory over his All England Club conqueror, Ivan Lendl, in the final of the Tokyo Indoor event on carpet. In a hard-fought contest, Edberg recovered from the disappointment of losing the first-set tie-break by seven points to four to claim the next two sets 6–4, 6–4 and rack up his sixth title of the year. Continuing on the tournament treadmill, Edberg tasted further success just two weeks later in Stockholm, winning the title there for the second time by overcoming his fellow Swede Jonas Svensson in four sets, 7–5, 6–2, 4–6, 6–4. By any standard, and certainly by comparison with previous years, 1987 was a superb year for Edberg. He had successfully defended his Australian Open title and reached a further ten finals, winning six of them. True enough, he had yet to capture other majors but, aged twenty-one, he had two Grand Slam titles and a total of sixteen tournament victories to his credit. Contemplating his lot at the end of 1987, Edberg could be pleased, if not yet satisfied with the results of his labours.

In 1988, Edberg could not repeat his earlier successes at the Australian Open but he did lift his first title of the year in February. In Rotterdam, he won the event on carpet, triumphing over Miloslav Mečíř in straight sets 7–6 (7–5), 6–2. His success in the Netherlands was then followed by the relative disappointment of final-round loss in Dallas to Boris Becker, a thumping 6–2, 6–2 loss to John McEnroe in Tokyo and yet another beating by Becker in the Queen's Club final, where the German prevailed in a sharply fluctuating encounter, 6–1, 3–6, 6–3. It had been particularly galling for Edberg to double fault to lose the Queen's Club match and he would have entered Wimbledon with mixed emotions: pleasure in the consistency of his run of final appearances and frustration with the defeats, notably by Becker.

Seeded third at Wimbledon in 1988, Edberg duly reached the semi-finals, where he probably expected to face his fellow Swede Mats Wilander the man who had won the Australian Open and the French Open that year and who in September would go on to take the US Open title. However, it was not to be. Wilander fell at the quarter-final stage to Miloslav Mečíř. As reported in

Bud Collins's *Total Encyclopaedia of Tennis*, Wilander candidly observed, 'My style is not suited to this surface. If we played three of the four majors on clay, maybe I'd have a chance for the Slam.' So Edberg was to face Mečíř instead and it was a titanic struggle. The Czech, doubtless brimming with confidence from his dispatch of Wilander yet still the underdog with nothing to lose, stormed to a two-set lead, 6–4, 6–2. At 3–3 in the third set, Edberg fell behind 0–40 before somehow digging deep to turn the set and the match around, eventually winning 4–6, 2–6, 6–4, 6–3, 6–4. Edberg had experienced a tough passage but he was through to his first final at Wimbledon and what was to prove the first of three consecutive finals that would feature Edberg and Boris Becker. John Barrett has pointed out that this was the first time that two men had contested three successive singles finals since the abolition in 1922 of the challenge round whereby the previous year's winner was automatically placed in the following year's final to take on the new challenger. On paper, although Becker was seeded sixth and Edberg third, the German seemed to enter the match as the favourite. The pair had met in six previous finals and Becker had won five of them, including their only grass-court duel to date, at the Queen's Club three weeks earlier. Moreover, Becker had eliminated the defending champion, Pat Cash, and the great Ivan Lendl en route to the final.

As it turned out, the 1988 final was first delayed by rain and, having been started, was interrupted again, at which point Becker led 5–4 in the first set, play then being suspended until the following day. On the Monday, John Barrett notes that 'the atmosphere was flat' and he suggests that this situation impacted more on Becker than it did on Edberg. Sure enough, Becker won the first set but Edberg attacked unremittingly, serving and volleying with great skill and intelligence to ride out the winner 4–6, 7–6 (7–2), 6–4, 6–2. This was Edberg's third Grand Slam title, and surely the sweetest to that point, and naturally it was the highlight of his season. The remainder of the year was relatively uneventful but the Swede was runner-up to Mats Wilander in Cincinnati, where his fellow countryman shaved their three-set battle 7–6 (7–5) in the final set, and Edberg won the Basel title for the third time in October, beating the Swiss Jakob Hlasek 7–5, 6–3, 3–6, 6–2.

The early months of 1989 were marked by final appearances in Scottsdale, USA and Tokyo. In the first, in March, Edberg was blown away by Ivan Lendl 6–2, 6–3. The second, however, six weeks later in Tokyo, was a different affair. Played on a hard court, like the previous encounter, Edberg outlasted Lendl 6–2, 2–6, 6–4 to claim his first title of 1989 and the twentieth of his career.

Of course, Edberg had by now proved himself both at the Australian Open and at Wimbledon, but he had yet to taste success at the French Open and the US Open. He eagerly sought the prize in Paris. He secured safe passage to the final by beating Becker in the semi-final. His last test was against the seventeen-year-old American Michael Chang. A slight figure of 5ft 8in., weighing an estimated 135lb, Chang, seeded fifteenth, had fought back from two sets down to score a stunning victory over Ivan Lendl, 4–6, 4–6, 6–3, 6–3, 6–3. Edberg, more than six years Chang's senior and appearing in his fourth Slam final compared with the American's debut showing, must have been a hot favourite. Moreover, Edberg led by two sets to one and gained a break of serve to lead 2–0 in the final set, but the irrepressible youngster was not to be denied. Chang came through 6–2 in the fifth set to become, at seventeen years three months, the youngest male winner of a Slam title. As any tennis fan knows, what counts is who wins the big points. Edberg enjoyed twenty-six break points that day but he won just six of them, as Bud Collins faithfully records. Gracious as ever, Edberg paid tribute to Chang for the quality of his play and his magnificent fighting spirit, but it must have been a huge disappointment for the Swede. At Wimbledon, seeded two, Edberg made his way to the final but was, in John Barrett's words, 'rather flat' as Becker, firing on all cylinders, crushed him 6–0, 7–6 (7–1), 6–4.

The blow of his heavy loss at Wimbledon was followed for Edberg by three near-misses. In August, in Cincinnati, for the second successive year, he was beaten in the final by a tight deciding set tie-break, seven points to five, this time by the American Brad Gilbert. Then in October in Basel, another American, Jim Courier, edged him in five sets 7–6 (8–6), 3–6, 2–6, 6–0, 7–5 to take the title and, a month later, in the final of the Paris Indoor, Becker was once again Edberg's nemesis as the German eased to a straight-sets win 6–4, 6–3, 6–3 to clinch the trophy. In December, however, there was more than respite for Edberg as he won the prestigious Grand Prix Masters title in New York on carpet, and he must have derived some satisfaction from beating Becker 4–6, 7–6 (8–6), 6–3, 6–1 to take the prize.

In 1985 Edberg had won the Australian Open and defended it successfully at the first opportunity in 1987. In 1988, he had donned the Wimbledon crown. By comparison, 1989 had been frustrating. Sure enough, he had two titles to his name, in Tokyo and New York – the second being of particular significance – but defeat by Chang must have rankled and Edberg would have been mightily disappointed to lose to Becker at the All England Club.

1990 was an altogether better and more uplifting year for Edberg. For the first time in three years, he reached the final of the Australian Open, this time with a superb performance to overcome Mats Wilander in the semi-final. Sadly, Edberg tore an abdominal muscle in the third set of his contest with Ivan Lendl and was forced to default, the Czech leading 4–6, 7–6 (7–3), 5–2. Lendl had his second Australian Open title in a row and Edberg had to wait and work to recover from his injury.

Just over seven weeks later, Edberg, duly recovered, was in winning form again. He reached the final in Indian Wells, and triumphed in an enthralling four-set battle against the then rising young American Andre Agassi, the margin 6–4, 5–7, 7–6 (7–1), 7–6 (8–6). A fortnight later, roles were reversed in the Key Biscayne final, also on a hard court, where Agassi was the victor 6–1, 6–4, 0–6, 6–2. Thereafter, Edberg notched up a string of successes. Victory over Aaron Krickstein to win the Tokyo Outdoor title was followed by the exhilaration of a return to form at the All England Club. In the third, and last, of Edberg's Wimbledon finals against

Boris Becker, the Swede made it 2–1 in his favour. It was quite some match, characterised by formidable serve-and-volley tennis. Edberg raced through the first two sets 6–2, 6–2. Becker fought back to win the third and fourth sets 6–3, 6–3 but Edberg held his nerve and came back to win 6–4 in the final set. His joy at winning his second Wimbledon title was enhanced when, the following month, he dislodged Ivan Lendl to become world number one.

Buoyed by Wimbledon victory and status as world number one, Edberg had a scintillating spell in August, beating Michael Chang to win the Los Angeles title, thrashing Brad Gilbert 6–1, 6–1 in Cincinnati to avenge the previous year's defeat and to lift the title for the second time, and then beating the Croatian Goran Ivanišević 7–6, 6–3 to win the tournament in Long Island. October saw Edberg twice succumb to Boris Becker, first in the Sydney Indoor final and, three weeks later, in the Stockholm final, but Edberg won the Paris Indoor tournament on carpet in November, albeit tinged with the disappointment that Boris Becker retired injured at three games all in the first set. In the ATP World Tour championships in Frankfurt, Edberg reached the final but was beaten in four sets by Andre Agassi. Looked at as a whole, it had been a fine year for Edberg, with positives greatly outweighing negatives. He had been runner-up in the Australian Open, won Wimbledon again, and contested no fewer than ten further finals, winning six of them. Most satisfyingly of all, Edberg had ended 1990 ranked world number one.

If 1990 had been a fine year for Edberg, so too, albeit in a different setting, was 1991. Just as the previous year Edberg had reached multiple finals, he did so eight times in 1991. Victory in the Stuttgart tournament on carpet against Jonas Svensson was backed up by victory in Tokyo on a hard court over Ivan Lendl and a resounding success over the American David Wheaton to win the grass-court title at the Queen's Club. Edberg was unable to repeat his Wimbledon successes of 1988 and 1990. Seeded number one, he fell in the semi-final to the 22-year-old German Michael Stich, who confirmed his arrival in the highest echelons of the game and stunned the tennis world by proceeding to dispose of Boris Becker in straight sets in that year's final. However, Edberg, after losing the Long Island final to Ivan Lendl in late August, went to New York for the US Open itching to win the other major title besides the French Open which had hitherto eluded him. The tournament was memorable on more than one count. First, Boris Becker was unexpectedly beaten in the third round by a man then ranked only forty-five in the world, Dutchman Paul Haarhuis. Secondly, Jimmy Connors, aged thirty-nine, reached the semi-final but was dispatched by his fellow American Jim Courier 6–3, 6–3, 6–2. Courier was almost eighteen years younger and it showed that day.

Edberg could probably see that the field was opening up nicely for him and he took advantage. He thrust aside Michael Chang and Javier Sánchez and then took care of Ivan Lendl in the semi-finals to square up to Jim Courier, who had slayed the magnificent Jimmy Connors in the final. It was a classic back court against forecourt confrontation, Courier remorseless from the baseline, Edberg probably the finest natural volleyer of his or any generation. In the event, I won't say it was a non-event for that would disrespect the avalanche unleashed by Edberg. He was simply brilliant – his 'finest hour', as John Barrett put it – up against the impressive 21-year-old Floridian. Courier had no answers as Edberg, performing at the peak of his outstanding powers, slaughtered the young American 6–2, 6–4, 6–0. Bud Collins reminds us that Edberg himself described his performance that day as 'the best match I've ever played'.

That victory, and its emphatic character, represented not merely the highlight of the year for Edberg but, alongside his Wimbledon triumphs, the pinnacle of his career. In October Edberg enjoyed back-to-back successes at the Sydney Indoor over the American Brad Gilbert, whom he demolished 6–2, 6–2, 6–2 and then at the Tokyo Indoor on carpet in a three-set tussle with another American, Derrick Rostagno. The latter victory was Edberg's second success at the event, but the first for four years.

In Stockholm a fortnight later, Edberg had to settle for runner-up status as Boris Becker finished strongly to win their five-set battle 3–6, 6–4, 1–6, 6–2, 6–2. Without doubt, however, the year had been a big success for the Swede. He had won six finals of the eight he played, won his first US Open title, put together a 76–17 winning record, garnered a record $2,363,575 in prize money and became, as Bud Collins points out, 'only the fifth player in the era to finish number one for consecutive seasons', Connors, Borg, McEnroe and Lendl being the others then able to boast that feat.

1992 saw Edberg start by reaching his fourth Australian Open final, though this time Courier took his measure in four sets, winning 6–3, 3–6, 6–4, 6–2. A month later, Edberg was runner-up to Goran Ivanišević over four sets in the Stuttgart Indoor event, but in May the Swede won his first title of 1992 and the thirty-fifth of his career by coming from behind to beat Michael Stich 5–7, 6–4, 6–1 in Hamburg. He still had no joy at the French Open and at Wimbledon, seeded to reach the final, he fell to the big-serving Ivanišević in the quarter-final. However, he found form, auspiciously enough, in New Haven, just before the US Open, overcoming the American MaliVai Washington 7–6 (7–4), 6–1 to lift the trophy. Yet easily the biggest cheer from Edberg's support-ers was for his performance at the US Open. Bud Collins points out that Edberg played three successive five-set matches at the event – against Richard Krajicek, Ivan Lendl and Michael Chang – each taking over four hours. Indeed, his victory over Chang 6–7 (3–7), 7–5, 7–6 (7–3), 5–7, 6–4 was the longest match either man played – and exceeded the five hours twelve minutes that Pancho Gonzales had required to beat Charlie Pasarell at Wimbledon twenty-three years earlier. In the final, Edberg had the singular satisfaction of defending his title successfully by beating the 1990 victor, Pete Sampras, 3–6, 6–4, 7–6 (7–5), 6–2. Bud Collins reminds us that to take the title, Edberg was required to play nineteen out of a possible twenty sets in the last four rounds of the event. Apparently the only precedent for this was in 1896, when Bob Wrenn went through a similar experience. Edberg's sixth and final Slam victory, in which it took him just under three hours to beat the man who was soon to dominate the men's game for much of the decade to follow, was very special. Edberg sacrificed the number one slot in the world rankings but it had been a splendid season for the Swede. He reached one further final that year, losing in the Sydney Indoor tournament in October to Goran Ivanišević.

Thereafter, Edberg enjoyed intermittent success, winning the third clay-court title of his career in Madrid in 1993, triumphing in Doha, Stuttgart and Washington in 1994 over Paul Haarhuis, Goran Ivanišević and Jason Stoltenberg respectively. The last tour singles title, the forty-second of his career, came in January 1995 in Doha, where he defeated his fellow Swede Magnus Larsson in straight sets 7–6 (7–4), 6–1. From 1993 to 1996 Edberg featured in eleven singles finals, winning five of them. In 1996 he retired from the professional tour, a tour he had joined thirteen years earlier and in which he had been the most successful Swede since Björn Borg. Mats Wilander had won seven Slams to Edberg's six and been a superb performer. Yet Edberg had won more titles and held the number one slot for a good deal longer. By any yardstick – titles won, performances given, consistency shown – his career was a monumental success.

What made Edberg a great champion and how great a champion was he? In common with countless other players, Edberg was technically sound, very fit and prone to no major weaknesses. In a sense, such a state of affairs is a necessary condition for any player to win a major title. To win six, to reach the final of all four major tournaments, to win forty-two ranking events, to hold the number one slot for seventy-two weeks and even to stay in the top ten for ten years and the top five for nine, required more than simply an impeccable backhand and a capacity to play great serve-and-volley tennis. It required huge mental strength. Edberg was equable of manner but no one should mistake that for being laidback – far from it. He was cool under pressure, steely in his determination, utterly focused on the job to be done and on the need to impose his game on that of his opponent. Ability and self-belief – the capacity to hit great shots and the willingness to back himself instinctively to make the right judgements – were crucial. As with the other great champions in this book, Edberg knew which points mattered most and, far more often than not, he played them well, indeed, often to perfection.

That explains, insofar as it can ever be fully explained, why Edberg was a great champion. As to how great, each will form his or her own view. No player is perfect and there are two weaknesses of Edberg that spring to mind. First, as mentioned at the outset, he did not possess a first serve to compare with those of the very greatest servers, including some other champions in this book such as Tilden, Budge, Kramer, Gonzales or, from his or later eras, Borg, McEnroe, Becker, Sampras or Federer. Of course, the quality of his placement, the variety of spin he deployed, the phenomenal calibre of his volleying and his overall ability to craft winning points were such that he was in no way gravely disadvantaged as a result of that relative weakness. Nevertheless, measured against others and in terms of the pursuit of tour victories, he would have won more cheap points with a first service of the premier rank. Secondly, Edberg thrived on fast courts, notably hard courts, some carpet courts, and grass courts. He was never as comfortable on clay and won only three of his forty-two titles on that surface. Most disappointingly for him, he never managed to win the French Open, playing runner-up to Michael Chang in 1989, representing his best performance at that event. It is the most notable gap in his record and one that he shares with eight other greats described in these pages – namely Tilden, Kramer, Gonzales, Connors, McEnroe, Becker, Sampras and, so far, Djokovic. For all that, Edberg was a remarkable player, a joy to watch, a fabulous competitor, a wonderful sportsman and a lasting credit to the sport which he graced as a professional for thirteen years. In the words of John Barrett, Edberg was 'elegance personified'. In addition, 'he was the quiet achiever and modest to a degree'. That modesty does not detract from but rather serves to underline the greatness of Stefan Edberg.

Chapter Sixteen

Andre Agassi

ANDRE AGASSI WAS a hugely charismatic American tennis player who was amongst the leading competitors in the game from the early 1990s until the mid-2000s. His record undoubtedly puts him in the highest echelon of the sport, one of the all-time greats with outstanding accomplishments on his career score sheet. He won eight Grand Slam singles titles over a period of eleven years, including one Wimbledon, four Australian Opens (a distinction shared in the Open era only with Roger Federer and Novak Djokovic), two US Opens and one French Open. Agassi is one of only four male singles players to achieve the Career Grand Slam (all four Grand Slam tournaments) in the Open era and one of seven in the history of the sport. In modern times, the only other players to have achieved this feat are Rod Laver, Roger Federer and Rafael Nadal. In addition, Agassi is one of only two men to win the Career Golden Slam – all four majors plus the Olympic gold medal in singles – the other being Rafael Nadal. In one respect, however, his record of victories is unmatched. To date he is the only man to win the Career Golden Slam and the ATP World Tour finals, a trophy he won in 1990 before he had landed a Slam title. As well as winning eight Slams, Agassi was the losing finalist on seven occasions and he was also the three times runner-up in the Year-End Championship finals. He won seventeen Masters Series titles and lost in the final six times, and in total he won sixty singles titles on the Grand Prix and ATP tour, amassing over \$31 million in prize money. On top of all of those personal achievements, he was twice part of the winning US Davis Cup team – in 1990 and 1992.

A right-handed player with a two-handed backhand, Agassi was by modern standards not a tall man, 5ft 11in., but he could generate immense power off the ground, at his peak proved to be as fit as any of his contemporaries and, by dint of his appearance – initially, long, flowing hair, later a shaved head and preference for unusual shorts and colourful outfits – came to be one of the most alluring and talked-about players of all time. Repeated injuries, including sciatica, vertebral displacement and a bone spur, ultimately led him to retire from professional tennis in September 2006.

Born 29 April 1970 in Las Vegas, Nevada, Andre Kirk Agassi is the youngest son of Mike and Betty Agassi. His father is a former Olympic boxer for Iran and is of Armenian descent and his mother is a survivor of breast cancer. Agassi has three older siblings, Rita – who was the last and estranged wife of the American tennis legend from the late 1940s to the early 1960s, Pancho Gonzales – Philip and Tami.

From an extremely early age, Mike Agassi had Andre playing tennis and he had resolved that his son would become the best player in the world. In his startling autobiography, Agassi reveals just how utterly focused his dad was on rearing him for supremacy in tennis. In his words: 'My father says that if I hit 2,500 balls each day I'll hit 17,500 each week and at the end of one year I'll have hit nearly one million balls. He believes in math. Numbers, he says, don't lie. A child who hits one million balls each year will be unbeatable.'

The sheer intensity of the practice sessions to which Agassi senior subjected young Andre, quite regardless of whether his son wanted to undertake them, is stupefying, and the picture this childhood induction presents is different from that of any of the other players covered in these pages. Again, Andre Agassi gives us the most explicit account: 'My father stays behind me. I rarely see him, only hear him, day and night, yelling in my ear,' as young

Agassi battles with the ball machine churning out balls at him at a rapid rate. His father's intolerance of error is made plain, but there is one type of error more intolerable, almost damnable, to Agassi senior than any other: 'Nothing sends my father into a rage like hitting a ball into the net. He dislikes when I hit the ball wide, he yells when I hit a ball long, but when I muff a ball into the net, he foams at the mouth.'

Mike Agassi's determination to propel his youngest child on the path to tennis stardom was absolute, to the extent that it motivated his purchase of a family home. He bought the property he did because the backyard was the right size to accommodate the tennis court he resolved to build. His father had Andre aged four hitting with tennis greats who were passing through town, beginning with Jimmy Connors. The latter informed Mike that Andre was sure to become a very good player. So far from graciously accepting the sign of approval and confident prediction of one of the sport's all-time greats, Mike Agassi is alleged by his son to have responded, 'I already know that ... he's going to be number one in the world.' Naturally, when Andre begins to play competitively and win his first seven tournaments in the ten-and-under bracket, he is chuffed and could reasonably have expected some praise or encouragement. Rather, he tells his readers, 'My father has no reaction. I'm simply doing what I'm supposed to do.'

In a disclosure that provoked extensive media coverage when his autobiography *Open* was published in 2009, Agassi repeatedly claimed that he hated tennis from an early age and insisted that it was a recurring theme throughout his career. As a young boy, he says, 'I hate all the junior tournaments, but I hate nationals most of all because the stakes are higher.'

At the age of thirteen, Agassi senior decided that as his son had beaten all local and regional opponents and, as he was convinced that he could not teach his son anything more, he would henceforth go to the Nick Bollettieri tennis academy in Florida to develop his game. Andre did not want to go, indeed wanted very badly not to go, but Agassi senior's mind was made up, and go he did, initially for just three months, as that was all the family could afford. Yet after watching young Andre for thirty minutes, Bollettieri, a hugely experienced coach, told Agassi senior that his son was the most talented junior he had ever seen and would be housed and taught free of charge.

Young Agassi did not like it one bit. 'The constant pressure, the cut-throat competition, the total lack of adult supervision – it slowly turns us into animals.' That said, fearsome regime though it was, Agassi certainly progressed as a player and he turned professional in 1986. At his first US Open he lost to Britain's Jeremy Bates in four sets but, significantly, by the end of 1986, Agassi had risen to number ninety-one in the world and he was still only sixteen. The following year he won his first professional singles title in Ita Parica and he closed the year ranked twenty-fifth in the world. Midway through the year, of course, Agassi went to Wimbledon for the first time and, plainly, in common with Messrs Connors, McEnroe and, several decades earlier, Perry, the experience was not altogether to his taste. To put it bluntly, he found the attitude of the organisers prescriptive, pompous and proprietorial. In his words, 'Wimbledon officials appear to take a haughty, high-handed pleasure in telling players what to do and what not to do. I resent rules, but especially arbitrary rules. Why must I wear white? I don't want to wear white. Why should it matter to these people what I wear?'

It was an uncomfortable beginning to his relationship with the most famous tennis venue of all and Agassi was trounced by Henri Leconte 6–2, 6–1, 6–2 in the first round in 1987.

His success in Brazil later in the year provided a precious fillip to his confidence. That said, the single tournament success of the year certainly did not spawn complacency. Rather, it was accompanied by a hard-headed acknowledgement of weaknesses, not just strengths. Specifically, around this time Agassi noted that he was 'running out of steam' in long matches and, whereas other players may have been able to serve their way to easy points, his 'average' serve rendered this option impossible.

In light of that experience, Agassi worked hard to improve his physical strength, in particular his endurance. That need for work on his physical conditioning had been keenly felt after he suffered defeats in 1988 in the Indian Wells semi-final to Boris Becker, at the French Open in five sets to Mats Wilander and at the US Open where, having beaten Connors in the quarter-final, Agassi lost to Lendl in four sets, saying, 'I'm not able to stay with a man of Lendl's calibre.'

Agassi decided to skip Wimbledon – having already declined to play in the Australian Open at the beginning of the year – as he objected to its traditionalism in general and its insistence on 'predominantly white' clothing in particular. For all that he had a long way to go, Agassi had reached the semi-finals of two majors in 1988 – the French and the US Open – and he had won six tournaments, notably Memphis, the US Men's Clay Court Championships, Forest Hills WCT, Stuttgart Outdoor, the Volvo International and the Livingston Open. Agassi had accumulated $1 million in prize money more quickly than anybody else had done; he was ranked third behind Ivan Lendl at number two and the world number one, Mats Wilander. Both the ATP (i.e. his colleagues) and *Tennis* magazine named Agassi as Most Improved Player of the Year for 1988. Still only nineteen, Agassi beat Connors in the US Open quarter-final in five sets in 1989 – Connors by then was almost thirty-seven – but he could not at this stage progress beyond that point.

Agassi had recently met Gil Reyes, a gym owner in Las Vegas, and the meeting was auspicious. Gil became trainer, confidant, friend and, effectively, father figure to Agassi. It was a very important relationship. Gil devised for Agassi a far superior exercise regime based on 'building the muscles necessary for starting and stopping' of which any tennis player has to do a huge amount as a matter of course. Agassi recalls, 'I work with Gil throughout the fall of 1989. The gains are big, and our bond is strong. Eighteen years older than I, Gil can tell that he's a father figure.' His trainer threw himself into his role, attending to every aspect of his charge's physical well-being and leaving nothing to chance. Agassi was clearly favourably struck by the rigour of his trainer's approach. 'From the start,' Agassi declares, 'Gil keeps a careful record of my workouts. He buys a brown ledger and marks down every rep, every set, every exercise – every day. He records my weight, my diet, my pulse, my travel.'

As Agassi did not play in the Australian Open until midway through his professional career, his first Slam of 1990 was, as usual, the French Open and it was the stage for his first such final. In one sense, it was no surprise that Agassi should perform well on clay. It is a slow surface, serve-and-volley players tend to come to grief on it, and it was potentially fertile ground for a baseline player, which Agassi was par excellence. Before him, Björn Borg and, later on, even more spectacularly, Rafael Nadal had shown just how phenomenally successful a player endowed with supreme groundstrokes and in great physical shape could be. In another sense, however, it was not perhaps a surface quite made for Agassi. In the early part of his career, Agassi was a keen exponent of first strike tennis. He would look to end points quickly, returning serve to enormous effect, setting himself up for a winning shot without delay. He returned serve brilliantly, hit hard and deep, and specialised in piercing double-handed backhands down the line. However, where the ball comes off the court less quickly, it is more difficult to put it away for a winner and, allied to the lack of a point-winning serve, it might explain why Agassi struggled to achieve the breakthrough that he needed at the French Open.

In 1990, he was the favourite to win the final but he was pitched against an experienced and wily clay-court craftsman in Andrés Gómez. Ironically, in the 1990 final, Agassi opted for a gameplan of long rallies, slowing the match down, working to grind out points as he calculated that his older opponent, Gómez, would tire, especially if the match went to a fifth set. It seems that Gómez had also made that calculation and concluded from it that he should adopt a more aggressive approach, speeding the match up, taking risks, trying to finish points without tiring himself unduly. Gómez won the first set quickly and lost the second set quickly. Gómez became stronger and sharper, served better and took the next two sets to win his first and only Grand Slam title.

Once again, Agassi skipped Wimbledon in 1990 – the third successive year he had done so. Nowadays, the top players miss a major title only if they are unfit to play but at that time it was not uncommon for a player to miss a major, albeit that it tended only to be the clay-court specialists such as Eddie Dibbs and Harold Solomon who would give Wimbledon a wide berth.

Agassi rejoined battle at the US Open and overcame Boris Becker, the defending champion, in the semi-finals. In the final, Agassi met Pete Sampras. whom he had beaten comprehensively twelve months previously, persuading himself that Sampras was not destined to succeed at the top level. How wrong could he be? This time, Agassi was completely outplayed, succumbing in straight sets 6–4, 6–3, 6–2. Despite the disappointment of his two Slam defeats, they had been his first major finals, he had won his only Tennis Masters Cup (the precursor to today's Barclay's ATP World Tour finals), defeating the Swede Stefan Edberg in the process, and he had helped the USA to win its first Davis Cup since 1982.

In 1991, Agassi once again reached the final of the French Open and he must have hoped it would be a case of third time lucky. He was the favourite. He had previously beaten his fellow American Jim Courier. He had trained at the Bollettieri academy with Courier and seen himself – almost certainly with justifica-tion – as the better player and hotter prospect. Agassi took the first set 6–3, led 3–1 in the second set with a point for a double break of serve when rain stopped play. Courier returned after the delay and fought back to take the second set, levelling the contest. Agassi won the third set 6–2 but then, shockingly, proceeded to lose twelve of the first thirteen points in the fourth set, sacrific-ing it 6–1. In the fifth set, at four games apiece, Agassi lost his serve, leaving Courier with the chance to serve for the match. At this stage any observer would expect Agassi to make a last-ditch attempt at least to break back, yet his observation in his autobiography is stunning. As he put it, 'Now, all at once, I just want to lose. I can't explain it any other way.'

Even allowing for a degree of literary licence, this is evidence of mental frailty. When the going got tough and when Courier, to whom Agassi felt superior, kept coming back at him, his reaction was proof of his incompleteness as a player in 1991. Instead of engaging 100 per cent, fighting like a tiger and demonstrating the sheer 'never say die, whatever it takes I'll do it, I'm going to win however long this lasts' attitude one associates with so many of the great champions whose ranks Agassi was later to join, he simply checked out. For the second successive year in Roland Garros and for the third time in a Slam singles final, Agassi came off second best.

Having boycotted Wimbledon for three successive years, Agassi chose to play the event in 1991, prompting much speculation about what he would wear. Ultimately, as the All England Club had always insisted, and was still insisting – as it does to this day – on attire being predominantly white, there was little doubt what Agassi would do. He wore white. Having reached the quarter-final, Agassi appeared to be on course for a place in the semi-final as he led David Wheaton two sets to one and two breaks of serve in the fourth set. Just then, he pulled a muscle in his hip and was scarcely mobile as he finished the match, Wheaton walking away with the fourth and fifth sets.

Once again, in 1992, Agassi skipped the Australian Open. In Paris, at the French Open, success eluded him once more as he lost to Courier in the semi-final, though Agassi did notch up a confidence-boosting victory over Sampras. Nevertheless, after six years on the professional tour, Agassi had been three times a finalist, not to mention a string of quarter- and semi-final appearances, but he had yet to win his first Slam.

The breakthrough for Agassi came at Wimbledon, the venue that on first acquaintance he had so heartily disliked that he avoided it for the subsequent three years. In 1991 injury had foiled him, but this time he was fully fit. Yet, following a poor run of form, Agassi had dropped out of the top ten and was seeded only number twelve. As a result, the pressure on him was much reduced from when he had been tipped to win titles, only to fail to meet expectations. In the quarter-finals, Agassi faced his seasoned adversary Boris Becker, who had been a finalist in six of the previous seven Wimbledon singles. It was an almighty five-set contest spread over two days, but Agassi prevailed. In the semi-final Agassi was pitted against the former three-time Wimbledon champion and ex-world number one John McEnroe. Sure enough, McEnroe was one of the all-time greats, but his last triumph at the All England Club had been eight years earlier. He was unseeded, thirty-three years old, and approaching the end of his career. That said, he was all the more popular and Agassi had to mind his business efficiently to come through in three straight sets to reach the final. There he was to face the big-serving Croatian Goran Ivanišević, who had beaten Pete Sampras in the other semi-final.

Agassi was in for a fight and he knew it. He had been worsted by the Croatian in their previous two encounters. Ivanišević took the first set 7–6. Agassi hit back to win the second and third sets 6–4, 6–4. The Croatian then dramatically raised his level and steamrollered through the fourth set 6–1. Agassi survived a break point at 3–3 in the fifth set and in the tenth game of the set he broke the Ivanišević delivery to claim the match and the title. The elation was palpable. Agassi had won his first Grand Slam title in the home of tennis. He discloses in his autobiography that he telephoned his father, who expressed no congratulations but told Andre that he had no business losing the fourth set. Agassi reports that he responded that it was a good thing that he won the fifth, to which there was no spoken response, merely the sound of sniffling. His father was crying. He was proud. He just couldn't say so. Agassi concludes, 'I can't fault the man for not knowing how to say what's in his heart. It's the family curse.'

1993 was a very difficult year for Agassi. Injury-afflicted
for much of the first part of the year, he was back on court at
Wimbledon but succumbed in a five-set duel with Pete Sampras,
who went on to take the title. At the US Open he crashed out
in the first round to Thomas Enquist, and thereafter he needed
surgery on a damaged wrist.

In 1994, Agassi began the season with a new coach, Brad Gilbert,
and a revised approach to match play. Instead of trying to win
points very early, he opted for a more tactical gameplan in which
he would still strive to boss opponents about but would be in less
of a hurry. After all, once he had overcome injuries, his fitness
level matched anyone's and he could afford to wait a tad longer
in rallies for the best opportunity to finish points in his favour. He
did not come good at once, losing early at Roland Garros and the
All England Club. Rather, he seemed to find form in the North
American hard-court season, winning the Canadian Open and
building himself up neatly for an assault on the US Open. To win
would be a tough ask. By then, ranked twentieth and unseeded,
there would be challenging duels though relatively little pressure.
Agassi beat Robert Eriksson, Guy Forget and Wayne Ferreira to
reach the fourth round, where he faced Michael Chang and won
in five sets. His quarter-final victim was Thomas Muster and in
the semi-final he came up against Todd Martin, who had beaten
him at Wimbledon only two months earlier. An accurate server
and strong returner, who exploited a weak delivery to powerful effect, Martin was a tough opponent but Agassi concludes in
his autobiography that there were always factors in his favour.
'Martin is always better on grass than on hard court. This is my
surface. Also, like me, he's an underachiever. He's a fellow slave
to nerves. I understand the man I'm playing, therefore, understand him intimately.' He adds that Martin has a 'tick' whereby
if he glances in a particular direction he will serve there but if he
stares intently that way, he will serve in the opposite direction.
This is an invaluable telegraph to Agassi at key points. Martin, as
it transpired, was nervous and he underperformed so that Agassi

won in four sets. In the final, Agassi conquered the German star
Michael Stich, winning relatively comfortably, 6–1, 7–6, 7–5. It
was a superb end to the season for Agassi, his first Slam victory
for over two years, and achieved from an unseeded position.

Building on the late season momentum from 1994, Agassi
began 1995 resolved to play the Australian Open for the first
time, a decision vindicated then and on three further occasions in
years ahead. Agassi enjoyed the hard courts, welcomed the heat,
liked the people and felt altogether comfortable in Melbourne in
a way he could never match at Roland Garros and Wimbledon.
Playing well, he reached the final without dropping a set. There,
he met Pete Sampras in the second of their five Slam finals and
for the first time since the 1990 US Open. Agassi began poorly,
double faulting to lose the first set 6–4. Thereafter, Agassi noted
a drop in his opponent's level, broke twice to win the second
set 6–1 and saved set points before winning the third-set tie-
break by 8–6. Agassi battened down the hatches in the fourth
set, held serve efficiently, broke Sampras and rode out the winner
6–4. It was his third Slam but, equally importantly, his second
in succession and precious to Agassi as his first major final
triumph over Sampras.

In the aftermath of victory, Agassi, who maintained that he had
not previously been preoccupied with being number one, decided
that he thirsted for the top ranking. He worked exceptionally hard
with Gil on sharpening his conditioning, interspersing bursts of
power and speed with other exercises to tone him for the reality
of match play that required both pace and endurance. At Indian
Wells in 1995, Agassi lost to Sampras in three straight sets but
in the final at Key Biscayne he was the victor over his rival in a
deciding-set tie-breaker, defeating Sampras 3–6, 6–2, 7–6 (7–4).
On the back of that triumph, Agassi attained the world number
one ranking.

Reasonably enough, ambitions evolve. Agassi had wanted to
win Slams and had done so. He had aimed for the top spot and
reached it. Now he had in his sights the target of winning each

of the four Slams. He had won Wimbledon, the US Open and the Australian Open, but the French Open, where he had twice been a finalist in 1990 and 1991, was a prize he eyed ravenously, referring to his ambition to win all four as 'the true Holy Grail'.

Ambition notwithstanding, Agassi was denied again at the French Open in 1995. He began the tournament in great shape, physically and mentally. He cantered through the first four rounds at Roland Garros without dropping a set. In the quarter-final, he was pitched against Yevgeny Kafelnikov. Early on in the first set, reaching for a ball, Agassi revealed later that he felt a snap – his hip flexor – and it produced pain and hobbled his movement. He kept going but, despite leading briefly in the third set, lost in straight sets. At Wimbledon he progressed to the semi-final but lost in four sets to Boris Becker, a defeat he described in his autobiography as 'one of the most devastating of my life'. He swiftly avenged the loss to Becker by beating his German adversary in the semi-final of the US Open but then lost the final to Pete Sampras in four sets. So in 1995 he won one major, was runner-up in another, reached the semi-final of the third, and made the quarter-finals of the fourth. Of the defeats, the most easily explicable was in Paris, where injury hugely hampered his performance against Kafelnikov but, given his focus on attaining the Career Slam, it was a crushing disappointment. That said, the ledger for 1995 was strongly positive. He was ranked number one in the world for the first time in April 1995 and retained that status for thirty weeks. Across the year, he won seventy-three matches and lost only nine. He won three Masters Series titles – Cincinnati, Key Biscayne and the Canadian Open – and seven titles overall. What was more, he was a prominent figure in the US Davis Cup winning team, the third such triumph of his career.

Relatively speaking, 1996 was poor. Agassi was dumped out of the Australian Open in the semi-finals in straight sets, shocking readers years later by the admission in his autobiography that he had tanked because he did not fancy playing Boris Becker, who would have been his final opponent. In Paris, he lost early to Chris Woodruff and at Wimbledon, similarly, he crashed out to Doug Flach. At the US Open, he was again decisively beaten by Michael Chang. He had the consolation of retaining his titles in Cincinnati and Key Biscayne, and the most glorious moment of the year was when he won the Olympic singles gold medal in Atlanta, overcoming Sergi Bruguera of Spain.

If 1996 was disappointing, 1997 was miserable and frustrating alike. Agassi was plagued by a wrist injury, a failed drug test and a marriage to Brooke Shields that was on the rocks. He played just twenty-four matches in the year – eighty or so would be the norm – and failed to win a single serious title. By November he was ranked 141. Success eluded him, his interest had evaporated, his future looked bleak.

At the start of 1998 it was three years since Agassi had won a Slam tournament and he was obliged to play the Challenger Series Circuit – for players whose ranking would not gain them entry to the main tour events – if he was to climb back up the rankings ladder and to take a serious shot at big titles once again. Just as the lean years were evidence of his decline – personal problems, injury, loss of confidence, mental frailty – so the drastic steps he took to fight back were evidence of a strength of character one can but admire.

Working with Gil, Agassi undertook a rigorous training schedule, competed with a new intensity and won five titles in the process, as well as a further five performances as runner-up. He failed to recapture his top form in the majors but his ranking shot up from 110 to six. At last he appeared to be on the way back, and this was confirmed in the most satisfying form and venue imaginable when, in 1999, he recovered from two sets down to win the French Open title over Andrei Medvedev 1–6, 2–6, 6–4, 6–3, 6–4. At that time, Agassi was only the fifth male player to win all four major titles in his career, the others being Rod Laver – who did it twice in the same year – Fred Perry, Don Budge and Roy Emerson. Since then, Roger Federer and Rafael Nadal have performed the same feat.

Importantly, Agassi had won the titles on the three different surfaces of grass, hard courts and clay. Hard courts were his preferred surface, but he had demonstrated his adaptability as other great champions, including Gonzales, Rosewall, Borg, McEnroe and Sampras never managed. Rosewall did win Grand Slams on grass at the US Open and Australia and never had the opportunity to win one on hard, because by the time the US changed surface in 1978 he was forty-four and virtually retired. In the process, Agassi became the first male player to win the Career Golden Slam – the four majors plus Olympic singles gold. His reaction to his French Open triumph? 'I'm sobbing. I'm rubbing my head. I'm terrified by how good this feels. Winning isn't supposed to feel this good. Winning is never supposed to matter this much. But it does, it does, and I can't help it.'

Glory in Paris was followed by a good performance at Wimbledon, where Agassi reached the final only to be comprehensively defeated in straight sets by Pete Sampras. At the US Open, Agassi performed superbly winning the title, and his fifth Slam tournament by beating Todd Martin 6–4, 6–7, 6–7, 6–3, 6–2. Agassi ended the year ranked world number one, breaking the stranglehold Pete Sampras had enjoyed at the end of each year from 1993 to 1998.

2000 began with a second Australian Open title for Agassi as he overcame Pete Sampras in a five-set semi-final – despite being aced by his fellow American thirty-seven times – and then defeated Yevgeny Kafelnikov for the loss of a set in the final. Since Rod Laver in 1969, no male player had reached four consecutive Grand Slam finals. Agassi had now done so. At Wimbledon, Agassi progressed to the semi-finals, where he was outdone in a five-set thriller by Pat Rafter, but at the US Open he crashed out in the second round to Arnaud Clément. Subsequently, he reached the final of the Tennis Masters Cup in Lisbon, losing to Gustavo Kuerten.

Agassi enjoyed an auspicious start to 2001 of which he reveals he had had a premonition. Referring to the Australian Open, he says, 'I feel good when we land. I do love this place. I must have been an Aborigine in another life. I always feel at home here. I always enjoy walking into Rod Laver Arena playing under Laver's name. I bet Brad that I'm going to win the whole thing.'

So it proved.

In the final, he beat his US Open conqueror Arnaud Clément in straight sets. In the previous round he outlasted Pat Rafter in a five-set encounter, though in the Wimbledon semi-final it was Rafter's turn to win a tight contest, prevailing 8–6 in the fifth set. At the US Open, Agassi reached the semi-finals but was outgunned in four eyewateringly tight sets by Pete Sampras, who won 6–7, 7–6, 7–6, 7–6. Ending the year ranked number three in the world, he was the oldest player, aged thirty-one, to do so since Jimmy Connors at thirty-two had ended 1984 as world number two.

In 2002, Agassi won no major title. However, he won Masters Series finals in Miami over Roger Federer and Rome against Tommy Haas as well as Madrid by default. In addition, he won further tournaments in Scottsdale and Los Angeles and, importantly, ended the year ranked world number two.

The following year Agassi again won the Australian Open title – his fourth – to take his tally to eight Grand Slam titles. This remarkable victory made him the oldest player in thirty-one years to win a Grand Slam title and he quickly followed it up with victories in San José, Key Biscayne and Houston. In April 2003, Agassi regained the world number one slot, lost it shortly afterwards and recaptured it briefly in June 2003 until early September. In total he had been world number one for 101 weeks, and, after finishing runner-up to Roger Federer in the Tennis Masters Cup, he ended the year ranked number four in the world, the oldest player to finish the calendar year in the top five since Jimmy Connors, aged thirty-five, had been number four in 1987. It was a remarkable tribute to his talent, competitive instinct, sheer determination and the character needed to fight back from adversity. Agassi had won the last of his Slam titles, though it is to his enduring credit that, aged thirty-five, he reached the US Open final in 2005, where the

then world number one and dominant force in the game Roger
Federer beat him 6–3, 2–6, 7–6, 6–1 to land his second consecu-
tive US Open. It was fifteen years since Agassi had first been a
Slam finalist and thirteen years since he won his first major title.
At thirty-five he had still been able to compete at the highest level
in an intensely physical sport.

How should we assess Agassi? What should be ajudged his
strengths? Can we identify weaknesses?

First, his tally of Grand Slam titles, by no means the only or
even automatically the most important measure of greatness to
be considered, but a significant factor in an objective assessment,
puts Agassi firmly in the top drawer. Federer, Sampras, Nadal,
Laver, Emerson and Borg won more, but eight Slams represent an
immense achievement. That achievement is the more remarkable
for the fact that he won all four major titles, a feat matched in
the Open era only by Laver, Federer and Nadal. Added to that,
winning seventeen Masters Series titles – and bested in that regard
only by Federer and Nadal – as well as taking Olympic gold in
the singles surely makes for a title record that puts him in the
premier league.

Secondly, in terms of exceptional weapons, Agassi had
groundstrokes which equalled or surpassed those of any of his
contemporaries. His two-handed backhand was an exquisite
stroke – powerful, consistent and accurate. Taken on the rise and
struck with purpose and conviction, it inflicted real damage on
opponents, and his forehand was also a formidable shot which
Agassi took early and hit to all parts of the court. That combination of power and control was a staple feature of Agassi's game.
Nowhere was that more amply illustrated than in his return of
serve, which was the best in the game at the time and has probably been rivalled since only by those of Novak Djokovic and
Andy Murray.

Thirdly, it can be said to be a mark of greatness that, following
injury, loss of confidence and disastrous lapses of form, Agassi
clawed his way back from the outer fringes of professional tennis

– playing tournaments without ball boys/girls or audiences – to the pinnacle of the game. To go three and a half years winning no major title, to crash to number 141 in the world then to fight his way back to world number one, taking a further four Grand Slam titles, was outstanding. By definition, his form over those years was not consistent – he missed taking part in major titles altogether and suffered several early losses – but the fact remains that he ended the year in the top ten no fewer than sixteen times and held the number one slot for a total of 101 weeks. That represents a consistency which most players, including champions, would crave.

Fourthly, yes, Agassi had weaknesses. His service, though much better in later years, was never of the highest calibre. He could not win cheap points with it as Sampras did with his delivery and so many of the greats have done. Finally, Agassi did show signs of real mental frailty and self-doubt, not to mention periodic losses of interest. He needed to be in the right frame of mind to perform at his peak. That meant that all had to be well with him in his personal life, including with friends. He could not compartmentalise and simply shut out such issues to focus on the job in hand. He is scarcely alone in that, and it is not proffered as a big criticism but, inevitably, the fact that those issues got to him from time to time did impact upon his record. Nevertheless, his record was superb. He was an exceptional talent, a competitor of real character, and a player who both won all the great prizes and performed in the highest ranks of the game for over fifteen years. Agassi was not good. He was not very good. He was great.

Chapter Seventeen

Pete Sampras

MANY PROPOSITIONS IN tennis, as in life more generally, are arguable. The proposition that Pete Sampras is one of the all-time greats is not one of them. The record of this Greek-American phenomenon speaks for itself. In a foureen-year professional career, from 1988 to 2002, Sampras won fourteen Grand Slam singles titles – a record since surpassed only by Roger Federer – including seven Wimbledon trophies, five US Open triumphs and two Australian Open victories. He won the ATP Year End Championships five times – again, a record exceeded only by Roger Federer's sixth win in the tournament in 2011 – and a further forty-five ATP tournaments, eleven of which were the prestigious ATP Masters 1000 titles. Sampras held the world number one ranking for no fewer than 286 weeks – again, since bettered in 2012 by Roger Federer – and enjoyed that status at the end of the year for six successive years from 1993 to 1998, a feat unmatched by any player in the Open era. In winning his first Grand Slam title, the US Open, in 1990, Sampras was, at nineteen years twenty-eight days, the youngest player to win the title in history. In winning his last Grand Slam event, that same coveted US Open crown, in 2002, he was, at thirty-one, the oldest man to do so in over thirty years. When Pete Sampras retired from professional tennis he had earned $43 million prize money alone and notched up a lifetime winning percentage of 77.44 per cent, scoring 762 victories and suffering 222 defeats. The only omission from an otherwise stunning CV was the absence of a French Open title. Victory at that Slam had always eluded Sampras, who had never progressed beyond the semi-final at Roland Garros. However, the above list of achievements suffices to show why Sampras occupies a proud place in the tennis Hall of Fame.

Born in Potomac, Maryland, on 12 August 1971, Sampras is the third child of Sammy and Georgia Sampras, both of Greek origin. Pete, together with his older brother, Gus, and sister Stella and younger sister, Marion, were regular attendees at services at their local Greek Orthodox church. More significantly, however, Sampras, at the age of three, found a tennis racket in his basement and took to hitting balls against the wall for countless hours. In 1978, Sampras senior sold up and moved the entire family to Palos Verde, California, not least in order that the warmer climate there would enable young Pete to play more tennis. Sampras himself attests that, by the age of eight, he was 'serious about tennis'. As he showed signs of great talent and outstanding athleticism, Sampras senior invested both money and time in the development of his son's game. The family joined the Jack Kramer Club, and Sampras became ever more focused on the sport. Interestingly, unlike many players who are understandably preoccupied with their own performance and that of contemporary champions only, Sampras was fascinated by earlier tennis giants and, though a right-hander himself, he idolised the left-handed legend of the 1960s Rod Laver. In his own words, 'I was deeply impressed by how smoothly Laver played – even on grainy, black-and-white 16 millimetre film.'

Sampras was talent-spotted at the club by paediatrician and tennis enthusiast Peter Fischer, who coached him until 1989. Not content, however, with one coach, Sampras had three men on the job. Fischer worked on developing the Sampras service, Robert Lansdorp was the groundstroke coach, and Del Little was the footwork and balance specialist.

Reared on the Californian courts, Sampras was a tall lad who worked hard both at his tennis technique and at his physical fitness. He quickly established himself as a very capable all-court player who could hit powerfully off both wings, was not afraid to volley and had a competent service. As a young junior, he deployed a double-handed backhand, which was not at all unusual and had been used throughout their illustrious careers by both Jimmy Connors and Björn Borg, amongst other giants of the game.

Yet Fischer, who recognised in Sampras a prodigious talent whom he wanted to see climb to the peak of the game, persuaded him to switch to the one-handed backhand to maximise his eventual chance of winning Wimbledon. The rationale was simple. The grass courts at the All England Club played fast, competitors had less time to hit shots and, Fischer believed, a classic one-handed shot would prove more efficient and effective at the highest level. Whether the reasoning was correct or not we shall never know, because no one can say with certainty how Sampras would have coped at Wimbledon if he had persisted with the two-handed shot. What's more, it really does not matter. What is more important and revealing is that Sampras endured a protracted phase of defeats in junior tournaments as he struggled to master the single-handed back-hand, but he persisted. Tellingly, he later observed that he never 'choked' on court – in other words, he never failed to perform through loss of nerve – because the experience of losing whilst he was adjusting and refining his game taught him not to be afraid to lose.

Sampras is searingly candid on this point in his own autobiog-raphy. On switching to the one-handed backhand, he notes that he 'started losing to all kind of players', including his contempo-rary and subsequent Grand Slam winner Michael Chang, over whom he had previously had an edge but who now started to 'hammer' him. Yet he was determined to master the shot for his own ultimate benefit. Again, following Fischer's insistent advice, Sampras 'played up' beyond his age group. Critics said at the time that Sampras was copping out, ducking the pressure of battling with his contemporaries and taking the easy option of pitting himself against older players, to whom a loss would be natural and require no explanation. Fischer's conviction, however, was that Sampras should not worry at that stage how he fared against his peers but think long-term, striving to play the 'right' way and develop a game that would help him reach – and then remain competitive at – the highest level.

At school, Sampras was known as 'the tennis kid', but he was unconcerned by the tag. As he put it, 'In order to be great at something, it really needs to be the focus of your life.' Sampras maintained that as a teenager his 'toughest challenge was changing my mindset from grinder to attacker'. Solid and consistent ball-striking from the baseline can take a player a long way and in the 1970s, American defensive specialists Eddie Dibbs and Harold Solomon both enjoyed successful careers on the professional circuit. Ultimately, however, neither won big at the very highest level. To win Grand Slams, it is not enough to defend effectively and to force opponents into error. Rather, to be a champion at the highest level, a player must have attacking weapons with which to win points. Sampras was ever mindful to impose his game on others, and worked to build the serve, groundstrokes and net game that would allow him to do so.

Throughout his professional career, Sampras used just one racket type, the Wilson Pro Staff Original, strung with babolat natural gut, but, unlike his racket, his playing style changed and developed over time. He had long had the hallmark of an all-court player, with a forceful serve, strong groundstrokes and the capacity to put opponents in highly defensive positions. Over the years, however, he cultivated the skill of serve-and-volley play and, from the baseline, he would either employ the aggressive chip-and-charge strategy or aim to hit an attacking service return and follow it to the net. Perhaps most strikingly, he enjoyed a remarkable capacity for producing aces and other unreturnable serves on key points, even with his second delivery.

He possessed power, accuracy and terrific disguise, rendering his service one of the best of his own or any era. Serving against him, some players attempted to get the better of him by delivering a high 'kicker' serve out to the Sampras backhand in the hope that it would cause him either to make an error or to offer a short or directionless return.

Turning professional in 1988 at the age of sixteen and, having started the year at world number 893, he finished it ranked number 199. His first professional match was a defeat by Sammy Giammalva Jr at the Ebel US Pro Indoor tournament in Philadelphia. The disappointing start was followed just one week later by Sampras defeating two top-forty players at the Lipton International Players Championships in Miami. His auspicious debut was not matched by another defeat of a top-forty player for almost six months, when Sampras beat world number thirty-nine Michiel Schapers at a tournament in Rye Brook, New York shortly before the US Open. As if to underline his jagged and oscillating trajectory at this point, Sampras lost in five sets in the first round of the US Open to world number sixty-nine Jaime Yzaga of Peru and did not progress beyond the quarter-finals in his next three tournaments. That said, he did savour the consolation of securing wins over world number seventy-nine Jim Courier in their first contest and, more impressively, over world number eight Tim Mayotte.

In 1989, Sampras edged ahead and ended the year ranked eighty-first in the world. He lost in the first round at the Australian Open to Christian Saceanu, made the second round at the French Open only to be trounced by his arch-rival, seventeen-year-old Michael Chang, 6–1, 6–1, 6–1 in their first clash on the pro tour. Wimbledon also saw Sampras dumped out in round one by Todd Woodbridge in four sets but, at the US Open, Sampras claimed the scalp of the defending champion and fifth seed Mats Wilander in five sets, 5–7, 6–3, 1–6, 6–1, 6–4, before succumbing to world number thirteen Jay Berger in the last sixteen. This was the best performance to date by Sampras in a major tournament, though his bolstered spirits will have been dampened somewhat by his subsequent defeat in the first round of four consecutive tournaments to end the year. 1989 was a good, albeit not great, year for the rising star, but champions reach their zenith at different ages and we should remember that Sampras had then completed only two seasons on the ATP tour and was still only eighteen. Recalling that Sampras, under the influence of Fischer, was concerned not only with immediate match statistics but with the ongoing development of his game, we should note his own view that it was in the latter half of 1989 that he made real strides in building the quality of his service which was to prove the most formidable weapon in his match-winning armoury in years to come. In his own words, before that point, 'I got the ball to the right place, with decent power and spin, but the loose, whiplash swing, the explosive snap – these were yet to develop.'

1990 was the year of the quantum leap forward for Sampras. In Sydney, he reached the quarter-finals before falling to Mats Wilander and then, at the Australian Open, he overcame twelfth-ranked Tim Mayotte in the first round in five very tight sets, triumphing 12–10 in the decider, before losing to twelfth-seeded Yannick Noah in the fourth round in four sets. In February, Sampras pocketed his first professional singles title at the Ebel US Pro Indoor in Philadelphia, where he defeated sixth-ranked Andre Agassi, eighth-ranked Mayotte and eighteenth-ranked Andrés Gómez in the final. There was a piquancy about the fact that the home of his professional debut two years earlier, where he had lost at the first hurdle, was the stage for his first tournament triumph. Achieving it entailed beating top-flight competitors and earned Sampras the additional reward of entry into the ranks of the world's top twenty for the first time. Weeks later, he came up against Ivan Lendl in the semi-finals of the indoor tournament in Milan and observed, 'Ivan simply overpowered me.'

Sampras did not contest the French Open and, once again, he lost in the first round at Wimbledon. He then played seven weeks on the spin on North American hard courts. He beat John McEnroe in the last eight of the Canadian Open, then lost to Michael Chang in the last four. He also reached the semi-finals in Los Angeles before falling to world number two Stefan Edberg. In his next three tournaments, Sampras did not progress beyond the quarter-finals.

Then, in September 1990, came the US Open. Sampras had certainly been advancing. He had progressed deeper into tournaments and notched up some big wins over top-quality players, albeit that, in his words, he started his 'quest at Flushing Meadows as a dark horse'. He was, as he put it, on the radar of his rivals, the pundits and knowledgeable fans whilst in no sense being regarded as the favourite in the public mind to win the title. Psychologically, this was a great starting place for Sampras – regarded warily, perhaps even feared, by his rivals but not widely expected to win the title. So, again in the words of Sampras himself, 'there was no pressure'. What fortified and propelled Sampras forward in this testing fortnight was the knowledge that throughout 1990, he had been improving and was continuing to do so. As he said himself, 'I was slowly becoming a better mover and all-round athlete and my serve – already vastly improved – just kept getting better. There was no magic bullet, coaching or technique-wise. Suddenly the big serve was just there and getting bigger as the months passed.'

Sampras came through the early rounds of the tournament strongly, playing well and feeling comfortable. In the fourth round, he defeated Thomas Muster and then faced Ivan Lendl, a multiple Grand Slam winner and his nemesis in Milan, whom he greatly revered. This was one demanding assignment but Sampras was sanguine, reasoning that he had been on the receiving end of Lendl's 'A' game and could not, therefore, be in for a surprise. There was a more fundamental reason for his optimism. Sampras knew that in the six months since he had been blitzed by Lendl in Milan he had become a better player. Sampras knew that he was stronger and sharper, could put Lendl under pressure, and boasted an improved service. On the back of big serving and a supply of forehand winners, Sampras won the first two sets 6–4, 7–6. He admits that he then made the 'classic rookie mistake' of thinking he had the match won, ignoring the fact that he was up against a man with eight Grand Slam titles under his belt and who had been in the US Open final in each of the previous eight years. Lendl stormed back to take the next two sets 6–3, 6–4.

To his enduring credit, Sampras reveals that he felt no panic or fear but stayed calm and focused on effective serving. Delivering multiple aces enabled him to take the game to Lendl and to seek the necessary break of serve. Sampras took the deciding set 6–2. From his defeat of Lendl, Sampras continued to serve formidably, volley well, and return on the backhand side to great effect to sweep aside the then twentieth-ranked John McEnroe in four sets to reach a final with the fourth-ranked Andre Agassi.

Sampras went into the match with Agassi relaxed and confident. Serving hugely, moving Agassi around and hitting groundstrokes off both wings with real force and purpose, Sampras declares that the match, from his vantage point, was played in a fog of inevitability and invincibility. He won his maiden Grand Slam title with a comprehensive, straight-sets dismissal of Agassi for the loss of only nine games 6–4, 6–3, 6–2. Winning the Grand Slam Cup to complete his year, Sampras ended 1990 ranked number five in the world, a stratospheric rise of seventy-six places in just twelve months.

After that cherished victory at Flushing Meadows, Sampras realised that he would now have to cope, for the first time, with pressure. His game was still developing and his return game (especially on fast surfaces) and groundstrokes were causing him occasional difficulty. At the start of 1991, Sampras missed the Australian Open and lost in the finals of the pro indoor tournament in Philadelphia to Lendl. He was defeated in the second round at the Queen's Club tournament in London and then crashed out in the second round at Wimbledon. Even though Sampras served big and could volley well, he was at this stage by no means at his best on grass. Rather, as he observes, the surface 'baffled and frustrated' him, unlike the hard courts, where he was in his element.

Returning to the US Open as the defending champion, Sampras suffered a crushing quarter-final defeat by Jim Courier, succumbing with little resistance, 6–2, 7–6, 7–6. At the press conference afterwards, Sampras provoked controversy with his reaction to the loss by almost seeming to welcome it – even claiming that it felt like a 'tonne of bricks' had been lifted from his shoulders.

Told of this reaction, Courier caustically observed, 'There are a lot of guys out there wishing they had that load of bricks on their shoulders.' Jimmy Connors was still more disparaging: 'Here I am almost forty years old and busting my hump and these young guys are happy to be losing. I don't know about these kids anymore.' In retrospect, Sampras admitted that his character had 'become an issue'.

Two months after his eclipse by Courier in the US Open, Sampras bounced back to seize the first of his five titles at the ATP World Championship final, slaying Courier in four sets, 3–6, 7–6, 6–3, 6–4. His euphoria – or plain relief – was short-lived, however, as he was squarely beaten in the Davis Cup final in Lyon against France by Henri Leconte 6–4, 7–5, 6–4 and then, in four sets, by Guy Forget. At the end of the year, Sampras had slipped to number six in the world.

In 1992, having dismissed his coach, Joe Brandi, the previous year, Sampras hired former professional player Tim Gullikson, to guide him. Gullikson made a few technical adjustments to his game. He reckoned Sampras stood too far to his right when receiving serve, exposing too much of his backhand. He advised him to stand further to the left to send the signal that he was looking to hit a big forehand return. The advice appears to have been sound, as Sampras won his next thirty-two matches against left-handers who were especially inclined to serve out wide to the backhand side in the advantage court. Other refinements made at the urging of Gullikson included firming up his backhand volley and shortening his backhand slice motion in order to get more weight behind the shot.

Sampras accurately describes his results in the first half of 1992 as 'so-so'. He performed better on clay, reaching the semi-finals in Nice and the last eight at the Italian and French Opens. He fell to Brad Gilbert at the Queen's Club tournament, by then a well-established warm-up event for Wimbledon. At Wimbledon itself, Sampras reached the semi-finals and then lost in four sets to Goran Ivanišević, declaring that he was 'still hating the grass all the way'. He recalled that 'the tennis was lightning-fast; the balls were hard and they flew like bullets. Goran served me off the court, but that wasn't just because of his superior fire power – it was partly because I was a flawed competitor.'

In the run-up to the US Open, working with his new coach, Tim Gullikson, Sampras moved up a gear on his preferred American hard courts, winning in Cincinnati and Indianapolis, overcoming Edberg, Lendl, Becker and Courier in the process. Understandably, he arrived in New York brimming with confidence. Sampras progressed to the final to confront Stefan Edberg, the defending US Open champion. Sampras won the first set but concedes that from thereon it was 'a terrible struggle'. Edberg took the next three sets 6–4, 7–6, 6–2. Once again, it was the manner of his defeat and explanation of it that raised real questions. He told the press, 'As the match wore on, I was running out of gas. I was very, very tired, maybe more mentally than physically. Mentally I was telling myself that my body just couldn't do it and, as a result, it didn't.' Later, he said that the truth had been that he was unable or unwilling to 'dig deep'. He had played without heart. He packed it in. This led to months of soul-searching before he resolved that he had to be mentally tougher if he was to reach the top. He ended 1992 ranked number three. He wanted to become and remain number one. So the Edberg match was his Rubicon, the event that caused him to reappraise his attitude and work for 'a huge 1993'.

In January 1993, Sampras reached the semi-finals of the Australian Open, losing again to Stefan Edberg. In Paris, once again, he reached the quarter-final of the French Open. In April, Sampras was ranked number one in the world for the first time because, even though he had not won a Slam for two and a half years, he had racked up more ATP points than anyone else. He was vindicated and critics were silenced when he won his first Wimbledon title in July, overcoming Jim Courier 7–6, 7–6, 3–6, 6–3. Victory was achieved by persistent, precision serve-and-volley tennis and by what Sampras himself described as a 'newfound determination to close out the match'. A trademark running forehand pass enabled him to break Courier's serve in the sixth game of the fourth set and Sampras did not look back. He felt in retrospect that this match was 'not merely about playing well'. It was about 'legitimising' his character as a champion.

Buoyed by triumph and a sense of liberation – liberation from his previous status as a one-Slam man – Sampras went on to claim the US Open title in September, crushing Frenchman Cedric Pioline 6–4, 6–4, 6–3. He ended 1993 as world number one and became the first player since the advent of the ATP to serve more than 1,000 aces in a season. From there, he went on to lift the trophy at the Australian Open, defeating Todd Martin in straight sets and then, back at Wimbledon in July 1994, he saw off Goran Ivanišević 7–6, 7–6, 6–0. After almost three years without a Grand Slam under his belt, a fortified, mature and mentally tough Sampras had picked up four such titles in twelve months. Despite the temporary setback of defeat in the last sixteen of the US Open, Sampras ended 1994 as world number one.

At the 1995 Australian Open, coach Tim Gullikson was rushed to hospital with what would prove to be the symptoms of an ultimately fatal brain tumour. Rocked by this shattering news,

Sampras battled his way to the final where he lost to Agassi. Paul Annacone subsequently took over as Sampras's full-time coach. By now, fast-playing grass courts were his best surface. The combination of awesome serve-and-volley execution, a versatile all-round game, and ferocious competitive instinct, including utter self-belief, led to Slam victories at Wimbledon in four sets over Boris Becker and at the US Open in four sets over Agassi. Victory for Sampras in all three of his matches and success for his country in the Davis Cup final over Russia in Moscow rounded off another superb year. Now with seven Grand Slams to his name, Sampras ended the year as world number one for the third year in a row.

1996 began with disappointment in the form of defeat by Mark Philippoussis in the third round of the Australian Open. At Roland Garros, Sampras reached the semi-finals, his best performance at his least favoured Slam, the French Open. More significantly, after three successive triumphs at Wimbledon, Sampras bowed out in straight sets to the tall, big-serving Dutchmen, Richard Krajcek 7–5, 7–6, 6–4. Yet Sampras by now had the game and the belief to recover from adversity much more readily than four or five years earlier. He came from two sets to one down to defeat Àlex Corretja in a fifth-set tie-break and went on to lift the US Open crown with a straight sets victory over Michael Chang in the final. Success at Flushing Meadows was followed up when Sampras prevailed in a Herculean five set battle with Boris Becker, winning 3–6, 7–6, 7–6, 6–7, 6–4 to claim the ATP World Tour championships, and end the year for the fourth successive year as world number one.

In January 1997, Sampras won his second Australian Open title, and in July he secured his fourth Wimbledon crown. That year, Sampras won singles titles in San Jose, Philadelphia, Cincinnati, Munich and Paris, and the ATP World Tour finals in Germany. In the process, he became the only player to win both the Grand Slam Cup and the ATP World Tour championships in the same year. Once again, he ended the year as world number one.

In 1998, Sampras lost his Australian Open title, and made no headway at the French Open, but he retained his Wimbledon title (the fifth of them), outlasting Goran Ivanišević over five sets and reached the semi-finals of the US Open before losing in five sets to Pat Rafter, who went on to win the title. Despite being chased for the number one spot by Chilean Marcelo Ríos, Sampras ended 1998 as world number one for the sixth successive year. Without a shadow of a doubt, Sampras was the dominant figure in the men's game, with eleven Grand Slam titles to his name.

1999 got off to a poor start as Sampras withdrew from the Australian Open and did not win a title in the opening months of the year. However, he won the Stella Artois championships at the Queen's Club and his sixth Wimbledon crown with a virtuoso demolition of Agassi, 6–3, 6–4, 7–5. This brought Sampras his twelfth Grand Slam title, matching the record set in the 1960s by Australian supremo Roy Emerson. Ironically, given that he had thwarted Agassi on the All England Club turf, he lost his number-one perch to Agassi the next day when ATP tour rankings were updated.

His ranking was harmed by withdrawal from the Australian and US Opens, where he had performed strongly the previous years and by the resurgence of Agassi. That said, Sampras defeated Agassi to win the season-ending championships for the fifth and final time, ending the year as world number three.

In 2000, Sampras lost in the Australian Open semi-final to Agassi, but claimed his seventh Wimbledon title and thirteenth Grand Slam trophy with a four-set win over Pat Rafter. This was the eighth consecutive win for Sampras in a Grand Slam final. Thereafter, he had a fallow period of over two years without another title. He was worsted in the US Open finals in 2000 and 2001 by Marat Safin and Lleyton Hewitt respectively, just as Roger Federer, a decade later, was to go from January 2010 to July 2012 without claiming a Grand Slam title. Indeed, it was to the nineteen-year-old Federer, when seeking an eighth Wimbledon crown in 2001, that Sampras succumbed in an epic five-set encounter, 6–7, 7–5, 4–6, 7–6, 5–7. Even though he did not enjoy quite the same staggering success on court, he married American actress Bridgette Wilson on 30 September 2000 and was as contented as at any other time.

In 2002, Sampras crashed out in the second round at Wimbledon to George Bastl of Switzerland and endured indifferent form in the lead-up to the US Open. There, Sampras was utterly focused, determined to claim one more big prize. Reaching his third successive US Open final, and his eighth overall, it was fitting that he faced the greatest rival of his career, Andre Agassi. Sampras, at thirty-one, faced Agassi, thirty-two, and Sampras it was who emerged victorious in four sets, 6–3, 6–4, 5–7, 6–4. This turned out to be the last tour match of Sampras's illustrious career and it earned him a record fourteenth Grand Slam title.

By any yardstick, Sampras enjoyed a quite exceptional career. Sure, he suffered adversity and never managed to win the French Open. That said, his record in the Slams was unsurpassed at the time and he had a winning record over the vast majority of his contemporaries. He prevailed over Boris Becker, Michael Chang, Stefan Edberg, Todd Martin, Thomas Muster, Mark Philippoussis, Pat Rafter and Andre Agassi more often than they defeated him. He also enjoyed a winning record over Ivan Lendl and John McEnroe, though it is only fair to point out that they were more than a decade older and not, therefore, his direct contemporaries.

His fellow competitors have showered him with tributes. It is appropriate to conclude this chapter with just a selection. Tony Roche, when Sampras surpassed Emerson's Grand Slam record said, 'It's an unbelievable achievement to break Roy Emerson's record. Sampras will go down as the greatest player of all time.' Boris Becker, himself winner of six Grand Slam titles, concluded in 1997, 'For me, he was always the most complete player. He has the power, he has the speed, he has the touch. He is the best player ever.' John McEnroe, seven times Grand Slam winner and former world number one, declared: 'I put him in the godlike stratosphere with Laver and Borg.'

Chapter Eighteen

Roger Federer

FACTS DON'T LIE – Roger Federer is unarguably amongst the greatest of the great. On any reckoning, he has a staggering track record. He has won a record seventeen Grand Slam titles, breaking the previous all-time male record of fourteen by Pete Sampras. Those seventeen victories were notched up over a span of thirty-seven majors from Wimbledon in 2003 to Wimbledon in 2012. He has won seven Wimbledon titles (five in succession from 2003 to 2007 and again in 2009 and 2012), five US Opens (consecutively from 2004 to 2008), four Australian Opens (2004, 2006, 2007 and 2010) and one French Open in 2009. Federer is the sixth of seven men to win all four Grand Slam titles during his career, with Fred Perry, Don Budge, Rod Laver, Roy Emerson, Andre Agasssi and Rafael Nadal being the others. He is only the fourth man in the Open era to do so, also equalling Andre Agassi's feat of triumphing in all those Slams on three different surfaces of hard courts, clay and grass. He has appeared in an all-time male record of twenty-four Grand Slam finals, beating the previous record of nineteen by Ivan Lendl. Federer has won the ATP World Tour finals six times (2003, 2004, 2006, 2007, 2010 and 2011) and is the only player to have won the finals undefeated more than once, astonishingly doing so no fewer than five times. In addition, Federer has won twenty Masters Series titles. Until he lost the world number one ranking to Rafael Nadal on 18 August 2008, Federer was the top-ranked player for a record 237 weeks, and in total he has held that ranking for 302 weeks. Since turning professional in 1998, Federer has pocketed over \$80 million in prize money.

To someone who has never seen Roger Federer play tennis, but who understands just the basics of the game, it is as well to encapsulate his distinction. He has one of the finest services in the game – not the fastest – in that he can hit it superbly straight up the 'T' or angled to the side of the service box. He can hit it hard and flat or deliver it with slice, topspin or kick, variously career- ing away from his opponent or racing furiously into his body. In common with most great exponents of the service, Federer excels by a virtuous mix of consistency and variety. That consistency and variety are the result of a first-class technique in the form of a superb service action – including weight transfer – which maximises power, direction and control and the imagination and intelligence to mix it up and thereby keep opponents guessing.

A vital part of a player's armoury is the second service – hence the old tennis adage 'You're only as good as your second serve' – and Federer's is probably as strong and dependable as any in the game today. Here he relies upon spin, placement, length and consistency. Such a high-quality second delivery is both invaluable in itself and liberating for Federer, who knows that he can afford to go for the extra pace with the first ball, safe in the knowledge that he has an excellent back-up if the first delivery fails.

A strong service is necessary but not sufficient. It has to be buttressed by real prowess in several other aspects of the game, including shot-making, defensive skill and sheer athleticism.

Federer's signature shot is a devastating forehand. Described by the late American writer David Foster Wallace as a 'liquid whip', Federer deploys the stroke to crushing effect, spraying his opponents around the court with a comparatively flat drive, hit hard and placed to all parts of the court with a remarkable length, precision and accuracy. His cross-court forehand is formi- dable, but Federer can equally hit piercingly down the line and he is at ease both with the conventional drive and with the so-called inside-out shot. The stock in trade of a top player is the ability to hit groundstrokes deep into the opponent's court, forcing him onto the defensive and making it difficult to counter-punch. Yet variety is of the essence and, alongside the standard fare of hitting deep, Federer has mastered the art of using all the angles of the court either to hit outright winners or to force his opponent out of position and thereby pave the way for the killer blow. Federer does this beautifully with the forehand, hitting the ball usually with some controlling topspin, wide to the right-hander's forehand but often pitched only a few feet beyond the service line. An opponent who is positioned either at the baseline or behind it has to scamper to reach it, either failing to return or doing so but leaving a simple shot for Federer to drive a winner to a wide-open court. Sometimes this tactic is deployed to the right-hander's backhand side and will similarly pose terrible problems for all but the most agile and dextrous of foes.

The backhand is undoubtedly the weaker wing yet it is still a top-quality shot. Federer can drive the backhand hard and flat, and when he steps in to take the ball on the rise and attack it he can achieve superb results. More commonly, he will wait slightly longer and hit the backhand from waist height, imparting a topspin that both gives some control and presents a challenge to an opponent, especially when Federer keeps driving to a good length. Yet the flat and topspin drives, though useful, especially when attempting passing shots against an opponent coming to, or camping on, the net, are only part of his armoury. He also boasts a vicious sliced backhand and, now and again, he applies side-spin, helping to keep the ball low and rendering it very difficult for an opponent to return the ball with any interest. As with the forehand, the staple diet is to hit deep, but with both topspin and slice, Federer will often use the short angles of the court, creating room for what can be a decisive winner with his next shot.

In receiving service, Federer is as able as anyone in the game at anticipating, reaching and returning most of his opponents' deliveries, and with the backhand he frequently does so with a chipped shot which lands fairly short. This can be deceptive to the viewer, looking like easy meat for an opponent, when in fact the ball has spin on it and sits low, making it tough for a player to dig it out and generate either a winning drive or an effective net approach shot. Yet, in tennis, as in every sport, competitors work to famil-iarise themselves with each other's game and to develop answers to problems posed. In 2008, 2009 and 2010, some opponents, notably Nadal, Robin Söderling, Novak Djokovic and Tomáš Berdych, became accustomed to the chipped backhand and were not fazed by it but hit back with real power and effectiveness, especially on the forehand side. It was noteworthy that in the final match of the 2010 World Tour finals against Nadal, Federer wisely strove to depend less on the chipped return, mixing up his play with more backhand service returns taken early and directed either down the line to the Nadal backhand or cross-court, using a short angle, to the forehand. This was visibly more effective.

Critics will argue that the Federer backhand is more prone to break down under extreme pressure. This is true but only the best players can place Federer under such pressure with any frequency. The opponent over the years who has posed the biggest problem for Federer by hitting topspin drives repeatedly to his backhand is Nadal. Part of the Federer greatness, true of other players, is his ability and determination to impose himself on an opponent and to conduct the business of the match on his own terms. He has found it much harder to do that to Nadal, especially on slower surfaces, as the Spaniard has directed heavy fire to the Federer backhand, often thereby taking control of points.

Federer's prowess at the net is immense. The ever greater abil-ity of players to return serve with force and effectiveness has meant that Federer, in common with his rivals, does not serve and volley with any frequency. He judges that the risk of being passed is too great, although occasionally he will deploy the tactic to take the opponent by surprise, perhaps sacrificing some pace on the service for the accuracy of his placement and setting himself up for a straightforward volley. Far more often, however, Federer plays the volley when he has manufactured a favourable

situation within the rally and plays a net approach shot which
should enable him to finish off the point with a powerful volley
with either the forehand or backhand side. He is very solid from
either wing, can hit deep or short and can deploy angle as effectively as any competitor.

One of the characteristics of great players which the ordinary
club player most admires is the way in which they apparently do
the most difficult things with consummate ease. A good example
is the high backhand volley or backhand smash. It is probably
the hardest shot in the game, requiring a judicious combination
of reach, balance, a strong wrist, effective weight transfer and the
intuitive sense of where to direct the ball. The Federer backhand
smash is a textbook example of the genre and the fact that he
executes it, as with every shot he plays, so apparently effortlessly
is a delight to his fans.

In addition, at the net, Federer excels at the conventional forehand smash or, as it is sometimes called, the overhead. Ideally,
the shot is very simply put away after a strong previous shot
has forced an opponent to throw up a last-ditch defensive lob.
However, that is by no means always the case. Sometimes an
opponent will manage a much higher or deeper lob and it is a
real challenge to put the ball away cleanly for a winner. Federer
will rarely allow the ball to bounce – if he is up against a sting-
ing topspin lob, letting it bounce is simply not an option – and
is remarkably fleet of foot to position himself and adept in his
timing to dispatch the ball successfully.

In service, forehad, backhand, volleys and overhead, Federer
is a brilliant practitioner of his art. Yet, keenly conscious that it
is always possible to learn more, and invariably necessary to get
better because opponents will, Federer has added to his arsenal in
recent years. The dropshot has become a weapon, opening up a
rich seam of points to be won. It appears that Federer has applied
himself to the task of fashioning a well-disguised dropshot, which
he can hit from his forehand or backhand wing with a dose of
underspin so that it plops over the net and promptly dies whilst

an opponent struggles mightily even to reach it, let alone make anything by way of an effective return. Naturally, the effectiveness of a shot lies in its execution and, perhaps more so than with any other shot in tennis, crucial to that effective execution is disguise. That disguise is achieved by taking the racket back as for a normal drive and adjusting the racket face and action only at the last moment. Success also depends upon surprise, i.e. using the shot sparingly as an occasional example of haute cuisine on the tennis court, rather than the regular meat and two veg which are the norm. A player who emails his intention to use the dropshot will find that it is reached and slammed home by his opponent. Similarly, a player who overuses the dropshot, notably in a low-percentage situation from the back of the court, is signalling inadvertently that he is losing patience or nerve, has no real sense of how otherwise to conduct the rally and is clutching at straws. On off days, Federer has failed with the dropshot, usually by under- or overhitting it. More often, however, he uses the weapon intelligently and to supreme effect.

Another shot that Federer plays with great skill is the lob. It is an essential part of the equipment of any serious player. Forced into a corner or otherwise out of position, a player will throw up a lob. This is done with a number of possibilities in mind. Federer can execute that defensive shot with great skill but he can also deploy the shot with topspin as an attacking stroke with which to win points.

Good, even exceptional footwork and wider physical fitness are vital to a professional player's chances of getting to and staying at the top. A player has to be constantly on the move, contriving to be in a position to play the shot of his choice, to run down an awkwardly placed shot from an opponent, to proceed with balance maintained to the net, periodically to retreat from the net with the agility and positioning required to play another shot or, at the most basic level, to be able to run – and run, and run – across and around the court in rallies of fifteen or twenty shots or more.

Many commentators have noted admiringly the superb footwork of Federer. Of course, that footwork benefits from his ability to anticipate his opponent's next move, which is in part a matter of instinct and talent, in part a matter of having studied opponents' patterns of play and in part a matter of eyeing an opponent like a hawk to gain a split-second's notice of what shot he will play next and where it will be directed.

Anticipation is vital but, on its own, not enough. Speed and stamina are crucial. Federer has cultivated both. That application, together with the sheer grace, finesse and economy with which Federer plays tennis, has certainly helped him to scale the heights in his career. Yet they also explain his quite remarkable consistency and relative freedom from injury since he turned professional more than fifteen years ago.

Described above are the attributes of Federer, the great champion. But where did he begin? What are the landmarks? How has he established his supremacy and ensured pride of place in the history books of tennis?

By modern standards, he took up the sport relatively late, first playing at the age of eight. He is said to have shown early promise, winning two national under-twelve titles in 1993. Two years later, Federer joined the Swiss Tennis national development programme and in 1995 he moved to his host family, Christinets, in Ecublens, on Lake Geneva. Interestingly, Roger Federer's website states that he initially struggled and was 'the youngest and weakest player in the training centre'. However, he worked hard and in 1998 he won the Wimbledon's boys' singles and he reached the final of the US Open junior tournament, where he lost in straight sets to David Nalbandian, one of his main rivals in those early years. Federer won four other ITF junior tournaments including the prized Orange Bowl and, on the back of that victory, he ended 1998 aged seventeen as the junior world number one. From those auspicious beginnings it was natural for Federer, the rising teenager who wanted to get to the top, to turn professional and he did so in 1998. Over the next four years, he made steady if not spectacular advances. He reached his first professional tour final at the Marseille Open in 2000. He won the Milan indoor tournament in 2001, his first title victory on the professional tour. In the same year, he reached the quarter-final of the French Open and the quarter-final of Wimbledon. The following year Federer reached the final of the Miami Masters, losing in four sets to Andre Agassi, and he notched up his first Masters Series event victory in Hamburg, defeating Marat Safin in straight sets. This was not merely a tonic but a milestone on his path to pre-eminence, because it made Federer a top-ten player for the first time. Between 1998 and 2002, Federer reached ten singles finals, winning four and losing six.

Those results were important stage posts but perhaps the most seminal moment in that period, and certainly that which thrust him into the consciousness of British tennis fans, was that Wimbledon quarter-final against Pete Sampras. The significance of the achieve-ment can scarcely be overstated. The then 29-year-old Sampras was the seven times Wimbledon champion, the defending champion, the number one seed and world number one, and the man widely regarded as one of the greatest players, even perhaps the greatest player, ever to set foot on a tennis court. Sampras was the legend that Federer later became. Few could have anticipated that Federer, talented and impressive performer as he was proving, would slay the supreme Sampras, even though Sampras had struggled in his second-round match, defeating the British player Barry Cowan only in five sets. The fifteenth-seeded Federer had also survived a five-set ordeal in the second round, prevailing over the Belgian Xavier Malisse. Federer and Sampras slugged it out over five hard-fought sets, the match advantage swaying back and forth, but Federer even-tually triumphed, 7–6, 5–7, 6–4, 6–7, 7–5, vanquishing a champion whom he had long admired and booking his place in the quarter-finals. There, Federer was promptly halted in his tracks, defeated by the sixth seed and British number one Tim Henman in four sets. Nevertheless, Federer had taken a huge scalp in Sampras and he started to be talked about as a future champion.

Disappointingly for the nineteen-year-old Federer, he was unable quickly to build on his success against Sampras by securing advances in the subsequent Grand Slam titles in 2001 or 2002. In the US Open in Flushing Meadows, Federer, seeded thirteenth, duly reached his expected place in the fourth round only to be thrashed by Andre Agassi 6–1, 6–2, 6–4. In the 2002 Australian Open, he fell to Tommy Haas.

Later that year, Federer, now seeded eighth, was unexpectedly knocked out in the first round of the French Open. At Wimbledon, seeded seventh and therefore expected to progress to the quarter-finals, Federer was dumped out of the championship in the first round by Mario Ančić.

At the 2002 US Open, Federer lost in the last sixteen, and in the 2003 Australian Open he fell at the same stage to David Nalbandian. At the French Open, he lost in the fourth round.

Nearly two years after Federer had reached the quarter-final at Wimbledon with that audacious and scintillating victory over the legendary Pete Sampras, Federer had failed to gain forward momentum in a major tournament and, worse, had under-performed, as measured by his seeding in four of the seven Grand Slam tournaments since his dispatch of Sampras.

The seven Grand Slams from Wimbledon 2001 to the French Open in 2003 had been won by Goran Ivanišević, Lleyton Hewitt, Thomas Johanssen, Albert Costa, Pete Sampras, Andre Agassi and Juan Carlos Ferrero. By the time of Wimbledon 2003, Ivanišević and Sampras had effectively left the field, Costa was viewed as a clay-court specialist, and only Lleyton Hewitt, Andre Agassi and Juan Carlos Ferrero were seeded above the fourth-ranked Federer. Hewitt was catapulted out of the tournament in the first round, Agassi and Ferrero in the fourth. A revitalised, stronger and more formidable Roger Federer made his move. Dropping only one set throughout the fortnight, namely in the third round to the 21-year-old American Mardy Fish, Federer beat the big-serving American Andy Roddick in straight sets in the semi-final, 7–6, 6–3, 6–3, and overcame the unseeded Australian Mark Philippoussis 7–6, 6–2, 7–6 in the final to win his first Wimbledon title and indeed his first Grand Slam event. Though he could not back up his Slam success at the US Open, he did win his first ATP World Tour final.

Federer entered 2004 brimming with confidence and a deep-rooted conviction that there were many more titles for the taking. Seeded two at the Australian Open, the number one seed being the defending champion Andy Roddick, Federer breezed through his first three opponents without dropping a set, before meeting the former Wimbledon champion Lleyton Hewitt, to be treated lightly at anyone's peril and without question one of the most tenacious fighters on the court in this or any generation. Losing the first set 6–4, Federer then turned up the heat and took the next three sets for the sacrifice of only seven games. In the quarter-finals, Federer conquered his long-time rival David Nalbandian, dismissing the Argentinian in four sets, 7–5, 6–4, 5–7, 6–3. Thereafter, Federer's passage to his second Grand Slam title was as smooth as he could possibly have wished. He beat Juan Carlos Ferrero in straight sets in the semi-final and Marat Safin 7–6, 6–4, 6–2 in the final.

Success in Melbourne was followed by a blip in the French Open, where Federer submitted to Gustavo Kuerten in the third round, the last time for more than nine years he was defeated so early in a major tournament.

At Wimbledon, Federer, now the world number one, played with an assurance that was fast becoming awesome. He cruised through the first four rounds in straight sets, and dropped only one set to Lleyton Hewitt en route to the final. Federer was then pitted against Andy Roddick. and he lost the first set before taking the next three to garner his second successive Wimbledon crown and the third Grand Slam title of his career. Though neither Federer nor anyone else was to know it at the time, the Wimbledon victory was also significant in marking the beginning of Federer's record streak of reaching twenty-three consecutive Grand Slam semi-finals.

By now, Federer had established not invincibility but dominance, winning three of the previous five Grand Slam titles. He went to the US Open determined to consolidate that record, and did just that. He lost a set to the Cypriot Marcos Baghdatis in the second round and came through a humdinger of a five-set match against Andre Agassi in the quarter-finals, winning 6–3 in the fifth set but, from then on, it was plain sailing. Federer disposed of Britain's Tim Henman easily in the semi-final and overcame Lleyton Hewitt with the unusual but ultimately comfortable scoreline 6–0, 7–6, 6–0 in the final. Federer had pocketed his fourth Grand Slam title at the age of twenty-three and, in November, he won the World Tour finals for the second successive year.

Federer fell at the semi-final hurdle in the 2005 Australian Open, which was won by Marat Safin. At the French Open in Paris, Federer succumbed in the semi-finals to Rafael Nadal, but he soon returned to his winning ways on his favourite turf at Wimbledon. Throughout the tournament, Federer sacrificed only one set, to Nicolas Kiefer, in the third round, crushing Fernando González in the last eight, Lleyton Hewitt in the semi-finals and Andy Roddick 6–2, 7–6, 6–4 in the final. Federer had secured his fifth Grand Slam title and his third Wimbledon singles trophy. By now, every player on the professional circuit had to recognise that he was the biggest cheese in the game, the man to watch, to admire and to strive against the odds to beat.

Having again successfully defended his Wimbledon title, Federer went to New York in pursuit of a second successive US Open. Federer sailed through the first three rounds without losing a set; prevailed in four sets against Nicolas Kiefer, who had briefly challenged him two months earlier at Wimbledon; trounced David Nalbandian, who had often tested or worsted him in the past, losing a mere seven games; and then overcame Lleyton Hewitt in four sets in the semi-final. At the last hurdle, Federer beat a truly great former champion, Andre Agassi, by 6–1 in the fourth set. Just over two years on from winning his first major at Wimbledon, Federer had racked up his sixth Grand Slam title.

Just as 2005 ended in style for the Swiss maestro, so 2006 began in similar vein. Yet the Australian Open confronted

Federer with a number of exacting encounters. True enough, he sauntered through the first three rounds without losing a set, but that ease of progress was not destined to continue. In the last sixteen, Federer held on in a tough, topsy-turvy match against the German, Tommy Haas. Having raced to a two-set lead, Federer was then pegged back to two sets apiece before riding out the winner 6–2 in the fifth set. In the quarter-final, Federer outdid the Russian Nikolay Davydenko in four sets, winning two hard-fought tie-breaks in the process. For the third Slam in succession, Federer came up against Nicolas Kiefer, this time in the semi-final, emerging victorious in four sets. In the final, Federer dropped the first set to Marcos Baghdatis, took the second by the same margin, 7–5, and then romped to the finishing post by taking the last two sets 6–0, 6–2.

The next Grand Slam in the annual calendar is the French Open. Although the tournament had never been his happiest hunting ground, Federer had reached the semi-finals in 2005 and this year he was to go one better. Winning six matches to reach the final, Federer was beaten by Rafael Nadal in four sets. Doubtless disappointed to lose, Federer was starting to demonstrate that although Nadal was deservedly earning the sobriquet the King of Clay, he was at least the second in line to the throne.

Moreover, a month later at Wimbledon, Federer had the opportunity to inflict revenge on Nadal and add to his growing Grand Slam trophy cupboard. Making light work of every opponent from the first round to the semi-finals, Federer needed to play only one tie-break in those six rounds over the Wimbledon fortnight. Then came the final against Rafael Nadal, now clearly establishing himself as the main challenger to the Federer supremacy. It was no walkover, even though Federer won the opening set to love, but the Swiss prevailed in four sets and was now the proud possessor of no fewer than eight Grand Slam titles, including four Wimbledon championships in a row.

In 2004, Federer had won three out of four Grand Slam titles. Now, in 2006, as he approached the US Open, he was bidding to do the same. The tournament was a triumph for Federer and it followed the well-trodden path of previous Slams. Indeed, Federer cantered to the quarter-finals without losing a set, supremely confident, and the undisputed master of his opponents. In the quarter-final, he dropped a set to the talented if erratic American, James Blake. In the semi-finals, he clinically disposed of Nikolay Davydenko and in the final, facing a former champion in Andy Roddick, Federer came through in four sets to clinch his third straight US Open title and the ninth major title of his career. After another outstanding year, the joy was complete for Federer when he won the World Tour finals in November.

Roger Federer entered 2007 as the undisputed colossus of competitive tennis. He had not won everything but he had won more than anyone else. The old adage that nothing succeeds like success applies to tennis as to so many other areas of human endeavour. Fortified by his ever increasing tally of major titles, not to mention the other tournaments he was winning, Federer must have approached 2007 confident in the expectation that he would achieve new triumphs. That confidence was to be amply justified.

In Melbourne at the Australian Open, Federer accomplished his most remarkable feat yet. As defending champion, Federer won the title for the third time and in doing so he became the first man since Björn Borg in 1976 to win a Grand Slam tournament without losing a set. Staggeringly, in the semi-finals, he beat his old adversary, Andy Roddick, for the loss of only six games 6–4, 6–0, 6–2 and disposed of the tenth seed, Fernando González, 7–6, 6–4, 6–4. This was the tenth Slam for Federer and the ease and margin of his victory must have provided an especially warm glow.

Once again, it must have been as chastening for Federer as it was predictable that the run of major victories was not sustained at Roland Garros. For the second successive year, Federer won six matches on the trot to reach the final but he was again vanquished in four sets by Rafael Nadal, the now 21-year-old Spaniard who had his measure on the clay court.

Undaunted, Federer had only a few weeks to wait before he got his own back on Nadal. He advanced through the Wimbledon draw in characteristically businesslike fashion, reaching the quarter-finals without losing a set, surrendering one set to Juan Carlos Ferrero and brushing aside the challenge of the gifted but quixotic Frenchman Richard Gasquet in straight sets in the semi-final. His final opponent was Nadal. It was a ferociously competitive match and much tighter than their encounter twelve months earlier. It went the distance and Federer triumphed in five sets 7–6, 4–6, 7–6, 2–6, 6–2, the closest and most arduous Grand Slam final of the eleven he had won or thirteen he had played.

In New York in September in the US Open, Federer was again victorious, beating Novak Djokovic in the final. To crown another fabulous year, he won the World Tour finals tournament for the fourth time. For the third consecutive year, he ended the year as world number one.

The run of success in major titles was truly phenomenal. Since the summer of 2005, Federer had reached the final of ten successive Grand Slam tournaments, winning eight of them. The streak could not continue indefinitely and it was broken in January 2008 at the Australian Open when Federer fell in the semi-final to Novak Djokovic, who went on to take the title. By the stratospheric standards Federer had now established and set himself, it was a failure, but he need not berate himself. At the French Open, he took his customary place in the final but a combination of very windy conditions and the still greater clay-court superiority of Rafael Nadal inflicted probably the heaviest defeat of his career as Federer limply succumbed 6–1, 6–3, 6–0.

At Wimbledon, Federer set out to beat Björn Borg's record of five successive titles but it was not to be. He marched all the way from the first round to the final without losing a set, but in the previous twelve months there had been one change. Nadal had improved and, conscious that he had consistently beaten Federer on clay but never on grass, had devoted himself utterly to winning against the maestro on Centre Court. Some commentators felt that Nadal had started to gain a psychological hold on Federer and to sow seeds of doubt in his mind about his capacity to cope with his young Spanish challenger. This theory gained credence when Nadal took the first two sets with comparative ease, 6–4, 6–4. But Federer is a proud man, hugely resourceful, a great champion and a formidable competitor. He had no intention of meekly submitting. On the contrary, he dug deep and clawed his way back winning the next two sets in hard tiebreaks to level the match. The final set was nip and tuck, without a break of serve, until Nadal struck, breaking the Federer serve at seven games all and serving out for the championship. The story of the match was, of course, the triumph of Nadal, the end of five years of Federer hegemony at Wimbledon, and the suspicion that this could mark the changing of the guard at the top of the men's game – as, in retrospect, it did. Nevertheless, Federer had made a superb contribution to what many regarded as the greatest final in Wimbledon history, lasting four hours and forty-eight minutes, interrupted by two rain delays and stretching over seven hours. The following month, Nadal eclipsed Federer when he was installed as the new world number one. Federer was left to rue his defeat and to reflect that he had won none of the three majors of the year and that he would have one last chance to plug the gap in 2008 by fending off his rivals at the US Open in September.

Federer had a point to prove. He had not run out of steam. No one should be so rash or impertinent as to write him off. He faced a tough match in the last sixteen, requiring five sets to put away the wily Russian Igor Andreev 6–3 in the final set, and in the semi-finals he overcame Novak Djokovic in four sets. Most commentators would have expected Federer to meet Nadal in the final but the latter succumbed to a superb performance by Britain's Andy Murray, who defeated Nadal 6–2, 7–6, 4–6, 6–4 to reach his first Grand Slam final at the age of twenty-one. It was very much an open question who would win, because Murray had built up a winning record in head-to-head matches against Federer. However, many observers have noted that Federer is a

different man in the majors, partly because the stakes are higher
and his thirst to win is greater, partly because he tends to be
stronger over five sets than three, and partly because he has built
up vast experience in playing big matches. Doubtless all these
factors played their part and Federer dismissed Murray with relative ease in three sets. 6–2, 7–5, 6–2 was the score and Federer
had banked his thirteenth Grand Slam title.

For the sixth year in a row, Federer had won a major tournament and he now needed to win just one more to match the
all-time record of fourteen Slams held by Pete Sampras. It had not
been his best year but, even so, Federer had reached the final in
three out of the four big titles and had triumphed once.

Federer began 2009 as the world number two, with Nadal
in pole position. That ranking appeared to be confirmed when
they met at the Australian Open. There, Federer, three times the
champion in 2004, 2006, and 2007, reached the final, the eighteenth Grand Slam final of his career. Always coming from behind,
Federer took the match into a fifth set but was outdone by Nadal,
who won it 6–2. Federer was in tears. He was devastated to be
defeated in another Slam final at what had previously been a
successful tournament for him and which had never before been
conquered by Nadal. Federer was good but not good enough.

Yet Federer bounced back at the French Open in Paris. This was
the one Grand Slam title he had never won. He had been defeated
four times there by Nadal. First in the semi-finals in 2005 and then
in 2006, 2007 and 2008 in the final. There is no denying that clay
is not Federer's best surface, but the idea that he cannot perform
on it is preposterous. He was then a three-time finalist, foiled only
by the finest clay-court player since Björn Borg, and in my view
the best ever on that surface. Once again Federer reached the final
but, to everyone's surprise, Nadal did not: he was dumped out
of the tournament by the rising Swede Robin Söderling in four
sets, 6–2, 6–7, 6–4, 7–6. On reaching the quarter-finals, Söderling
won two more matches in order to face Federer. The omens were
encouraging for Federer, who had never lost to the Swede, and

this final was no exception. Federer won comfortably in straight sets, 6–1, 7–6, 6–4. This was the sweetest of victories. The French Open had always eluded him and he never lost sight of the goal to win it. Of course, the triumph would have been still greater if he had beaten Nadal to win the title, but in head-to-head competition, players can by definition play only those whom they are pitched against, not those whom they are not. Federer had now won each of the majors. The record was complete. In the process, he had matched the Pete Sampras tally of fourteen major titles. True enough, he had never won the Grand Slam of all four major titles in one year, but in the Open era only Rod Laver had that distinction, last achieved in 1969. Federer was a winner again and he could be well pleased with his work.

Wimbledon 2009 was bereft of Nadal, who had been diagnosed with knee tendonitis. Federer progressed seamlessly through the first two rounds, dropped a set to the German Philipp Kohlschreiber in the third round and dismissed Robin Söderling in straight sets to reach the quarter-final. There Federer met and disposed of Ivo Karlović in straight sets before visiting a similar fate on Tommy Haas in the semi-finals. Federer might have expected to face Andy Murray or Juan Martín del Potro but del Potro was beaten in the second round by Lleyton Hewitt and Andy Murray was overcome in four closely fought sets by Andy Roddick, who powered his way to the final. Federer enjoyed an overwhelming advantage over Roddick, whom he had beaten consistently for several years.

The pundits were united in the expectation that Federer would win and win easily. In fact, the final was an epic, a titanic struggle between the multiple Grand Slam winner Federer and the awesome server Andy Roddick, who yearned to win Wimbledon and add to his single Slam victory notched up in the US Open six years earlier.

Roddick took the first set and had four successive set points to take the second set in the tie-break. Astonishingly, he could take none of them and Federer squared the match at one set all.

They split the next two sets and slugged out the final set (no tie-break) with no break of serve until Federer led 15–14 and broke the Roddick serve to take the match and the title. It was one of the most exciting finals in years. Federer served fifty aces and, despite a superb showing by Roddick, gave the impression of being unwilling even to contemplate the possibility of defeat. Victory delivered the sixth Wimbledon title for Federer, and meant that with fifteen Grand Slam titles he had now surpassed Pete Sampras, who had notched up fourteen.

On the back of the Wimbledon success, there appeared to be a strong prospect of victory in the US Open. Federer reached the final with a comfortable victory over Novak Djokovic which will probably be best remembered for the sublime hotdog shot that Federer played. Djokovic had lobbed the ball over Federer's head and the most one would have expected would be for Federer somehow to scrape it back – but no. He drove the ball between his legs back over Djokovic's side of the net, right past his opponent, deep into the court for a clean winner. Federer, usually expressionless, erupted with joy. The crowd were ecstatic and Djokovic sportingly acknowledged what had been an unanswerable stroke of genius.

Federer was the favourite to win the final, partly because he was the world number one but also on account of sheer big-match experience. This was del Potro's first and, so far, only Slam final. Yet Federer was unable consistently to impose himself on his opponent, whose game is characterised by a ferocious serve and extremely powerful, largely flat groundstrokes which he sprays remorselessly around the court. Federer led by a set to love and two sets to one, but he could not bury del Potro who finally prevailed 6–2 in the final set. It was a disappointment for Federer but not a disaster. He had appeared in all four major finals of 2009, winning two and losing two. That was a better record than anyone else and, in addition, he had won two Masters tournaments: in Madrid over Nadal and in Cincinnati over Djokovic, ending the year as world number one for the fifth consecutive year.

At the 2010 Australian Open many tennis aficionados might have hoped that a fully fit and rejuvenated Rafael Nadal would meet Roger Federer, who had proved in 2009 that he was still performing at the highest level. Yet it was not to be. Nadal, trailing 6–3, 7–6, 3–0 to Andy Murray, retired with a right knee injury and Murray then defeated Marin Čilić to reach his second Grand Slam final.

For his part, after dropping the opening set of his campaign to Igo Andreev, Federer was advancing with growing confidence. Beating Andreev in four sets, he then brushed aside his next three opponents, Victor Hănescu, Albert Montanés and Lleyton Hewitt, without a hint of difficulty. He then came back from a set and a break down to defeat Nikolay Davydenko, and in the semi-final he pulverised Jo-Wilfried Tsonga 6–2, 6–3, 6–2.

Thus, the final pitched Federer against Murray, a rematch between the rivals who had contested the US Open final sixteen months earlier. Some observers thought that Murray, growing in confidence and experience, would overcome Federer, but in fact the result was little different from their encounter in New York. Federer served well, was aggressive, and quickly took control, winning 6–3, 6–4, 7–6 to clinch the title, his sixteenth Grand Slam victory. This was his fourth Australian Open victory and the best start to the year that Federer had enjoyed since 2007.

After such an auspicious start to the year – winning another major for the loss of only two sets – Federer fans must have hoped, even expected, that the run would continue. Yet the opposite happened. At the French Open Federer produced a majestic first set against Robin Söderling in their quarter-final, but was then comprehensively outplayed, thereby failing for the first time in six years to reach the semi-final of a major tournament.

At Wimbledon, Federer suffered a similar fate. After surviving a two-set deficit to Colombian, Alexandro Falla, in the first round, Federer reached the quarter-finals, where he lost to Tomáš Berdych. Federer was curiously error prone and frankly out-hit by an opponent who felt from the start that he could and would prevail. The attributes that had served Federer so well over the last seven years, namely bossing his opponent about the court from the start or raising his game to seize back control from an audacious challenger, simply deserted him. He had nothing left in the tank and subsequently suggested that he was struggling with a bad back. This was the second major in a row in which Federer had unexpectedly crashed out and defeat inevitably prompted speculation that he was on his way out of the game or, at any rate, in terminal decline.

Further disappointment was in store at the US Open. There was no catastrophe. Federer progressed to the semi-finals, defeating a string of opponents and wreaking straight-sets revenge on Söderling, who had thwarted him at Roland Garros. Come the semi-final against Djokovic, however, he was outdone. The match went to five sets and at 5–4 up in the fifth he led 15–40 on the Djokovic serve but was unable to finish off his opponent and ended up losing the set 7–5 and, with it, the match. Defeat was a bitter pill, perhaps the more so because victory was within his grasp. Inevitably, defeat fuelled a growing sense that Federer had lost his way, could no longer win tight matches at the highest level, and did not evoke in opponents the respect and foreboding which had for years been a secret weapon in Federer's favour.

Relief and, indeed, exhilaration were provided by the World Tour finals in London in November. As though he was keeping the best until last, Federer played superbly throughout the week. He won his group, beating David Ferrer, Andy Murray and Robin Söderling in straight sets, booking his semi-final slot against Djokovic, whom he comprehensively outplayed 6–1, 6–4. It was some consolation for the wounding defeat he had sustained at Flushing Meadows and, more importantly, it booked his ticket for the final. In the other semi-final, a thrilling contest between Nadal and Andy Murray produced a final-set tie-break and victory for Nadal after nearly three hours on court. The stage was set for yet another duel between the old rivals. Federer struck first, winning the opening set 6–3, Nadal responded by taking the second by the same margin and, appropriately enough, a final set was required to separate the gladiators. Federer broke the Nadal serve early in the third set and Nadal, who had experienced a far more testing semi-final, looked exhausted. He had nothing left. There was little bite in his shots in that third set and Federer was motoring. He finished the match off quickly enough, winning the final set 6–1, securing his fifth World Tour final crown and equalling the record of Sampras and Agassi, the only other players to have won the title on five occasions.

If 2010 was a year of mixed fortunes for Federer, 2011 was worse. At the Australian Open, Federer waded through the opening rounds with comparative comfort and, observing an apparently injured Rafael Nadal succumb to David Ferrer, he must have been optimistic about his chances. Yet, in the semi-finals, his conqueror at the US Open the previous autumn, Novak Djokovic, plainly had other ideas. The opening set was hard fought, but Djokovic took it on the tie-break. The story of the second set, however, was illustrative of a bigger problem for Federer over the past couple of years. Fighting back from the disappointment of the first set and raising his game for the purpose, Federer raced to a 5–2 lead but he failed to press home his advantage, lost his serve twice in succession and saw Djokovic snatch the set from him 7–5. With one break of serve, Djokovic took the third set 6–4, completing a clinical demolition job. Federer's hopes of adding to his sixteen Slam titles were dashed at the fourth major in succession.

Even the most stridently partisan of Federer supporters would be unlikely to pin their hopes on victory at the French Open, but Federer did better than might have been expected. Reaching the semi-finals, he relished the prospect of another show-down with Djokovic. The odds favoured the latter, who had beaten Federer in their last three tussles, had undoubtedly gone up a gear over the previous six months and had not lost a single match in 2011. But Federer wanted to avenge those defeats and to book another battle with Nadal. Federer played extremely well, serving strongly and, as he had often failed to do in 2010 and 2011, taking his chances. Federer took the first two sets, a below-par Djokovic won the third and Federer clinched victory with an ace in the tie-break of the fourth set. It was a gratifying win and put Federer in the twenty-third Slam final of his illustrious career.

Victory over Nadal would have been the biggest single deal of his career to date, but on clay, against probably the finest ever exponent of the game on that surface, it was always going to prove a tall order. Federer started like a man possessed, shaking Nadal by stepping in, taking the ball on the rise and hitting with force and accuracy to all parts of the court. At 5–2 up in the first set, on the Nadal serve, Federer had a set point, hit a drop shot just wide and thereafter went on to lose the set. Nadal won the second set and it was a mark not merely of Federer's skill but of his character too that he eked out success in the third set tie-break. Nadal promptly raised his level and won match and title with a 6–1 margin in the fourth set. Once again, defeat was a disappointment but hardly a surprise, and securing victory over Djokovic and a twenty-third Slam final were worthwhile consolation prizes for Federer.

Interestingly, although most of the media were justifiably focused on the sensation that Djokovic had been in the first half of 2011, there were some grounds for thinking that Federer might triumph at Wimbledon. He cantered through the first three rounds without loss before dropping the opening-set tie-break to Mikhail Youzhny in the last sixteen and then taking control. What followed was, for Federer and his fans alike, surprising and heartbreaking in equal measure. Up against the mercurial Frenchman Jo-Wilfried Tsonga, whom he had usually beaten, Federer predictably took the first two sets and seemed destined for an uncomplicated victory. But Tsonga, far from wilting, found his range in every department – on serve, off the ground and at the net – and blasted Federer 6–4, 6–4, 6–4 in the next three sets. Never before in his career had Federer lost a match when he had led two sets to love. For the second successive year, Federer had been knocked out in the quarter-final, left to rue what might have been, to ponder what chance of winning another Grand Slam and to look to the US Open. There, he was again thwarted. In an extraordinary rerun of the 2010 semi-final, Federer reached the last four and faced Djokovic. Playing sublimely, Federer took the first two sets, but Djokovic fought back to level the match at two sets apiece. Federer served for the match at 5–3 and had two match points at 40–15 but Djokovic went for broke, wrested the match back to 5–5 and then broke again and served out to win the contest 7–5 in the final set.

The media are forever the most fickle of friends but they could be forgiven for suspecting that Federer was on the way out. First eclipsed as world number one by Nadal, since overtaken by Djokovic as number two, he was now dismissed unexpectedly from his favourite and most successful tournaments. It is not that 2011 was a debacle or even very bad. Federer won one title at the start of the year. He reached the semis of the Australian Open, the final at the French Open, the quarter-final at Wimbledon and the semi-final of the US Open. Most professional tennis players would regard such a show as the apogee of achievement. But there's the rub: Federer is not 'most professional tennis players'. He is, and has come to be judged by others besides himself, exceptional. By the standards he has set, three-quarters of 2010 and virtually all of 2011 fell short.

2012 was a very different story. After losing in the Australian Open semi-final to Nadal, Federer went on a winning spree lasting six months. This included tournament victories in Rotterdam, Dubai, Indian Wells, Madrid and Cincinnati. Most importantly, however, Federer won his seventh Wimbledon title, beating Djokovic in the semi-final and Andy Murray in the final. This was his seventeenth major title but the first since January 2010. He also took the Olympic silver medal and was the losing finalist in four tournaments.

Sadly, 2013 was a year of disappointment with only one tournament win – in Halle – and early exits at Wimbledon and the

US Open. The only modest silver lining in the cloud was Federer's performance at the World Tour finals in November. He reached the semi-final stage after coming from behind to beat del Potro 4–6, 7–6, 7–5.

What has gone wrong? First, Djokovic has improved sharply and that improvement accounts in part for three defeats of Federer in major titles. Secondly, other players of a certain ilk, notably those with strong serves and huge power off the ground, no longer in awe of the maestro, have combined greater patience with the ability to out-hit Federer. Thirdly, although Federer has not uttered a syllable to suggest it, it looks as though he has lost that absolute faith in himself to triumph in the biggest and most closely fought matches. Put bluntly, it is thought by many that he is gripped by self-doubt. In recent years, he has squandered match points and lost to Baghdatis, Tsonga, Berdych, Djokovic and Monfils. Matches in top-flight tennis frequently turn on a few points, rarely more than half a dozen. Federer used to play his best on those points. Now he is not consistently doing so. Finally, there is a lingering suspicion that Federer no longer has the overpowering desire to win that he had of old. He has turned thirty-two, won seventy-eight titles, notched up more prize money than anyone else in history and secured more Grand Slams, but he has a wife and twin four-year-olds, with a second set of twins born in May 2014. Perhaps, say the doubters, the hunger is no longer there. He has nothing left to prove. Whilst it may be tough for Federer to motivate himself for smaller events, the possibility of adding to his collection of majors is surely motivation enough. He continues to compete and it would be foolhardy to write him off. I believe he can win another Slam, although realistically it will have to be in the next year or two and a string of them seems a distant hope.

At the start of 2014, Federer announced that Stefan Edberg, six times Grand Slam title winner and his childhood hero, would join his coaching team. Only time will tell whether the addition of the Swede to his camp, full fitness and his own prodigious efforts will help him to win big titles once again. In early January, Federer reached the final in Brisbane, only to lose unexpectedly to former Wimbledon champion Lleyton Hewitt. At the Australian Open in Melbourne, he reached the semi-final for the eleventh successive year, notching up notable victories over Jo-Wilfried Tsonga in straight sets and Andy Murray in four sets before succumbing to Nadal. Subsequently, he won the Dubai title for the sixth time, beating both Djokovic and Berdych. In addition, he reached Masters 1000 finals in Indian Wells and Monte Carlo and has risen to number four in the world rankings. There are certainly signs that Federer has raised his level and, no doubt influenced by Edberg, one of the greatest net players of all time, he is coming in to the net much more than in recent years. The greatness of Federer is assured. The only issue is whether it can now be extended.

Chapter Nineteen

Rafael Nadal

RAFAEL NADAL IS unquestionably one of the all-time greats in the history of tennis. At the time of writing, he is ranked world number one. He has won thirteen Grand Slam titles (eight French Opens, two Wimbledons, one US Open and one Australian Open), twenty-six Masters 1000 Titles and sixty-one singles titles. He has also won the Olympic singles gold medal (2008) and he has earned over $64 million in prize money alone. It was in 2010, aged twenty-four, that Nadal became only the seventh player in the Open era and the youngest ever to complete a career Slam, i.e. winning each of the four Grand Slam tournaments, and from 2005 to 2011 he was ranked in the world's top two.

Nadal has won a record eight French Opens, including four in succession from 2005 to 2008, and a further four from 2010 to 2013. He is only the third male player in the Open era to have won the French Open and Wimbledon in the same year. He was the first Spaniard to win the Australian Open in 2009 and he is both the first and, to date, the only player to win three consecutive Grand Slam tournaments on three different surfaces – clay, grass and hard court in the same year, namely 2010. Nadal has helped Spain to lift the Davis Cup no fewer than four times and he also owns the record for the longest single-surface winning streak in the Open era, having won eighty-one consecutive matches on clay from April 2005 to May 2007. Indeed, although a prolific winner on all surfaces, Nadal has been especially successful on clay courts. He has a 36–4 record in clay-court tournament finals and a 67–1 record in best-of-five-set matches on clay. As of October 2012, Nadal enjoyed a career record of 583 singles wins, and only 122 losses, a success rate of 82.7 per cent.

Let us now take a closer look at Nadal. It is instructive to note how he developed his taste for tennis, what playing style and career course he adopted and followed and, in particular, why he has proved such a formidable competitor. Rafael Nadal, nicknamed Rafa, was born in Manacor, Mallorca, Spain on 3 June 1986 and he still lives there today. His father, Sebastian, was the business partner with two brothers in a restaurant called Sa Punta, and owner of a glass and windows company, Vidres Mallorca. His mother, Ana Maria, and father separated in 2009. He has a younger sister, Maria Isabel, and his coach for the last twenty-two years has been his uncle, Toni Nadal, himself a former professional tennis player. Rafa started playing tennis at the age of four, with Uncle Toni. Of his early experiences of tennis, Nadal recalls in his autobiography, 'Toni says that at first I found tennis boring. But being in a group helped, and it's what made possible everything that followed.' Nadal is open and explicit about Uncle Toni: 'Toni was hard on me ... Toni never let up ... maybe if I hadn't loved playing the game, I wouldn't have put up with my uncle. And I loved him too, as I still do and always will.' Renowned for his close relationship with his family, Nadal observes, 'For all the discipline, I had an amazingly happy and warm life as a child, and maybe that is why I was able to put up with the harsh treatment I received from Toni.' He maintains that, without in any way diminishing the role of his uncle, 'The principal driving force in my life has been my father, who, along with my mother, created a happy and stable home base without which I would not be the tennis player I am.' Specifically, Nadal insists that his desire to succeed, together with the knowledge that you have to work hard to fulfil your ambitions, can be traced to his family.

As a keen young player, under the tutelage of Uncle Toni, Nadal scored some notable early victories, becoming Balearic

Islands Under-12 Champion aged eight and winning the Spanish National Under-12 and -14 titles in 1997 and 2000. In these early years, three facts are perhaps of particular interest. First, noticing that, at eight, Nadal was hitting forehand shots with two hands, Uncle Toni urged him to play left-handed, believing that it would give him a natural advantage on a tennis court, as he would mainly compete against right-handers and that they could find playing against a left-hander more awkward and challenging. Secondly, when, at the age of twelve, Nadal won both the Spanish and European tennis titles in his age group, he was also a keen footballer and his father decided that young Rafa must choose between the two sports, not least so that his schoolwork did not suffer unduly. Nadal chose tennis, dropped football and in so doing started to develop that single-minded focus on his goal that has defined his career ever since. Thirdly, at fourteen, the Spanish Tennis Federation suggested that Nadal leave Mallorca and move to Barcelona to continue his tennis training. The family declined this request, partly out of concern for his education but also, tellingly, because Uncle Toni did not accept that it was necessary to go there, the US, or anywhere else in order 'to be a good athlete', insisting instead, 'You can do it from your home.'

Working dedicatedly with Uncle Toni accompanied by fitness trainer and fellow Manacor resident Rafael Maymo, Nadal developed and honed the rudiments of his tennis game. His basic approach is to stand behind the baseline and to hit aggressive groundstrokes, with heavy topspin, to cover the court through powerful anticipation and fast footwork, and to prevail either by crafting opportunities for winning shots or by forcing opponents into errors. Nadal is renowned for his supreme defensive qualities, his magnificent athleticism and his skill as a ferocious counter-puncher. Like Pete Sampras, Nadal hits effectively on the run and has an enviable ability to create winning shots from apparently defensive, disadvantageous positions. He excels too in the use of the dropshot.

Deploying a full Western grip forehand, his technique has been described as a 'lasso-whip' follow-through, whereby his left arm finishes above his left shoulder, although he is able to use a more orthodox swing and to hit the ball deep and flat. The staple shot, however, is with huge topspin, averaging 3,200 perambulations per minute, compared with 2,700 by Federer and between 1,800 and 1,900 by predecessors Pete Sampras and Andre Agassi. Lest this seems a dry, 'techie' point of no great relevance, the reader should be in no doubt of its significance. Although most of Nadal's shots land short, often well short of the baseline, the very high bounces achieved by his forehands – at the shoulder level of opponents or higher – limit or altogether remove any advantage that an opponent would gain from a short ball. Moreover, the technique, deployed remorselessly, can impose great strain on opponents, especially when the ball is hit high to the backhand side of a right-hander, when that right-hander hits the backhand with one hand. In these early years, these strong foundations of a counter-puncher's game were put in place and the only notable weakness in Nadal's armoury was a relatively poor service, especially the second delivery.

Nadal turned professional in 2001 and, aged fifteen, reached the second round at that year's Seville Challenger tournament. The following year, 2002, still shy of sixteen, he scored his first victory on the ATP circuit and he ended the year ranked 199 in the world. 2003 saw a very significant improvement as Nadal defeated former French Open champion Albert Costa in Monte Carlo, won his first Challenger title, reached the third round at Wimbledon – the youngest player since Boris Becker to do so – and entered the top fifty in the world. In 2004, Nadal defeated the then world number two, Andy Roddick, in the Davis Cup final, in which Spain triumphed over the USA. In so doing, Nadal became the youngest player (eighteen years six months) to record a singles win for the winning team in the Davis Cup.

This solid progress gave way to groundbreaking advance in 2005. Nadal began by reaching the fourth round of the Australian Open and continued two months later by reaching the final of the

Miami Masters, succumbing only in five sets to world number one Roger Federer. These were big milestones indeed. The year improved further as he then won twenty-four consecutive singles matches and, over the year, notched up a teenage record of eleven titles, including four ATP Masters shields. In the process, Nadal became the first teenager since Boris Becker in 1986 to finish the season as world number two. The crowning glory of the year was Nadal's capture of his first Grand Slam title, the French Open. Achieving that new pinnacle required Nadal to defeat the number one seed and world number one Roger Federer in the semi-final, and victory at Roland Garros was the scene-setter for multiple triumphs in the years to follow. As a footnote, it is interesting, in light of the fascinating rivalry that was to develop with Roger Federer, that in 2005 both Nadal and Federer won eleven singles titles, including four Masters Series titles, and that Nadal won seventy-nine matches, bettered only by Federer's eighty-one.

2006 was again a successful year for Nadal. On the clay courts of Europe he won all four tournaments he played, notching up twenty-four match victories in the process. Given that defending a title won the previous year is the stiffest of tests, Nadal could be mighty proud to win the French Open again, his second Grand Slam triumph, besting Roger Federer in four sets in the final. After bouncing back when only two points from defeat to American qualifier Robert Kendrick in the second round at Wimbledon, Nadal upped his game and beat Andre Agassi and three further opponents, all in straight sets, to reach his first Wimbledon final where he was soundly beaten, but by no means thrashed, 6–0, 7–6, 6–7, 6–3, by Roger Federer, who thereby won his fourth consecutive Wimbledon title. At the year-ending Tennis Masters Cup, Nadal reached the semi-finals before losing once more to Federer, this time 6–4, 7–5. Nevertheless, he ended the year ranked world number two and with four victories scored over Federer. Indeed, in a sign of just how big a threat he had become, Nadal was the only player then to have beaten Federer more than once since the latter became world number one.

2007 started modestly for Nadal, including with defeat in the quarter-finals of the Australian Open, but he won the Masters tournament in Indian Wells and went on to claim three clay-court titles before falling to Federer in the final of the Hamburg Masters, ending a phenomenal 81-match winning streak on clay, a single-surface success record unbeaten in the Open era. Peaking at just the right time, Nadal claimed his third straight French Open title in June, overcoming Federer once again in the final. At Wimbledon, Nadal made it to the final for the second successive year, this time stretching Federer to the limit as Federer took the match and title with a 6–2 final-set win. Over the year, Nadal won six titles, ending the year as world number two, a ranking he had then held for 128 consecutive weeks since 25 July 2005.

2008 was a scintillating year for Nadal. He won eight titles – an impressive feat to be sure – but the statistics do not begin to tell the story. In January he reached the semi-finals of the Australian Open for the first time, albeit suffering an overwhelming straight-sets defeat by razor-sharp Jo-Wilfried Tsonga. Weeks later, he reached the final of the Miami Masters for the second time. Thereafter, Nadal went into overdrive, winning four clay-court titles, defeating Federer in three finals. In the French Open final, he not only defeated Federer in three straight sets but sacrificed only four games in the process. This was his fourth consecutive title victory at Roland Garros and he thereby became, alongside Borg, Federer and Sampras, only the fourth player in the Open era to achieve such a success spree in one Grand Slam tournament.

Nadal won his first grass-court title in the Queen's Club in London and entered Wimbledon on a 23-match-winning streak. Nadal reached the final for the third year in a row to face his conqueror in each of the two years, Roger Federer. In the longest final in Wimbledon history, Nadal prevailed 9–7 in the fifth set. The scalp was of seismic significance. Nadal had won his first Wimbledon, proving that he could triumph on grass as that other legendary clay-court player Björn Borg had done three decades earlier. Indeed, it was Nadal's first Slam on a surface other than clay. Furthermore, he proved that he could beat the great Roger Federer on the surface he had dominated for five years. Nadal did not achieve the same success at the US Open, falling to Andy Murray in the semi-final. Yet, to put the icing on the cake of an exceptional year, Nadal won the Olympic singles gold medal in Beijing, defeating the Chilean Fernando González in the final. Nadal went on to help Spain reach the semi-finals of the Davis Cup. Sadly, in November, he was forced to withdraw from the year-ending Tennis Masters Cup in Shanghai owing to tendonitis of the knee and he felt compelled to withdraw from Spain's Davis Cup final against Argentina for the same reason. These real disappointments notwithstanding, it was a groundbreaking year for Nadal who had snatched the world number one ranking from Federer in August and held it as the year closed.

In 2009, Nadal won his first hard-court Grand Slam at the end of January in Melbourne, defeating fellow countryman Fernando Verdasco in a five-set semi-final encounter lasting over five hours, then triumphing over Roger Federer in the final, also in five sets. As well as becoming the first Spaniard to win the Australian Open, Nadal became the first male player simultaneously to hold three Grand Slam singles titles on three different surfaces.

Shortly after his success Down Under, Nadal suffered a knee injury in Rotterdam and pulled out of a tournament in Dubai the following week. In March, he played Davis Cup tennis against Serbia, defeating both Janko Tipsarević and Novak Djokovic, and then proceeded to win his thirteenth Masters 1000 series tournament at Indian Wells. From there, Nadal notched up further titles in Monte Carlo, Barcelona and Rome before losing in the Madrid Masters final 6–4, 6–4 to Roger Federer.

In Paris, seeking his fifth consecutive French Open, Nadal was unexpectedly defeated in the fourth round by the Swede Robin Söderling, 6–2, 6–7, 6–4, 7–6. To date, this is the only loss Nadal has ever suffered at the French Open.

Shortly afterwards, Nadal revealed that he was suffering from tendonitis in both knees and he withdrew from the Wimbledon

Championship, which was won by Roger Federer. Nadal sacrificed the number-one slot to Federer in July and, although he recovered fitness sufficiently to play at the US Open in Flushing Meadows, Nadal was trounced in the semi-final by Juan Martín del Potro 6–2, 6–2, 6–2. Moreover, he fared no better at the World Tour finals in London, losing all three of his matches in straight sets – to Robin Söderling, Nikolay Davydenko (the eventual winner) and Novak Djokovic. In December, Nadal derived satisfaction from winning his rubbers in the successful Davis Cup final against the Czech Republic. 2009 had its high points, notably at the beginning and end, but the year was marred by defeat, injury and his parents' separation.

If 2009 was a year of mixed fortunes for Nadal, 2010 was excellent. He won no fewer than seven titles, including three Slams. However, the start was not auspicious. At the Australian Open, Nadal retired with knee trouble in the quarter-finals when trailing two sets and 3–0 to Andy Murray. Following a brief rest and recovery, Nadal reached the semi-finals of both Indian Wells and the Sony Eriksson Open, but suffered disappointing defeats respectively to Ivan Ljubičić and Andy Roddick. His year first caught fire at his favoured hunting ground of the Monte Carlo Masters in Monaco, where Nadal won the title for the sixth consecutive year, conceding only twenty games in six matches and not dropping a set. Thereafter, Nadal won the Rome and Madrid Masters, overcoming David Ferrer in Italy and Roger Federer in Spain before moving on to Paris. There, he reclaimed his French Open title, defeating his conqueror in 2009, Robin Söderling, in straight sets. Victory was sweet as Nadal became the first man both to win three Masters Series tournaments on clay and to take the French Open. In the process, he reclaimed his spot as world number one.

Injury had forced him to miss Wimbledon in 2009, but this time Nadal was out to regain the title he had first claimed in 2008. It was hard going in the early rounds as Nadal was taken to five sets by Dutchman Robin Haase in the second round and by German

Philipp Petzschner in the third. Thereafter, Nadal progressed to the final, dropping only one more set – to Robin Söderling – and then comprehensively dispatched the Czech Tomáš Berdych 6–3, 7–5, 6–4 to lift his eighth Grand Slam title.

At this point, Nadal had won three of the four Slams since his first triumph in 2005 in Roland Garros, but the US Open had always eluded him. 2010 was to be different. Playing at his outstanding best, Nadal went through six rounds to the final without dropping a set and defeated Novak Djokovic in the final in four sets, 6–4, 5–7, 6–4, 6–2, completing a career Golden Slam (all four Slams plus the Olympic singles gold medal). Nadal lifted one further title, the Japan Open, and, for the first time, he reached the final of the ATP World Tour finals at the O2 arena, where he succumbed to Roger Federer 6–3, 3–6, 6–1. It had been a formidable season in which Nadal joined Mats Wilander to become only the second player to win Slams on three different surfaces at least twice, and he ended the year as world number one.

After the rich harvest of 2010, it would be tough the following year to maintain such an ascendancy, and Nadal did not do so. It was by no means a poor year, just not as outstanding as 2008 or 2010. Nadal won three titles, including the French Open, Barcelona, and the Monte Carlo Masters for the seventh time, but he struggled against two opponents above all: injury and Novak Djokovic. In the Australian Open he suffered what appeared to be a hamstring injury against David Ferrer, who defeated him in straight sets in their quarter-final encounter. At Indian Wells, Nadal made the final but lost to Djokovic in three sets. The pattern repeated itself at the Sony Eriksson Open, with Nadal again succumbing to Djokovic, this time in a third-set tie-break. Once again, in Madrid, Nadal lost in the final to Djokovic. He then suffered a further loss in the Rome Masters to Djokovic but in June he won his sixth French Open title, with a four-set defeat of Roger Federer in the final. At Wimbledon, Nadal again reached the final, but lost in four sets to Djokovic, his fifth consecutive defeat in 2011 at the hands of the Serb. As a result, Djokovic seized the world number one slot and Nadal was pegged back at number two. The pattern of the year continued at the US Open: Nadal reached the final, Djokovic beat him. At the ATP World Tour finals, never Nadal's ideal setting – the indoor courts have tended to work better for Federer – the Spaniard was trounced by Federer and lost to Jo-Wilfried Tsonga, thereby exiting the tournament. Nadal had notched up important victories, but for the first time in six years neither he nor Federer had dominated. Djokovic had done so.

2012 was a disappointing and, above all, a frustrating year for Nadal. The season got off to a poor start at the Qatar Open when Nadal, playing well below his best, lost in the semi-finals in straight sets to the mercurial Frenchman Gaël Monfils. Performing altogether more sharply, Nadal overcame both Tomáš Berdych and Roger Federer to reach the final of the Australian Open. There, he succumbed in a Herculean struggle against Novak Djokovic in five sets, the match time of five hours and fifty-three minutes setting a Slam record. Defeat was especially galling for Nadal, who had led 4–2 in the final set before losing it 7–5. Disappointment continued at the Masters 1000 event at Indian Wells, where Nadal reached the semi-finals only to be comprehensively beaten in straight sets by Roger Federer, who proceeded to win the title. In Miami, Nadal made it to the semi-finals but withdrew from his keenly anticipated encounter with Andy Murray, owing to problems with one of his knees. After that setback, Nadal revived his spirits by taking the Monte Carlo Rolex Masters title for the eighth straight year, ending a sequence of seven losses to Djokovic with a clinical 6–3, 6–1 dismissal of his Serb rival. The better results continued in Barcelona, where Nadal won the tournament for the seventh time in eight years, defeating his doughty fellow Spaniard David Ferrer 7–6, 7–5 in the final. In the Madrid Masters, on a controversial blue clay surface which he and many other players found slippery and uncongenial, Nadal crashed out in the third round to Fernando

Verdasco by a margin of 7–5 in the deciding set, after squandering a 4–0 third-set lead over a player who had never previously beaten him in thirteen contests. In Rome, Nadal again met Novak Djokovic and was victorious 7–5, 6–3, bagging his sixth Rome title. Most importantly, for it was to be his biggest achievement of the year, Nadal won an outright record seventh French Open title, clinching victory over Djokovic in four sets. This was the third successive win over the Serbian and must have encouraged Nadal to hope that he had reasserted dominance over Djokovic and, very likely, of the rankings.

In fact, triumph in Paris was quickly followed by disappointment and, ultimately, by frustration. At Halle, the pre-Wimbledon grass-court tournament in Germany, Nadal was unexpectedly dumped out in the quarter-finals 6–3, 6–4 by Philipp Kohlschreiber. This minor disappointment was swiftly followed by the major blow of defeat in the second round at Wimbledon by the Czech player Lukáš Rosol, ranked number 100 in the world, in a captivating five-set contest. This was the first time in seven years that Nadal had failed to advance to the third round of a Grand Slam tournament. Rosol had played out of his skin and could not reproduce that form in his next match, submitting to Philipp Kohlschreiber. That said, the defeat was a wounding blow for Nadal, who pulled out of the 2012 Olympics the following month, blaming tendonitis in his knee. This must have been hugely frustrating for Nadal, who would dearly have loved to repeat his Olympic triumph of 2008. Nadal subsequently missed the US Open and the ATP World Tour finals, ending 2012 ranked fourth.

Despite the toll of injury in 2012 and his displacement as world number one by Djokovic and Federer, Rafael Nadal is undeniably one of the most successful players of his or any generation. In any case, in 2013, Nadal reminded us of his greatness by returning from injury stronger than ever. Back as world number one, he won a long string of titles in 2013, including his eighth French Open and his second US Open. His service improved, his groundstrokes are, if anything, even more penetrating, and he is keeping a formidable length with them.

Many professionals can and do perform brilliantly, so what are the elements in his make-up that have elevated Nadal to the pinnacle of his sport? And what, if any, are his weaknesses? The strengths are formidable. First, Nadal is a superb ball-striker who hits with ferocious force and spin, imposing immense pressure on opponents by the sheer unrelenting consistency and bite of his groundstrokes. These are ordinarily driven to a good length, often well-angled, and calculated to oppress opponents, putting them in positions where they cannot attack, but rather will yield errors or short balls from which he can score easy winners. Secondly, Nadal has developed the capacity to play well on all surfaces – clay, hard courts and grass – showing himself frighteningly competent at the baseline, reliable at the net and blessed with great hands to pick up and manoeuvre the ball in his chosen direction. The latter enabled Nadal to change the direction of shots, to use angles subtly and to win cheap points by use of the drop shot. Thirdly, when not injured, Nadal has staggering stamina and an awesome appetite for covering the court and defending supremely. Fourthly, there is no player in the modern game with better concentration or a finer capacity for playing the big points well. On even the ordinary points, Nadal gives no quarter, displays the most ruthless focus and, almost certainly, 'psyches' opponents entirely legitimately, by making them work for every single point. When the critical points of a match come, Nadal's entire attitude and demeanour suggest that there is no way he will admit the possibility of losing. Quite simply, he is remorseless. His sheer mental resilience and resolve can be soul-destroying for his competitors.

Nadal's only obvious weaknesses have been a less than brilliant service and vulnerability to injury. The latter is exacerbated by the way Nadal plays, throwing himself into every shot and deploying a technique on groundstrokes that strains both arms and knees. If Nadal is unlucky, his proneness to injury could be career-ending, although to date it has merely been career-damaging. If not, he could still enjoy five years or more at the top of the game. He boasts a winning record against each of his major rivals. He is already thought by many to be the greatest clay-court player ever. He seems set to be judged amongst the finest competitors in the history of the game.

Chapter Twenty

Novak Djokovic

AT THE TIME of writing, Novak Djokovic, the Serbian tennis supremo, is the number two ranked player in the world. Still only twenty-six, he has won six Grand Slam singles titles, including four Australian Opens, one Wimbledon and one US Open. He ended both 2011 and 2012 as world number one and relinquished the top slot to Rafael Nadal only in the latter part of 2013. By winning three Grand Slam finals in 2011, Djokovic became the fifth player in the Open era to achieve that success in a calendar year. On reaching the final of the French Open in 2012 – even though he was runner-up – Djokovic became only the ninth player in the Open era to reach the final of all four Grand Slam singles tournaments, and he was only the fifth to do so in five consecutive such titles. A member of the Serbian team which won the 2010 Davis Cup, Djokovic was the Olympic singles bronze medallist in 2008 and he has won eighteen Masters Series 1,000 titles – including a record five in 2011 – affording him fourth place in the Masters Series winning stakes since the advent of the Series in 1990. Unsurprisingly, Djokovic has won a plethora of awards in recognition of his play and sportsmanship, and to date he is the only man in the Open era to win three consecutive Australian Open titles. To do so, he overcame Britain's Andy Murray in 2011 and 2013 and the great Spanish champion Rafael Nadal in 2012.

Born 22 May 1987 in Belgrade to Srđjan and Dijana Djokovic, Novak caught the tennis bug at the tender age of four. Aged six, he was observed by Yugoslav tennis legend Jelena Genčić at Mount Kopaonik, where his parents ran a fast food restaurant. Genčić enthused that he was the 'greatest talent' she had seen 'since Monica Seles'. They proceeded to work together for six years until he moved the Pilić Tennis Academy in Obversch to build upon his progress. A mere four years later, still only fourteen, Djokovic began to compete internationally at junior level.

In common with many, perhaps most, top players today, Djokovic is best described as an all-court player, the foundation of whose game is forceful baseline play, characterised by depth, power and consistency. The length of Djokovic's groundstrokes, notably his return of serve, is remarkable, though over the years he has also developed and refined the capacity to use the short angles of the court, hitting both forehands and backhands there, either winning points outright or taking opponents hopelessly out of position. His forehand is excellent but, by common consent, his backhand is even better, a double-handed shot hit with power and precision both up the line and across the court. He is exceptionally agile, moving superbly to cover the court and to defend effectively. Indeed, his movement is so sharp that he is not only able to get back balls that would elude other players but, very often, to produce winning strokes from defensive positions. His service, for a time in 2009 a notable weakness in his game, is now a great strength: the first delivery hard and flat, yielding him many cheap points, and the second hit with kick or slice, often forcing opponents onto the defensive. If the Djokovic serve is very good, his return of serve is frankly outstanding. He can hit the block or chip return as competently as anyone but, whether sliced, topspun or hit flat, the most striking features of his returns are their consistency and length. In short, he rarely concedes the point with an unforced error and, more often than not, his return cancels out the initial advantage possessed by a server and puts Djokovic on at least level terms with his opponent at the start of the point. This inevitably puts opponents under immense pressure, as they are rarely able to break his serve and know that they will almost invariably be obliged to work very hard to hold their own.

No less an authority on the game than John McEnroe believes Djokovic to be the greatest returner ever seen in men's singles. The Serb maestro also volleys competently and is relatively sound overhead, though he is not, and would not claim to be, the greatest exemplar in either department. Djokovic lobs the ball to great effect, typically with topspin and especially effectively off the backhand wing. He has also developed the dropshot. It is deployed with mixed results. More often than not, it is a point winner, exquisitely executed. If it is hit when it is not a percentage play or Djokovic is facing pressure, it can backfire on him.

Djokovic was a very good junior player, but by no means the outstanding performer of his generation. In 2001, he was part of the junior Davis Cup team for the Federal Republic of Yugoslavia, reaching the final but losing his singles match. He put together a win–loss record of 40–11 in singles and the highlight of his junior career was to reach the semi-final of the 2004 Australian Open.

Turning professional in 2003, Djokovic did not immediately qualify to participate in the high-ranking events of the men's game. Rather, as was the regular experience of dozens, if not hundreds, of other would-be champions, Djokovic performed in Futures and Challenger tournaments, rungs below the elite professional circuit. Between 2003 and 2005, Djokovic won three of each category of event, a solid foundation for the advance he was about to make.

In 2005, the Serb achieved a major breakthrough by qualifying for the Australian Open, the first Grand Slam event in which he had participated. He was then resoundingly defeated in the first round, though there was no disgrace in the then seventeen-year-old Djokovic succumbing to the ultimate victor in the tournament, Marat Safin, 6–0, 6–2, 6–1. Subsequently, Djokovic reached the third round at Wimbledon and the US Open and he also played in four Masters Series tournaments, for two of which he had to play qualifying rounds and in one of which he advanced to the third round. 2005, though not outstanding, was a very solid year in the development of Novak Djokovic's career, and he improved on it in 2006, reaching the quarter-finals of the French Open – his first such quarter-final and an impressive achievement on the very demanding clay courts of Roland Garros. That performance, coupled with his progression to the last sixteen at Wimbledon, propelled Djokovic into the world's top forty singles players for the first time. His play sharpened and self-confidence enhanced by his performance in those two major competitions, Djokovic won his first ATP title at the Dutch Open in Amersfoort without sacrificing a set. He added a second title at the Open d'Moselle in Metz, and broke into the top twenty for the first time. In the course of that highly successful year, Djokovic also reached the quarter-finals of the Madrid Masters, then an indoor hard-court tournament, and it was a maiden appearance in the last eight of such a tournament.

Any player who reaches the top twenty, as Djokovic, only nineteen, had just done, would naturally aspire to climb to the next echelon – the top ten – sooner rather than later.

Djokovic got his 2007 campaign off to a positive start with victory in the ATP tournament in Adelaide. He performed solidly enough at the Australian Open but was outplayed in straight sets by the ultimate champion, Roger Federer, in the fourth round. The Masters tournaments that came just a few weeks after the Australian Open were highly significant for the rising Serb star. At Indian Wells, California – a Masters 1000 event peppered with top-flight competitors – Djokovic reached the final, losing to Rafael Nadal. Shortly afterwards, in Miami, at a similar such Masters 1000 event, Djokovic defeated Nadal in the last eight and went on to win the title. These successes elevated him to the top ten.

In addition to playing in the Davis Cup for his country, Djokovic competed in Monte Carlo, losing in the third round to the Spaniard David Ferrer; in the Estoril Open, which he won by beating the Frenchman Richard Gasquet; and in Rome and Hamburg, where he was a quarter-finalist. Most importantly,

Djokovic secured a real career breakthrough by reaching the semi-final of a Grand Slam, the French Open, going one better than the previous year. He lost to Rafael Nadal, who was to win the title for the third successive time – at the time of writing he has won it eight times – and who is now widely regarded as the greatest clay-court player of all time.

Proving, as if proof were needed, that his progress in Paris had not been a quirky one-off but rather that he was thrusting closer to the top, Djokovic reached the semi-finals at Wimbledon. To do so he needed every ounce of his skill, determination and match-playing quality to overcome the popular Cypriot Marcos Baghdatis in five sets over five hours. That victory might well have taken its toll, for Djokovic then retired in the third set of his semi-final encounter with Rafael Nadal, citing an elbow injury. This must have been a disappointment as he had won the first set and lost the second, so the match remained competitive.

Post-Wimbledon, Djokovic triumphed at the Masters Series Rogers Cup in Montreal. This was a notable achievement in any circumstances but dramatically magnified by the fact that to do so Djokovic overcame the world's number three, two, and one, respectively Andy Roddick, Rafael Nadal, and Roger Federer in the last three rounds of the tournament. No one had accomplished this feat of worsting the top three in the same event since Boris Becker had done so thirteen years earlier. At least as noteworthy was that Djokovic joined Tomáš Berdych, as they were then the only two players to have beaten both Federer and Nadal since they had become the two highest-ranking players in the men's game. The other tournament highlights of the year for Djokovic were his first Grand Slam final, the US Open, where he was beaten in straight sets by Roger Federer, and his fifth title of the year in Vienna, where he defeated the Swiss Stanislas Wawrinka. Djokovic ended the year as world number three and, in recognition of his increasing success, he received the Golden Badge Award for the best athlete in Serbia, with the Olympic Committee of Serbia also declaring him the best athlete.

Clearly Djokovic was knocking on the door of Grand Slam success; the Swedish legend Björn Borg, underlining the seriousness of the Serb's challenge to the dominant duo of Federer and Nadal, declared that the Serb was 'definitely a contender to win a Grand Slam'. It had not happened in New York, but Djokovic went all the way at the 2008 Australian Open. The previous September, Djokovic had reached the US Open final without losing a set and he repeated that commanding performance in Melbourne, overcoming the top seed and three-time defending champion Roger Federer in straight sets in the semi-final. That victory alone created a record, as Djokovic was the youngest player, still only twenty, to have reached the semi-finals in all four Grand Slams. He then won the final by dispatching the entertaining but unpredictable Frenchman Jo-Wilfried Tsonga in four sets. This was Djokovic's first Grand Slam title. This was Serbia's first Grand Slam singles title. This was also the first time in three years that a Grand Slam singles title was not won by Federer or Nadal. Those giants of the game had carved up the previous eleven such Slams between them.

A semi-final loser to Andy Roddick in Dubai, Djokovic then claimed his ninth and tenth career singles titles in Indian Wells and Rome. At the French Open in Roland Garros, Djokovic reached the semi-final for the second time but again lost to Nadal. After such a strong start to the year, Wimbledon was a setback for Djokovic. Seeded third, he was beaten in the second round by former Grand Slam winner Marat Safin. Thereafter he was defeated in the last eight of the Rogers Cup in Toronto and in the final of the Cincinnati Masters, on both occasions falling victim to Britain's Andy Murray. Disappointed though Djokovic must have been not to add to his title tally, he will have drawn some comfort in Cincinnati from his semi-final victory over Rafael Nadal.

Defeated in the semi-final of the Beijing Olympics by Nadal, Djokovic overcame the loser of the other semi-final, the American James Blake, and thereby won a bronze medal. At the US Open,

Djokovic reached the semi-finals but was beaten by Roger Federer in four sets. As the season drew to a close, Djokovic was the defeated finalist in Thailand, where Jo-Wilfried Tsonga scored a straight-sets win. However, perhaps more significantly, Djokovic won the prestigious Tennis Masters Cup title – now the World Tour finals – for the first time, defeating the highly resourceful and capable Russian Nikolay Davydenko to claim the trophy.

By the high standards Djokovic had now set and attained, the beginning of 2009 was underwhelming for the Serb. Defeated by the talented Latvian Ernests Gulbis in the opening round in Brisbane, Djokovic was defeated in the semi-finals in New South Wales by Jarkko Nieminen and he failed to retain his Australian Open title, retiring from his quarter-final match against the American Andy Roddick. Further disappointment came in the Marseille semi-final, where he was beaten by Tsonga, but in late February Djokovic claimed his twelfth career title in Dubai with victory over the indefatigable David Ferrer. At Indian Wells, Djokovic fell at the quarter-final stage to Roddick, and in Miami he conquered Roger Federer in the semi-finals but fell short of Andy Murray in the final. In Masters 1000 events in Monte Carlo and Rome, Djokovic reached the finals but was defeated each time. Victory at the Serbia Open gave Djokovic his second title of the year and at the Madrid Open he reached the semi-finals and held three match points against Rafael Nadal, but after four hours and three minutes, he succumbed to the Spaniard. That defeat must have been a wrench but it will have paled into insignificance alongside his loss in the third round of the French Open to the German Philipp Kohlschreiber. Despite winning two titles in 2009 and reaching a clutch of finals and semi-finals, failure to reach his seeded position i.e. semi-finals in Paris, coming on top of his under-performance at the Australian Open, must have been intensely frustrating.

Further disappointment was in store in the grass-court season. Djokovic reached the final of the Gerry Weber Open but was beaten by the hugely experienced German and former world number two Tommy Haas. The experience was repeated in the quarter-finals at Wimbledon, as Haas once again defeated the Serb.

In Cincinnati, Djokovic scored a notable victory over Rafael Nadal to reach the semi-finals but was beaten in the final by Roger Federer. At the US Open, Djokovic performed strongly, reaching the semi-finals for the sacrifice of only two sets, but was beaten in straight sets by Roger Federer.

After the US Open, Djokovic enjoyed a relatively strong finish to the year. He won his third title of the year by claiming the China Open and his fourth by defeating Roger Federer in the latter's backyard, the Swiss Indoors in Basel. Victories over Nadal and Gaël Monfils secured for Djokovic his first Masters 1000 title of the year, the BNP Paribas Masters. Ending 2009 as world number three for the third successive year, Djokovic had reached ten finals and won five of them. Moreover, he had played ninety-seven matches, winning seventy-eight and losing nineteen. It had been a strong year, the sole – but significant – caveat to which was that he had not added another Grand Slam title or reached a final.

In 2010, Djokovic was defeated in the quarter-finals of the Australian Open by Jo-Wilfried Tsonga in five sets, but he rose for the first time to world number two. A semi-finalist in Rotterdam, defeated by the Russian Mikhail Youzhny, Djokovic got his own back in Dubai, winning the final against Youzhny, and thereby his first trophy of the year. Playing for Serbia in the Davis Cup rubber in Belgrade against the USA, Djokovic steered his country to a 3–2 victory and its first quarter-final appearance by winning both of his singles ties, against Sam Querrey and John Isner. Unsuccessful in Indian Wells and Miami, Djokovic parted company with his coach, Todd Martin, and ventured forth to the clay courts but was beaten in the semi-finals in Monte Carlo and the quarter-finals in Rome by Fernando Verdasco. He retired in the quarter-finals of the Serbia Open and, seeded to reach the semi-finals at the French Open, he was eliminated by the Austrian left-hander Jürgen Melzer in five sets. At Wimbledon, Djokovic reached his expected place in the semi-finals but faced not Roger Federer but his assassin, Tomáš Berdych. The Czech prevailed in straight sets. Later, in Toronto, in the Rogers Cup, Djokovic reached the semi-finals but was defeated by Roger Federer.

In a sense, the US Open proved to be the most significant singles tournament for Djokovic. Courting disaster against his fellow Serb Viktor Troicki in the opening round in sweltering conditions that had often troubled Djokovic, he survived in five sets 6–3, 3–6, 2–6, 7–5, 6–3 and then marched imperiously through the next four rounds without dropping a set. In the semi-final, Djokovic served to stay in the match at 4–5 in the fifth set and trailed 40–15. He saved the two match points and went on to win his first victory over Federer at the US Open after losses to him in each of the three preceding years. Although Djokovic lost the final to Nadal in four sets, he will have received a big psychological boost from his defeat of the Swiss maestro.

Djokovic then helped Serbia to overcome the Czech Republic to reach the Davis Cup final, retained the China Open and reached the semi-finals in Shanghai before succumbing to Federer. Similarly, at the Barclays ATP World Tour finals in London, Djokovic reached the semi-finals but was beaten 6–1, 6–4 by Federer. Towards the end of the year, Djokovic won both of his singles rubbers as Serbia defeated France to win the Davis Cup. This was of huge significance to Djokovic in terms of pride and morale and, ending the year again as world number three, Djokovic had embarked on a lengthy unbeaten run that went well into 2011.

2008 was momentous for Djokovic because he had notched up his first Grand Slam title. 2009 and 2010, as we have seen, saw the Serb win many tournaments and confirm his status as principal challenger to Messrs Federer and Nadal. Yet those two years had been frustrating for him as he had not backed up his initial Slam or quite reached the very pinnacle of his sport. That crucial stride was taken in 2011. At the Australian Open, Djokovic overcame Federer, the defending champion, in straight sets in the semi-final and meted out the same treatment to Andy Murray in the final. At the French Open, Djokovic fell short, beaten in four sets by an inspired Roger Federer in the semi-final, but, of monumental significance, Djokovic won the Wimbledon singles with a superb display against Rafel Nadal, winning 6–3 in the fourth set.

That achievement was then backed up by Djokovic's quite outstanding performance at the US Open. There, two matches were revealing of just how far Djokovic, who had shown some mental frailty in tight matches in earlier years, had travelled. In the semi-finals at Flushing Meadows, Roger Federer in the words of the American commentator Leif Shiras, 'controlled the real estate' for two sets, staying on the baseline, not retreating, but taking the ball on the rise, hustling Djokovic, firing winners and bossing around the younger man. Far from wilting, Djokovic hung in, capitalised on a slight dip in Federer's level, and quickly recovered to two sets apiece. Intriguingly, it was Federer who broke serve first in the final set and who led 5–3 with two match points at 40–15 on his own serve. Djokovic hit a superb winning forehand off a very respectable Federer first serve to save one and teased an error from the Swiss to save the other. Djokovic then broke back and broke again, going on to take the match 7–5 in the fifth set. That win was big – because it was against Federer, because it was for the second successive year from match points down and because it put him in a final in which once again he could attempt to demonstrate mastery over Nadal. That final produced play from both men, but particularly Djokovic, of such stunning quality – in terms of power, length, accuracy of groundstrokes and breathtaking physical endurance over long rallies – that the crowd 'oohed' and 'aahed' at regular intervals. Djokovic prevailed 6–2, 6–4, 6–7, 6–1 to lift his third Grand Slam title of the year, and his fourth in total. In addition in 2011, he had won another seven tournaments, including a record-breaking five Masters 1000 titles, and he had beaten the formidable Rafael Nadal six times on three different surfaces. All who observed Djokovic in 2011 must have realised that they were witnessing a sportsman at the peak of his powers.

Nadal himself described Djokovic's performances as 'probably the highest level of tennis I ever saw'. The Serb finished the season with a win–loss record of 70–6 and ranked number one in the world. No longer the young pretender yapping at the heels of Nadal and Federer, Djokovic had overtaken both of them.

He began 2012 by underlining how and why he had made the gigantic stride to the top of the world rankings. In the semi-final of the Australian Open, he squared up against Andy Murray, who offered vastly tougher resistance than in the 2011 final. Ultimately, after four hours and fifty minutes, Djokovic was victorious, recovering from two sets to one down, saving break points at 5–5 in the final set and taking it 7–5. This win itself demanded huge physical exertion and mental strength alike. Yet only forty-eight hours later, against an opponent as dogged, relentless and effective as any in modern times, Djokovic beat Rafael Nadal in five sets, 5–7, 6–4, 6–2, 6–7, 7–5, having trailed 4–2 in the final set. That match lasted five hours and fifty-three minutes, the longest Grand Slam final in the Open era. Thereafter, 2012 was still good for Djokovic but, perhaps almost inevitably after the near invincibility of 2011, not quite as good. A semi-final loser in Indian Wells, Djokovic won in Miami, lost in Monte Carlo and Rome to Nadal and, reaching the French Open final for the first time, lost to Nadal there too. That defeat in four sets was compounded by a similar four-set defeat at the hands of Roger Federer in the semi-finals at Wimbledon. Narrowly missing out on an Olympic medal, Djokovic retained his Rogers Cup title, lost in the Cincinnati Masters final to Federer, and was beaten in five sets in the US Open final by Andy Murray.

Following that reverse, he retained his China Open title, won the Shanghai Masters over Murray, and ended the year in style, winning the ATP World Tour finals in London with a tight straight-sets victory over Roger Federer. He had started the year as world number one, been knocked off his perch for four months by a resurgent Roger Federer and then ended 2012 where he started – on top of the world.

2013 started strongly for Djokovic as he won a record third consecutive Australian Open in January, defeating Andy Murray in the final in four sets, his sixth Grand Slam title. That was followed by another title in Dubai. At present, Djokovic continues to play with great assurance, although he knows that doing so requires constant application, constant focus and constant performance under pressure. In 2013 as a whole, Djokovic won a sprinkling of tournaments but was unable to win a Slam after the Australian Open. In the French Open, he lost an eyewateringly close semi-final to Nadal (9–7 in the final set); at Wimbledon he was runner-up to Andy Murray; at the US Open he was beaten in the final by Nadal in four sets. However, the Serb did enjoy the consolation of winning the World Tour finals at the O2 in November, coming through the group stage undefeated and beating Nadal in straight sets in the final.

For years, as we have seen, Djokovic stood at number three in the world, a fine player but, with a single Grand Slam to his credit, heavily outshone by Federer and Nadal alike. Today he stands above Federer and neck-and-neck with Nadal – which inevitably poses the question: what has changed? The simple answer is that, in the two years from 2011, he improved when they did not or, at the very least, improved more than they did. A fuller answer is required to illuminate the reader, as there is more than one factor involved.

First, Djokovic has ironed out the technical problems which bedevilled his service in earlier years. Improving the penetration, consistency and accuracy of his first and second deliveries alike, the service is no longer a burden to bear but a weapon to wield. By winning more cheap points and blunting opponents' attack, he has reduced the pressure on himself and increased the pressure on them.

Secondly, Djokovic has developed the best service return in the game. Over and over and over again, he returns opponents' services with interest, frequently achieving remarkable length and placing the onus on the server to press harder to produce something exceptional to win the point. This has a hugely wearing effect on opponents, often inducing errors and producing the service break Djokovic requires.

Thirdly, in addition to being a superb ball-striker when attacking, Djokovic has raised his fitness level to such an extent that he defends better than ever and probably better than anyone, with the possible exception of Andy Murray and Rafa Nadal. His footwork is so good that he is overwhelmingly in the right position; he is so fast that he can chase down and return balls that others would not reach, and his staggering stamina is such that he can play, even in intense heat, for four, five or six hours if required. This he simply could not do before 2011 and on occasions he had retired from exhaustion.

Fourthly, as the saying goes, success breeds success. He has acquired not complacency, which would be fatal, but the self-confidence, driven by the stubborn insistence on ultimate victory which impels him to keep going in adversity and to produce his best when he needs it most.

In short, he has come to acquire an aura, if not of invincibility, at any rate of unbreakability. Psychologically, this is a huge advantage and puts Djokovic in a wholly different place to the one he was in before 2011. If he remains fit, the Serb should have at least five more years playing at the highest level. No one knows which or how many titles he will win, but he has done enough already to prove that he is a big champion, an amazing competitor and one of the greats of the game.

The Greatest of the Greats

I HOPE THAT you have enjoyed reading about the 'greats' of men's tennis. If you are already a connoisseur, the chapters might each have been useful as a potted reminder of the phenomenal exploits of individual illustrious champions. If you are a general reader with some interest but not a compendious knowledge, they will perhaps have offered welcome enlightenment.

I said in the introduction to this book that the choice of the top twenty could not realistically be viewed as a matter of indisputable fact. Inevitably, the similarities of record between different players meant that the judgement as to whom to include (and therefore exclude) would be subjective and, ultimately, personal. That said, many readers could be forgiven for reacting to the book by saying, 'Yes, but what about X? Why wasn't he included?'

Let me start by placing the matter in context. Fifty-two men have won three or more Grand Slam singles titles. All but one of the champions celebrated in this book reached that total (mostly rather more). The only exception was Pancho Gonzales, who won two Slams as an amateur, turned professional – thereby rendering himself ineligible, as it transpired, to participate in Grand Slam tournaments for twenty years – and won fifteen professional Slams and was world professional champion for eight years. Ilie Năstase won two Slams and was a huge talent but I doubt that many commentators would complain at his exclusion from a list of twenty titans of men's tennis. Lleyton Hewitt and Andy Murray have both won two Slams and are still playing. The second of the

Slam successes for Hewitt was in 2002 but he is still competing and anything is possible. Andy Murray has notched up his dramatic successes in the last two years and only a fool would deny that he has a great chance in the next five years of adding, perhaps very significantly, to his total.

From the past, there is a rich galaxy of fine players who missed the cut for the top twenty. Bobby Riggs, the American, won three Slams and was highly regarded by no less an authority than Jack Kramer (as Vines had been). But Riggs was at the top relatively briefly and did not dominate in the way that Fred Perry, Don Budge or Bill Tilden did. Admirers of the great Tony Trabert, who won five Grand Slam singles titles, could argue for his recognition but I feel that, superb though he was, Gonzales and Hoad were more so. Ellsworth Vines was a notable champion of the 1930s who played a blistering game, and he is admired by many commentators. However, his title tally was modest and although he worsted Fred Perry in their head-to-head encounters, Perry achieved much greater success overall. The Australian Jack Crawford won six Slams but I confess to believing that players who have done so in the Open era – a more competitive era with a larger field of high-quality players than ever – are still more deserving of recognition. The same argument applies to the great French Musketeers, Jean Borotra, Henri Cochet and René Lacoste. The latter two each won seven of the ten Slam finals that they contested. John Newcombe, the big-serving Australian, also won seven Slam singles, five of them in the Open era, but others, to my mind, had a slight edge over him. The Swede Mats Wilander won seven of eleven Slam finals and was a superb performer but, from the same period, Edberg and Becker arguably did, overall, still better. The list of 'near misses' given above is by no means exhaustive, but it does demonstrate to the reader that the choice is not simple. For all that, I believe that every one of the top twenty was or is very special and deserves to be considered above the larger pack of champions not included.

Ah yes, but which of the champions, you might ask, is the greatest? A good place to start, and some believe also the best place to finish, is with an attempted comparison of players from the same generation. The first group is surely those who played before 1945 – namely, Bill Tilden, Fred Perry and Don Budge. Let us remind ourselves of their respective achievements. Tilden won ten Grand Slam singles titles and was twice a finalist in the French Open. In addition, he won four professional majors and was the losing finalist at the Wembley professional tournament three times. He also featured in the successful US Davis Cup team for seven consecutive years from 1920 to 1926. Generally recognised to be the first great champion, he won 138 career titles – albeit not recognised by the ATP, which did not then exist – and boasted a career win–loss record of 907–62, or 93.6 per cent. He scarcely lost a match over a period of seven years and his record is frankly awesome.

What are we to make of Perry and Budge? Budge states in his memoir that 'after enduring Vines's power game, I never felt any real pressure against Perry'. Perry was a year and a half older than Vines but won his first Slam (the US Open) in 1933, compared with the maiden victory of Vines in 1931, also at the US Open. In the head-to-head battle, Perry played Vines in 1937 and 1938 no fewer than 162 times, Vines winning eighty-eight matches and Perry seventy-four. Yet the head-to-head record is not the only guide to who was the better player. Also relevant is the overall level of success. At the risk of sticking my neck out, I would argue that Perry, with eight Slam titles as an amateur and two as a runner-up, together with the fact that he won all four majors, is slightly greater than Vines. Despite taking all four titles, Perry did not dominate the sport to the extent Tilden did and therefore ranks below the first great champion.

Budge won six Grand Slam singles titles as an amateur. In addition, he claimed four professional majors, made up of two US Pro titles, a Wembley Pro and a French Pro. Most importantly, amongst those victories, he won the Grand Slam of all four major titles in the same year, 1938, two days before he turned twenty-three. To this day, he is the youngest holder of the Grand Slam distinction and only Rod Laver has since achieved it (twice). In the head-to-head stakes, Budge overcame Vines by twenty-two matches to seventeen and Perry by twenty-eight matches to eight. After 1942, Budge joined the US Army Air Force and subsequently he tore a shoulder muscle, suffering irreparable damage and later being overtaken by Bobby Riggs. Budge was demonstrably superior to both Vines and Perry. Budge was more than twenty-two years junior to Tilden and, though Budge got much the better of their contests, the head-to-head between Budge and Tilden is by no means conclusive. Tilden was at the top for longer but Budge won the Grand Slam and probably faced a greater range of high-class opponents. For me, the balance of evidence suggests that of this great group Budge should be ranked first, followed by Tilden and then Perry.

The next collection of titans comprises Jack Kramer, Pancho Gonzales, Ken Rosewall, Lew Hoad, Roy Emerson and Rod Laver. Again, just as Budge was not a direct contemporary of Tilden, Kramer (the eldest of this second group) and Laver (the youngest) were more than seventeen years apart. The first fascinating comparison is between Kramer and Gonzales. As we saw earlier, they were not friends; sometimes they could be even said to be enemies. Kramer, writing in 1979, is generally complimentary about Gonzales and clearly respected him as one of the greats, though he made it clear that he considered himself to be the greater player. Let us take another look.

Jack Kramer won three Grand Slam singles titles as an amateur and a further two professional majors. His amateur career was suspended for six years by World War II, otherwise Kramer might well have won major titles long before the age of twenty-five, when he first won the US Championships. Kramer turned professional to take on Bobby Riggs and won their tour but, more importantly, he thumped Gonzales by ninety-six matches to twenty-seven. Game, set, and match to Kramer...

Well, actually, no. Kramer had been the established pro champion for over two years. Gonzales, only twenty-one, was just joining the pro ranks and had by no means reached his peak. If Kramer's amateur title haul was comparatively modest at three majors, a record then interrupted by war and concluded by turning professional, the trophy title of Gonzales as an amateur was even more modest. He won two Slam singles, both at the US Open, and he never won Wimbledon, the Australian Open or the French Open.

However, there is an especially good explanation in Gonzales's case. He turned professional in 1949 and was then barred from competing in any of the four major championships until the advent of the Open era in 1968, by which time he was forty and past his best. Yet, as a professional, he won fifteen major titles – eight US Pros (including seven in succession), four Wembley Pros and three Tournaments of Champions. Just as he never managed to win the French title as an amateur – reaching only the semi-final twice, in 1949 and, incredibly, in 1968 – so he did not win the French Pro title but was twice the losing finalist. Gonzales won far more than Kramer and stayed at the top for much longer. Bud Collins is said to have observed, 'If I had to choose someone to play for my life, it would be Pancho Gonzales.' Both were tennis giants. Kramer probably achieved far more for the game by promoting professional tennis and pressing for an end to the artificial barrier between professionals and amateurs, leading to the Open era. Yet this book is about champion players and, for me, Gonzales was the greater champion.

Ken Rosewall won eight Grand Slam singles titles over a period of seventeen years from the age of nineteen to a couple of months before he turned thirty-six. He was also a losing finalist at Wimbledon four times – in 1954, 1956, 1970 and 1974. He won fifteen professional majors, two US Pro, five Wembley Pro and eight French Pro (including seven in a row). He also won the WCT Tour finals twice, defeating Rod Laver on both occasions. He won an estimated 133 career titles, was world number one in the early 1960s and stayed in the top twenty for twenty-five years. His record of consistent achievement is, to this day, quite extraordinary. Although he never won Wimbledon, he could certainly play on grass, as his success in the Australian Open and US Open – both played on grass at the time – clearly proves.

Lew Hoad won four Grand Slam singles titles. In addition, he won the Tournament of Champions as a professional in 1959 and was the runner-up in seven professional major finals in the US, UK and France. As we saw in Chapter Seven, Hoad was the most offensive of players, constantly on the attack, a brilliant shot-maker and, when on song, widely thought to be unplayable. Jack Kramer compared him with Ellsworth Vines and many other commentators have emphasised the breathtaking brilliance of Hoad at his best. Yet, quite apart from the fact that between 1955 and 1964 he trailed Rosewall by forty-five matches to twenty-five, his overall record does not compare favourably with that of Rosewall. Even allowing for his back troubles over the years, Hoad was nowhere near as consistent a performer as Rosewall or Gonzales and was not able to continue playing at the highest level as long as Gonzales, Rosewall or Laver.

As we saw in Chapter Eight, Roy Emerson set a new record of twelve Grand Slam singles titles – unsurpassed until Pete Sampras bettered it in 2000 – and was a big figure in the sport. That said, the fact that so many of his major titles were won as an amateur when the best players had turned professional inevitably puts him at a disadvantage in any comparisons with other players. Ken Rosewall and Rod Laver were undoubtedly his superiors. In the Open era, Rosewll led Emerson three matches to one and Laver by the even more striking margin of 4:1. Unfortunately, I can find no evidence of the head-to-head record between Emerson and Hoad. Laver, who played both many times, rates Hoad above Emerson. On the other hand, statistically, in terms of Slams, Emerson is ahead. In terms of overall quality of play and performance at their peaks, I would place Hoad above Emerson.

Rod Laver won eleven Grand Slam singles titles as an amateur. Yet the single most important fact about Rod Laver and the major titles is that he won the Grand Slam – all four majors in the same year – not once, but twice. He did it in 1962 before he turned professional and he did it again on his return to the All England Club in the second year of the Open era. He also won eight professional majors, three in the US, four in the UK and one in France. He won an estimated 200 career titles (though only forty-one have been recognised by the ATP) and he was part of a winning Australian Davis Cup team five times, in 1959 to 1962 and then again in 1973. Rosewall stayed at the top of the game longer and won Slam finals over a period of seventeen years compared with Laver's nine but Laver led Rosewall in their head-to-head by seventy-nine matches to sixty-three. Overall, to my mind, Laver's record is better on account of his winning the Grand Slam twice. Only two players in history have won the Grand Slam. Budge did it twenty-four years before Laver first achieved it. In the forty-four years since Laver won it for the second time, no one has managed it. Of the six greats just assessed, Emerson surely ranks sixth, Hoad fifth and Kramer fourth. Gonzales and Rosewall both have fantastic records. The 'titles won' criterion points to Rosewall but Gonzales was world professional champion for eight years and is thought to have enjoyed a head-to-head superiority over Rosewall of 107 to 75. For me, Gonzales just pips Rosewall, so Laver, Gonzales, Rosewall, Kramer, Hoad and Emerson should be placed in that order.

I tend to view Connors, Borg, McEnroe and Lendl as a quartet. Although not precise contemporaries – and head-to-head comparisons should always allow for that – they played in the same era and can readily be compared.

Connors won eight Slams, Borg eleven, McEnroe seven and Lendl eight. Connors won three of the four major titles, failing only to capture the French Open in which four semi-final appearances were his best performance. He is alone in winning the US Open on three different surfaces, was ranked world number one for a total of 268 weeks, won more singles titles (109) than any other man since the advent of Open tennis and won both the Tour finals and the WCT finals (the latter twice). His career win–loss record is second only to that of Björn Borg. In addition, he reached the quarter-final or better of no fewer than forty-one Grand Slam tournaments, matched only by Roger Federer.

Borg won three more Slams than Connors. The American did not win the French Open, but Borg did not win the Australian Open or the US Open, though he was runner-up in the latter four times. Borg also won the Tour finals twice and the WCT finals once. On the main professional tour, Borg and Connors played twenty-three times, Borg leading fifteen matches to eight. Borg was ranked world number one for 108 weeks – a far shorter period than Connors's 268 weeks – and he won sixty-four career titles, as against Connors's 109. The truth is that their records are different in a number of ways. Borg did much better at Wimbledon and at the French Open; Connors did better in the US. Borg achieved dramatic success over six years; Connors won major titles over nine. Borg effectively quit the sport a couple of years after winning his final Slam; Connors continued for well over a decade after he claimed his last major title. Connors is thought to have played 1,532 matches on the tour, Borg 735. For persistence at or near the top, Connors outdoes Borg. For victories at the highest level, Borg outdoes Connors. For two reasons, Borg is the greater champion. First, it is remarkable almost beyond words that a clay-court player trained himself to transition to grass so successfully that he won Wimbledon five times on the spin. This achievement has no contemporary parallel. Secondly, the fact that on three occasions (1978–80) Borg won the French Open on clay and followed up his success by victory at Wimbledon on grass only a month later is astonishing. Such success obviously required an unruffled, forensic and relentless focus on the job but it also demanded great adaptability between very different surfaces.

What are we to make of the claims of McEnroe? In terms of exquisite artistry and natural talent, McEnroe was greater than either of the above. His range of shot-making skills, what he could do with a ball and the sheer quality of his service and volleys at their best were superior to those of Connors and probably to those of Borg too. In terms of the statistics, McEnroe won seven majors and seventy-seven career titles. He also won the Tour finals three times – better than the Borg or Connors record – and the WCT finals no fewer than five times. His career win–loss record in singles was only marginally inferior to that of Borg and Connors but, perhaps most strikingly, he was a key member of the successful US Davis Cup team five times. His Slam singles triumphs were notched up over a shorter period than those of Borg, but he was at or close to the top for considerably longer as he retired in 1992, ranked twentieth in the world and aged thirty-three whereas Borg departed the scene aged twenty-six. On the other hand, McEnroe did not compete for anything like as long as Connors on the main tour. McEnroe was level 7–7 in his head-to-head rivalry with Borg and his overall singles record is less great than that of the Swede. In head-to-head terms he got the better of Connors to the tune of 20–14 but won fewer tournaments. It is tough to choose between these two titans but my sense is this: McEnroe was the more talented and, at his peak, a better player but Connors was the more successful. McEnroe had a greater abundance of gifts but did not always use them to full advantage. Connors exploited to the maximum every ounce of ability to the full, and was also probably the fitter of the two. If a part of greatness is the fulfilment of potential, Connors scored close to maximum points. McEnroe, the sometimes wayward genius, did not. Although his tantrums often distracted opponents, they also harmed him, either there and then in a match, e.g. the 1982 Wimbledon final, or subsequently. By a narrow head, therefore, Connors pips McEnroe.

Lendl also won eight majors and racked up ninety-four ATP Tour career titles, a record second only to Connors. He won the Tour finals five times and the WCT finals twice. His win–loss record was 1071–239, (81.8 per cent) – like Connors, he played a very large number of matches – and in the head-to-head with Connors he led 22–13, though Connors won their final-round encounters 4–2 and several of Lendl's victories came when

Connors was beyond his prime. Against McEnroe, Lendl had a 21–15 advantage. McEnroe will savour his defeats of Lendl in the US Open final in 1984 and the Volvo Masters final staged in January 1985. Yet the sweetest victory for Lendl – and the bitterest pill for McEnroe – was the French Open final in 1984. Coming from two sets behind and 4–2 down in the fourth set, Lendl eventually won their encounter 3–6, 2–6, 6–4, 7–5, 7–5. In 1985 at the US Open, Lendl prevailed over McEnroe in straight sets. Importantly, Lendl ended the year as world number one in 1985, 1986, 1987 and 1989 and held the top spot in total for 270 weeks, two weeks longer than Connors.

Lendl did not exert the seismic impact on tennis that Borg achieved and, to my mind, was not as outstanding. The comparison with Connors is arguable either way but my feeling is twofold. First, Connors was a big competitor in the game for longer. Secondly, Connors was not naturally a grass-court player – preferring hard courts – but albeit much less spectacularly than Borg, Connors came to terms with grass to the extent that he won Wimbledon twice. Lendl never came to be fully comfortable on grass and, by a modest degree, Connors's track record is superior, not least his extraordinary performance in Slams over nearly two decades. However, just as Connors outdoes McEnroe, so, I suggest, does Lendl. I preferred watching McEnroe who, leaving aside the histrionics which endeared him to some and repelled others, was as great a natural talent as any of the twenty, with the possible exception of Roger Federer. Of course Lendl had talent, but not the variety, touch or balletic quality of McEnroe. Lendl had a machine-like quality. The words indomitable, self-disciplined, remorseless – yes, even ruthless – spring to mind. Was Lendl as entertaining as McEnroe? No. Yet he won more by extracting every last ounce of advantage that he legitimately could out of the talent and commitment he exhibited, greatly improving his mental strength in order to do so. For that reason, he ranks ahead of McEnroe. Borg, Connors, Lendl and then McEnroe is my reading of the order of those great contemporaries.

Kramer and Gonzales disliked each other and there appears to have been mutual antipathy between Messrs Connors, McEnroe and Lendl. Doubtless such antipathy adds spice to a rivalry and is grist to the media mill, but there is no sign of such hostility between Boris Becker and Stefan Edberg, both of whom won six Slam singles titles. Theirs was a great rivalry, reflected not merely in their Slam encounters but in a total of thirty-five matches between the two players from 1984 to 1996. The pair were evenly matched and judging which of them was the better is not straightforward. Becker won the head-to-head battle by twenty-five matches to ten and all three of their Davis Cup clashes. On the other hand, Edberg was victorious in three of their four Grand Slam encounters and of their three successive Wimbledon finals, Edberg won two of them. In Becker's favour is the fact that he is the youngest man, aged just seventeen, to win the singles at Wimbledon and that, alongside his Slam successes, he won the Tour finals three times and the WCT finals once. Edberg won the Tour finals once and the Olympic singles bronze medal in 1988 (as well as the doubles). Becker won forty-nine career titles to Edberg's forty-two and had a modestly higher win–loss ratio of 76.9 per cent to 74.9 per cent. Yet Edberg, and this is perhaps significant, held the world number one ranking for seventy-two as against twelve weeks for Becker. In one sense, Becker might be regarded as the bigger of the titans in that he caused a sensation by the truly breathtaking achievement of winning Wimbledon so young. That victory attracted huge interest to Becker, often making life difficult for him by engendering absurdly high expectations of the man, as described in Chapter Fourteen. Yet it can be argued, as we saw earlier, that Becker, hugely success-ful though he was, might have been expected to win even more titles given his auspicious debut. Edberg was the less flamboyant character but he bestrode the peak of the mountain for some-what longer. In truth, there is precious little difference between them as champions, but that persistence as number one probably eases it for Edberg.

From the early 1990s to the early 2000s, the Sampras–Agassi rivalry was one to savour, not least because of their contrasting styles. Sampras, possessed of a cannonball serve, thrived on serve-and-volley play; Agassi was the greatest returner in the game and unsurpassed at his best from the back of the court. Sampras, as we saw, won fourteen Grand Slam singles titles to Agassi's eight and Sampras held the world number one ranking for 286 weeks, beating the Lendl record and overtaken only by Roger Federer in 2012. In the head-to-head, Sampras led 20–14, including winning three of their four Grand Slam encounters. Agassi was world number one for over 100 weeks and in one respect could claim superiority, namely that he did win each of the major titles whereas Sampras, ill at ease on clay courts, never won the French Open. Of course, at the time, the courts were somewhat faster, favouring the server, whereas the enhanced synthetic strings which later came to favour the returner had yet to be developed. Agassi might well have fared better in today's conditions and, at the very least, Sampras would have had to adapt or suffer. Yet we can judge credibly only by the circumstances they faced and, overall, Sampras had the advantage and was the more dominant champion.

Today's rivalry between Messrs Federer, Nadal and Djokovic (mentioned in that order because that was the order in which they first won major titles) differs from all of the others in that all three are still competing and their ranking in relation to each other and in the list of all-time greats is a potentially moveable feast. As of now, Federer has won seventeen major titles, including all four of the Slams, and seventy-eight career titles. He was ranked number one in the world for 302 weeks, an all-time record.

Rafael Nadal has won thirteen Slams, including all four of the major titles and sixty-three career titles, and he also won the Olympic singles gold medal in 2008. At the time of writing he had been world number one for a total of 116 weeks. Nadal leads Roger Federer in their head-to-head by twenty-three matches to ten and he has a 22–18 advantage over Novak Djokovic.

Djokovic has six Slam titles to his name but he has yet to win the French Open. He has won forty-one career titles and enjoyed a total of 101 weeks as world number one. Although the Serb has a modest deficit in matches with Rafael Nadal, he has won far more of their contests since the great leap forward in his career in 2011. Against Roger Federer, he trails at 16–18, Federer having won most of their matches before 2010 and Djokovic more often emerging victorious in the last three years.

At present, Federer has the best record in Slams, career titles and tenure at the very top and deserves to be ranked above the other two. Over the last four years, Nadal has been gaining ground, winning seven majors in that period to Federer's two. Nadal has yet to match Federer's overall record but that could yet change. Djokovic has proved superb since 2011 but has much ground still to make up if he is to rival the total accomplishments of the Swiss and the Spaniard.

In sport as a whole today, the interest in records and how the performance of one player or team compares with that of another is intense. Many sports fans are fascinated by the statistics and who is or was better than whom. Tennis is no exception and many readers will ask, 'Where should we rank the twenty titans of men's tennis, not merely within the generations but across them?' In short, what is the pecking order? Before even attempting to answer this question, there are a number of points, some immediately obvious and others less so, that need to be made. First, modern rackets are conducive to the easier generation of greater power than the comparatively leaden wooden rackets of forty years ago and vastly more so compared with the small-head wooden rackets of the Bill Tilden era. Moreover, alongside the capacity to produce much greater racket head speed from most shots, the synthetic strings which top players now tend to favour also make it easier for a player to hit hard but still control the ball than it was when gut strings were generally used.

Secondly, it is only fair to point out that the surfaces on which most tournaments are played have changed. In the past, more majors were played on grass. Today only Wimbledon takes place on turf, and the Australian and US Opens are played on hard courts. On the whole, surfaces are now slower and this has led to more baseline play and longer rallies.

Thirdly, we can but speculate as to how the likes of Tilden or Budge would have adapted to modern rackets and court conditions and, conversely, whether and, if so, to what extent a Borg, a Sampras, a Federer or a Nadal would have coped with the conditions of 1930s tennis.

Fourthly, sports science, diet awareness and the rigour and sophistication of fitness training regimes are far advanced on what they were fifty, let alone eighty, years ago. If he were competing today, Bill Tilden could not consume a steak and fried potatoes followed by ice cream an hour before squaring up against a super-fit gluten-free diet purist by the name of Novak Djokovic and expect to hold his own. However, it is perhaps reasonable to assume both that past titans would have been able to deploy superior rackets to their advantage and that, competing in a different era, they would have adjusted their diet and training regimes to stay competitive.

Just two further observations at this stage should be made. First, past champions might be thought to be at a disadvantage to today's giants and vice versa but in different ways. On the one hand, until relatively recently, many champions did not always play all of the Slams, either for reasons of journey distance or because they had won a particular Slam and didn't feel the need to repeat the experience. This was not irrational because the focus on breaking records did not apply, becoming a preoccupation of the top players only over the last thirty years or so. If they had chased umpteen titles, they might have won them. On the other hand, it can be argued that life is particularly tough for today's champions because the sheer depth of top-flight professional competitors is such that the leaders of the pack have to work excruciatingly hard to stay ahead of the ten, twenty, even thirty players behind them. Moreover, because there are over a hundred guys making some kind of living on the professional tour, a top ten player can lose to someone ranked fifty or even a hundred places below on a bad day for him and a good day for the challenger. That has happened at Wimbledon in 2012 and 2013, for example, to Nadal (twice) and Federer. Such a fate was unlikely to befall a Tilden, a Budge or a Kramer.

Second, there is much surely to be said for Jack Kramer's contention that whilst rackets, strings and court surfaces change, the basic ingredients of champions do not. Talent, hard work, sound temperament, the capacity to perform under pressure, to raise one's game to meet a threat, have been perennial requirements of great champions down the ages and remain so today. Moreover, it is possible to admire both the magnificence of earlier eras' champions and to cheer with equal fervour contemporary greats. For my part, I admire what Tilden did to make himself the best and I salute the achievements of the maestros in later decades. I confess that I do not share the view of those who bemoan today's game for its alleged lack of variety. To my mind, the quality of men's tennis today is outstanding and just as there have been golden eras in the past, what we are witnessing now is very special indeed. As a boy and young man in the 1970s and '80s, I was in awe of Connors, Borg, McEnroe and Lendl, to give but four examples, but I find it hard to exaggerate just how exquisite is the performance of today's champions.

All of the above said, there are only two methods for comparing past greats with present greats, both of them problematic. One of them is to deploy a narrow statistical approach of computing win–loss ratios and counting titles. This is a possible guide but deeply flawed. For years, Tilden faced little serious competition and enjoyed a flabbergasting level of match success, but it does not prove that he was better than, say, Rod Laver. A second method is to look both at records – tournaments won, performances delivered, consistency shown, dominance achieved in the sport – and at the conditions in which they were achieved – before offering what is inevitably a subjective, even speculative view, as to the respective greatness of the greats. Subject to the caveat that it can in no way be more than a piece of educated guesswork, my preference is for that second method. It is fun to ponder the order on court. This would be mine:

20. Roy Emerson
19. Lew Hoad
18. Boris Becker
17. Stefan Edberg
16. Novak Djokovic
15. Fred Perry
14. Jack Kramer
13. John McEnroe
12. Ivan Lendl
11. Jimmy Connors
10. Ken Rosewall
 9. Pancho Gonzales
 8. Andre Agassi
 7. Bill Tilden
 6. Björn Borg
 5. Pete Sampras
 4. Don Budge
 3. Rod Laver
 2. Rafael Nadal
 1. Roger Federer.

I am aware that virtually no one will agree completely with this assessment; that is part of the charm of the exercise. Indeed, it may not be long before I change my own mind, either because of the performance of a contemporary player or because the discussion which I seek to stimulate through this book obliges me to rethink my own rankings. I can already anticipate a lobby which will argue that I have penalised John McEnroe too harshly for not, as far as I am concerned, fulfilling a potential which might have allowed him up to twice the Grand Slam titles which he won, or that I have been too kind to Andre Agassi because of his achievement in winning all four major titles. Admirers of Björn Borg and Rod Laver will understandably stake a claim for their man to be considered the most able of all time. For most observers who are not dedicated historians of the sport, and certainly for a lot of younger fans, there is a natural tendency to think of current greats. Some may think that Novak Djokovic warrants a higher ranking, but I reckon that his slot is a fair reflection of his performance to date. This lack of agreement is the intrinsic consequence of a volume such as this, which it has been my immense personal pleasure to undertake. As you may expect from a Speaker of the House of Commons, I welcome the debate which I hope will now follow.

Further Reading

- *Big Bill Tilden: The Triumphs and the Tragedy*, Frank Deford (Simon & Schuster, 1975)
- *The Last Champion: The Life of Fred Perry*, Jon Henderson (Yellow Jersey, 2009)
- *Fred Perry: An Autobiography*, Fred Perry (Hutchinson, 1984)
- *Don Budge: A Tennis Memoir*, Don Budge (Viking, 1969)
- *The Game: My 40 Years in Tennis*, Jack Kramer and Frank Deford (André Deutsch, 1981)
- *Man with a Racket: The Autobiography of Pancho Gonzales*, as told to Cy Rice (Thomas Yoseloff, 1959)
- *Ken Rosewall, Twenty Years at the Top*, Peter Rowley with Ken Rosewall (Cassell Publishers Ltd, 1976)
- *Muscles: The Story of Ken Rosewall*, Ken Rosewall as told to Richard Naughton (The Slattery Media Group, 2012)
- *Golden Boy: The Life and Times of Lew Hoad, a Tennis Legend*, Larry Hodgson and Dudley Jones (DSM, 2001)
- *The Outsider: My Autobiography*, Jimmy Connors (Bantam Press, 2013)
- *High Strung: Björn Borg, John McEnroe and the Untold Story of Tennis's Fiercest Rivalry*, Stephen Tignor (HarperCollins, 2011)
- *Serious: The Autobiography*, John McEnroe (Little, Brown, 2002)
- *Open: An Autobiography*, Andre Agassi (HarperCollins, 2009)

- *Boris Becker's Tennis: The Making of a Champion*, Boris Breskvar with Ulrich Kaiser (Springfield Books, 1987)
- *The Player: The Autobiography*, Boris Becker with Robert Lübenoff and Helmut Sorge (Bantam Press, 2004)
- *A Champion's Mind: Lessons from a Life in Tennis*, Pete Sampras with Peter Bodo (Aurum Press, 2009)
- *Fantastic Federer: The Biography of the World's Greatest Tennis Player*, Chris Bowers (John Blake Publishing, 2006)
- *Federer: The Biography*, Chris Bowers (John Blake Publishing, 2013)
- *Roger Federer: Quest for Perfection*, René Stauffer (New Chapter Press, 2010)
- *Total Tennis: The Ultimate Tennis Encyclopedia*, Bud Collins (ed.) (SPORTClassic Books, revised edition, 2004)
- *Wimbledon: Gentlemen's Singles Champions 1877–2011*, John Barrett and Alan Little (Wimbledon Lawn Tennis Museum, 2006)
- *Tennis: Myth and Method*, Ellsworth Vines and Gene Vier (Viking, 1978)

Index

Agassi, Andre 69, 101, 110, 167, 182, 183, 184, 186, 198, 199, 205–22, 228, 230, 234, 235, 236, 239, 246, 247, 249, 259, 268, 269, 304, 308, 309
Agassi, Betty 206
Agassi, Mike 206, 208, 213
Agassi, Philip 206
Agassi, Rita 206
Agassi, Tami 206
Allison, Wilmer 28, 29
Amdur, Neil; 84
Ani, Mario 247
Anderson, Mal 97
Andreev, Igor 253, 257
Anger, Matt 174
Annacone, Paul 191, 234
Arraya, Pablo 161
Ashe, Arthur 105, 127, 130, 138, 140, 141, 150
Austin, Bunny 19, 22, 35

Bale, Stuart 180
Baghdatis, Marcos 249, 250, 262, 283
Baltzell, E. Digby 41
Barrett, John 88, 92, 97, 98, 99, 174, 190, 196, 197, 200, 203
Bates, Jeremy 208
Becker, Boris 51, 69, 141, 165, 166, 167, 171–88, 190, 192, 193, 194, 195, 196, 197, 198, 199, 200, 201, 203, 209, 211, 213, 216, 232, 234, 236, 268, 269, 283, 294, 303, 208
Becker, Elvira 171, 176
Becker, Karl-Heinz 172
Bellamy, Rex 83, 113
Berdych, Tomáš 242, 257, 262, 263, 273, 274, 283, 287
Bergelin, Lennart 139
Berger, Jay 227

Bernard, Marcel 103

Blake, James 251, 284

Borg, Björn 31, 41, 54, 99, 118, 121, 129, 130, 131, 132, 133, 135–45, 147,
    151, 152, 153, 157, 160, 161, 162, 169, 187, 201, 202, 203, 218, 220, 225,
    237, 251, 252, 254, 270, 284, 299, 300, 301, 302, 306, 307, 308, 309

Borotra, Jean 20, 294

Bosch, Günter 172

Brandi, Joe 231

Breskvar, Boris 172

Brett, Bob 183

Bridge, Peter 109

Bromwich, John 34, 35, 53, 95

Brook, Rye 227

Brown, Tom 49, 50

Bruguera, Sergi 184, 217

Budge, Don 11, 17, 29, 30, 33–42, 48, 53, 54, 62, 65, 68, 74, 96, 97, 101, 110,
    114, 118, 129, 203, 217, 239, 294, 295, 296, 299, 306, 307, 308

Bungert, Wilhelm 103

Carillo, Mary 160

Cash, Pat 165, 166, 176, 193, 196

Casel, Sergio 178

Chang, Michael 184, 185, 197, 198, 199, 200, 201, 203, 214, 217, 225, 227,
    229, 234, 236

Čilić, Marin 257

Clément, Arnaud 218, 219

Clerc, José Luis 161

Cochet, Henri 10, 11, 20, 23, 24, 294

Collins, Bud 35, 85, 99, 104, 166, 176, 196, 197, 200, 201, 297

Cooke, Elwood 48

Cooper, Ashley 97, 98

Connors, Gloria 122–3, 124, 126

Connors, Jimmy 31, 40, 51, 54, 69, 73, 86, 87, 99, 118, 121–33, 135, 140,
    141, 142, 143, 144, 147, 150, 153, 154, 159, 161, 162, 163, 165, 168, 169,
    175, 180, 194, 200, 201, 203, 207, 208, 209, 219, 225, 231, 299, 300, 301,
    302, 303, 307

Connors, 'Two-Mom' 122, 125, 126

Corretja, Àlex 234

Costa, Albert 247, 268

Courier, Jim 183, 184, 198, 200, 201, 211, 212, 227, 231, 232, 233

Cowan, Barry 246

Crawford, Jack 24, 25, 26, 28, 29, 34, 76, 92, 294

Cronin, Ned 67

Curren, Kevin 163, 175, 176, 192

Danzig, Allison 48, 78, 83
Darmon, Pierre 103
Davies, Mike 85, 116
Davidson, Owen 105
Davidson, Sven 96
Davydenko, Nikolay 240, 251, 257, 272, 285
De Morpurgo, Umberto 20
De Stefani, Giorgio 24
Del Potro, Juan Martín 255, 256, 262, 272
Dent, Phil 127, 128, 129
Deford, Frank 2, 3, 4, 5, 7, 8, 10, 12
Dempster, Hugh 24–5
Dibbs, Eddie 124, 126, 138, 211, 226
Drobn, Jaroslav 49, 50, 61, 62, 73, 77, 78, 86, 92, 93, 94, 95
Djokovic, Novak 69, 203, 205, 220, 242, 252, 253, 256, 258, 259, 260, 261,
    262, 263, 271, 272, 273, 274, 275, 279–92, 304, 305, 306, 308, 309
Djokovic, Srđjan 279
Dwyer, Don 147

Edberg, Stefan 51, 69, 166, 173, 178, 179, 180, 181, 182, 183, 185, 189–204,
    211, 229, 232, 233, 236, 262, 263, 294, 303, 308
Emerson, Roy 70, 95, 101–8, 114, 117, 118, 125, 145, 149, 217, 220, 235,
    236, 239, 296, 298, 299, 308
Enquist, Thomas 214
Eriksson, Robert 214
Evans, Richard 85

Falkenburg, Bob 61
Falla, Alexandro 257
Farquharson, Norman 23
Federer, Roger 41, 69, 83, 101, 110, 118, 119, 121, 122, 133, 135, 144, 145,
    151, 154, 159, 168, 190, 203, 205, 217, 219, 220, 223, 236, 239–63, 268,
    269, 270, 271, 272, 273, 274, 275, 282, 283, 284, 285, 286, 287, 288, 289,
    290, 300, 302, 304, 305, 306, 307, 308
Ferrer, David 258, 259, 272, 273, 274, 282, 285
Ferreira, Wayne 214
Ferrero, Juan Carlos 247, 248, 252
Fischer, Peter 224, 225, 228
Fish, Mardy 247
Fisher, Carl 3, 5
Fitzgerald, John 181
Flach, Dough 217
Flaherty, Vincent X. 67
Flam, Herbie 60
Forget, Guy 183, 214, 231

Froehling, Frank 103

Gallico, Paul 7
Gasquet, Richard 252, 282
Genčić, Jelena 280
Gerulaitis, Vitas 125, 142, 143, 151, 161, 162
Giammalva Jr, Sammy 227
Gilbert, Brad 182, 192, 198, 199, 200, 214, 219, 232
Gimeno, Andrés 82, 115
Gómez, Andrés 210–11, 228
Gonzales, Pancho 27, 38, 51, 53, 54, 57–71, 75, 80, 81, 82, 88, 92, 97, 98, 99, 115, 118, 151, 168, 190, 201, 203, 206, 218, 293, 294, 296, 297, 299, 303, 308
González, Fernando 249, 251, 271
Gorman, Tom 127
Grant, Bitsy 36
Gregory, Colin 21
Grimsby, Will 41
Guillermo, Vilas 131, 140, 142, 161, 162, 163
Gulbis, Ernests 285
Gullikson, Tim 151
Gullikson, Tom 231, 232, 233

Haarhuis, Paul 200, 202
Haas, Tommy 219, 247, 250, 255, 286
Haase, Robin 272
Hănescu, Victor 257
Harris, Jack 52
Harris, Joe 91
Hartwig, Rex 77, 94, 95, 96
Heldman, Julius 39, 113
Henderson, Jon 15, 16, 17, 22, 23, 25
Henman, Tim 246, 249
Hewitt, Bob 103, 126
Hewitt, Lleyton 235, 247, 248, 249, 255, 257, 263, 293, 294
Hillyard, Brame 26
Hippenstiel, Robin 45
Hlasek, Jakob 197
Hoad, Lew 66, 68, 71, 73, 78, 79, 80, 81, 82, 91–9, 114, 118, 139, 149, 294, 296, 298, 299, 308
Hollis, Charlie 111, 112
Hopman, Harry 35, 36, 77, 78, 93, 111, 149
Hoyles, Fred 152

Isner, John 286

Ivanišević , Goran 175, 184, 199, 201, 202, 213, 232, 233, 235, 247

James, Edward 152
Järryd, Anders 175, 177, 193
Johanssen, Thomas 247
Johnson, Lyndon B. 61
Johnston, 'Little' Bill 3, 7, 8, 9
Jones, Perry T. 60

Kafelnikov, Yevgeny 216, 218
Karjicek, Richard 201
Karlović, Ivo 255
Kendrick, Robert 269
Kerzner, Sol 157
Kiefer, Nicholas 249, 250
Kodeš, Jan 116, 125, 129
Kohlschreiber, Philipp 255, 275, 285
Korda, Petr 183
Kovacs, Frank 37, 49
Koželuh, Karel 11
Krajicek, Richard 234
Kramer, Jack 15, 26, 30, 31, 38, 40, 41, 43–56, 59, 63, 64, 65, 66, 67, 68, 69,
    80, 81, 87, 92, 98, 99, 118, 190, 203, 224, 294, 296, 297, 298, 299, 303,
    307, 308
Kriek, Johan 153, 174, 177, 191
Kuertem, Gustavo 218, 248
Kuhn, Ferdinand 25
Kühnen, Patrick 182
Kukuljevik, Francisco 35

Lacoste, René 294
Lansdorp, Robert 224
Larsen, Art 94
Larsson, Magnus 202
Laver, Bob 111
Laver, Lois 111
Laver, Melba 111
Laver, Rod 40, 41, 68, 69, 70, 74, 82, 83, 85, 86, 99, 101, 102, 103, 106,
    109–19, 130, 138, 139, 140, 145, 149, 205, 217, 218, 219, 220, 224, 237,
    239, 255, 296, 297, 298, 299, 307, 308, 309
Laver, Trevor 111
Leconte, Henri 174, 208, 231
Lendl, Ivan 31, 69, 118, 121, 132, 133, 135, 143, 144, 147, 153, 154, 155,
    157, 159–69, 177, 178, 181, 182, 183, 185, 194, 195, 196, 197, 198, 199,

200, 201, 209, 228, 229, 230, 232, 236, 239, 299, 301, 302, 303, 304, 307, 308
Lewis, Chris 153, 161
Little, Dell 224
Ljubičić, Ivan 272
Lott, George 22, 23, 25
Lundgren, Peter 181

McEnroe, John 41, 51, 69, 118, 121, 131, 132, 133, 135, 136, 137, 138, 139, 142, 143, 144, 147–57, 162, 163, 164, 165, 169, 175, 176, 180, 181, 187, 192, 194, 195, 201, 203, 208, 213, 218, 229, 230, 236, 237, 281, 299, 300, 301, 302, 303, 307, 308
McEnroe, John Patrick 147–8
McEnroe, Kay 147–8
McCauley, Jo 82
McGowan, Bill 149
McGregor, Ken 66, 76
Maciel, Francisco 191
Mackay, Barry 113, 114
McKinley, Chuck 103, 104, 114, 148
McNamara, Peter 163
McNamee, Paul 154, 163
Mako, Gene 35–6
Malisse, Xavier 246
Mark, Robert 102
Martin, Todd 214, 218, 233, 236, 286
Maskell, Dan 17, 18, 112
Maurer, Andreas 179
Mayer, Sandy 161
Maymo, Rafael 267
Mayotte, Tim 167, 173, 174, 181, 227, 228
Mečíř, Miloslav 165, 166, 180, 192, 195, 196
Medvedev, Andrei 217
Melzer, Jürgen, 286
Menzel, Roderich 24, 35
Merlin, André 24
Metreveli, Alex 127
Metzler, Paul; 41
Minton, Robert 23
Monfils, Gaël 262, 274, 286
Montanés, Albert 257
Mottram, Buster 139
Mulligan, Marty 114
Mulloy, Gardnar 61, 62, 79, 94, 95
Murray, Andy 15, 23, 220, 253, 254, 255, 257, 258, 261, 263, 271, 272, 274,

279, 284, 285, 288, 289, 290, 291, 293, 294
Muster, Thomas 214, 229, 236

Nadal, Ana Maria 266
Nadal, Rafael 31, 69, 99, 101, 110, 119, 138, 142, 144, 145, 151, 160, 169,
    205, 210, 217, 220, 239, 242, 249, 250, 251, 252, 253, 254, 255, 256, 257,
    258, 259, 260, 261, 263, 265–77, 279, 282, 283, 284, 285, 286, 287, 288,
    289, 290, 291, 304, 305, 306, 307, 308
Nadal, Sebastian 266, 267
Nadal, Toni 266, 267
Nalbandian, David 154, 245, 247, 248, 249
Năstase, Ilie 125, 127, 137, 140, 141, 142, 293
Naughton, Richard 79
Neale, Fraser 102, 114
Newcombe, John 73, 75, 84, 86, 87, 115, 119, 127, 190, 294
Nielsen, Kurt 76, 78
Noah, Yannick 144, 161, 162, 191, 192, 228
Norton, Brian 8, 9
Nyström, Joakim 174, 177, 194
Nüsslein, Hans 36

O'Neal, Tatum 155
Okker, Tom 127
Oliff, John 19
Olmedo, Alex 81, 114
Orantes, Manuel 106, 130, 140
Osuna, Rafael 103

Pails, Dinny 53, 65, 92
Palafox, Antonio 'Tony' 148–9
Panatta, Adriano 126, 141
Parke, J.C. 7
Parker, Frank 34, 49, 50, 60, 62, 65
Pasarell, Charlie 69, 70, 201
Pate, David 194
Patterson, Gerald 7, 8
Patty, Budge 62, 96, 97
Pecci, Víctor 142
Pernfors, Mikael 165
Perry, Fred 15–32, 36, 37, 60, 68, 74, 92, 93, 101, 208, 217, 239, 294, 295,
    296, 308
Perry, Samuel 15, 16, 17, 18, 20–21
Petzschner, Phillip 272
Pfister, Hank 174
Philippoussis, Mark 234, 236, 247

Pietrangeli, Nicola 104
Pilić, Niki 139, 140
Poulain, Frank 60
Price, S. L. 64

Querrey, Sam 286
Quist, Adrian 25, 29, 36, 91–2, 94, 96

Rafter, Pat 218, 219, 235, 236
Ralston, Dennis 104
Raymond, Lee 118
Reeves Walton, Josephine 2
Reyes, Gil 209, 210, 215, 217
Richardson, Ham 93, 95
Richey, Cliff 125, 156
Riggs, Bobby 37, 38, 47, 49, 51, 52, 53, 54, 63, 64, 65, 68, 294, 296
Riordan, Bill 125, 126
Ríos, Marcelo 235
Roche, Cliff 46, 47, 48
Roche, Tony 70, 83, 84, 104, 105, 106, 115, 116, 117, 236
Roddick, Andy 151, 247, 248, 249, 251, 255, 256, 268, 272, 283, 284, 285
Roberg, Percy 190
Rose, Mervyn 76
Rosewall, Ken 66, 67, 68, 71, 73–89, 91, 92, 93, 94, 95, 96, 97, 98, 99, 101, 106, 115, 116, 117, 118, 129, 130, 139, 149, 168, 218, 296, 297, 298, 299, 308
Rosewall, Robert 74, 75
Rosol, Lukáš 275
Rostagno, Derrick 200
Rowley, Peter 74, 85

Saceanu, Christian 227
Safin, Marat 235, 246, 248, 249, 281, 284
Sampras, Georgia 224
Sampras, Gus 224
Sampras, Marion 224
Sampras, Pete 41, 51, 69, 101, 118, 121, 135, 145, 149, 159, 167, 183, 184, 185, 186, 190, 191, 201, 203, 211, 212, 213, 214, 215, 216, 218, 219, 220, 221, 223–38, 239, 246, 247, 254, 255, 256, 259, 267, 268, 270, 298, 306, 308
Sampras, Sammy 224
Sampras, Stella 224
Sangster, Mike 103
Sánchez, Emilio 180
Sánchez, Javier 200

Santano, Manolo 103, 106
Savitt, Dick 94
Scanlon, Bill 173
Schapers, Michiel 227
Schroeder, Ted 59, 61, 62, 63, 64, 70, 176
Sedgman, Frank 51, 54, 65, 66, 71, 81, 94
Segura, Pancho 49, 54, 59, 65, 66, 81, 98, 123, 124, 125, 126, 127, 129
Seixas, Vic 62, 76, 78, 79, 94, 95
Shields, Brooke 217
Shields, Frank 28, 63
Shimizu, Zenzo 7, 10
Shiras, Leif 288
Simionescu, Mariana 143
Siemerink, Jan 185
Skeen, Dick 45
Smith, Red 76
Smith, Stan 86, 87, 127, 140
Söderling, Robin 242, 254, 255, 257, 258, 271, 272, 273
Solomon, Harold 126, 138, 161, 211, 226
Stadler, Roland 192
Staley, Jenny 96
Stanley, Roy 111
Steeb, Carl-Uwe 182
Stich, Michael 183, 199, 201, 215
Stockton, Dick 124, 127, 129
Stoefen, Les 37, 45
Stolle, Fred 103, 104
Stonltenberg, Jason 202
Sturgess, Eric 62, 92
Summers, Pop 17, 18, 19, 20
Svensson, Jonas 195, 199

Talbert, Bill 62, 79
Tanner, Roscoe 142
Taróczy, Balázs 160
Taylor, Roger 125, 140
Teacher, Brian 160
Teltscher, Eliot 160, 161
Throckmorton, Harold 3
Tignor, Stephen 136, 137
Tilden, Bill 1–14, 20, 23, 31, 36, 37, 41, 45, 47, 48, 61, 68, 92, 93, 118, 159, 203, 294, 295, 296, 305, 306, 307, 308
Tilden, Herbert 2, 4, 5
Tingay, Lance 98
Tipsarević, Janko 271

Ţiriac, Ion 125, 172, 174, 176, 187
Trabert, Tony 66, 67, 69, 71, 77, 78, 81, 95, 96, 294
Troiki, Viktor 287
Tsonga, Jo-Wilfried 257, 260, 262, 263, 270, 274, 284, 285, 286
Tunis, John R. 26

Van Horn, Welby 35
Verdasco, Fernando 271, 275, 286
Vines, Ellsworth 11, 21, 30, 33, 36, 38, 39, 40, 44, 45, 47, 48, 51, 54, 68, 92,
    93, 95, 96, 99, 294, 295, 296, 298
Volkov, Alexander 181, 183

Wallace, David Foster 240
Washington, MaliVai 201, 201
Wawrinka, Stanislas 283
Westphal, Michael 179
Wheaton, David 199, 212
Whitney, Eli 3
Whittaker, Tom 22
Wilander, Mats 153, 163, 164, 165, 166, 177, 179, 182, 191, 192, 193, 194,
    195, 196, 198, 202, 209, 227, 228, 273, 294
Wilson, Bridgette 236
Wood, Peggy 8
Wood, Sydney 21, 25, 28, 35
Woodruff, Chris 217

Youzhny, Mikhail 260, 286
Yzaga, Jaime 227